ENCOUNTERING RACE IN ALBANIA

ENCOUNTERING RACE IN ALBANIA

An Ethnography of the Communist Afterlife

Chelsi West Ohueri

CORNELL UNIVERSITY PRESS   ITHACA AND LONDON

Copyright © 2025 by Cornell University

All rights reserved. Except for brief quotations in a review, this book, or parts thereof, must not be reproduced in any form without permission in writing from the publisher. For information, address Cornell University Press, Sage House, 512 East State Street, Ithaca, New York 14850. Visit our website at cornellpress.cornell.edu.

First published 2025 by Cornell University Press

Librarians: A CIP catalog record for this book is available from the Library of Congress.

ISBN 9781501781865 (hardcover)
ISBN 9781501781872 (paperback)
ISBN 9781501781889 (epub)
ISBN 9781501781896 (pdf)

To Jaustin, Westlynn, and Amelia Brielle

Contents

Acknowledgments	ix
A Note on Language and Terminology	xix
Introduction	1
1. The Communist Afterlife	25
2. The Trial of the Anthropologist	57
3. Peripheral Whiteness	81
4. On Blackness: A Story in Six Names	109
5. A Question of Racism in Three Acts	148
Conclusion	184
Notes	193
References	199
Index	213

Acknowledgments

Writing is communal. I am the author of this book, but this book would not have been possible without the support, guidance, love, and encouragement from my wide community of family and friends. I am indebted to each and every one of you. I cannot list every single person, but I want to take some time to thank many of the people who have walked with me on this nearly twenty-year journey.

This research would not have possible without my extended "framily" in Albania who have shown me immense kindness and love for many years. To Berta Adhami: I am forever thankful for our chance encounter and how it blossomed into a lifelong friendship. Thank you to Klodi Hoti, Anisa Sokoli, Pjeter and Vitoria Çuni and their family, and all the families of Thethi and the Shala Valley that welcomed me in 2006 and 2007. Elvisa Sokoli has been a rock for me—thank you for all the apples, glasses of wine, and laughter that we have shared. Thank you to my first Albanian language teachers Kledi Shegani and Maklena Çabej. To Anila Xira, thank you my *zysha*, my friend, and a constant source of light and belly laughs. Thank you to Orkida Driza for your friendship and support. A big thank you to my friends Lauren and Landi Skora who have long supported me in this work and continue to regularly check in about it. And thank you to Lauren for being one of my first research assistants. Thank you to Klaudian Marku, my hairstylist and friend, who eagerly told me, "I know how to do Black hair" when I first showed up at *New Look Tina* in 2008—thank you to Tina and all of the stylists at the salon. A sincere thank you to Ikuko Fujimoto for being my fellow Albanian language learner and travel partner. I want to also thank a group of special friends who provided a support network in Albania: Sylvia Deskaj, Dylan Byrd, Cindy Eldridge, Dave Scott, and Taylor Hodges. You all mean so much to me. Thank you for all the chuckles, shenanigans, and memories over the years.

I am who I am because of the teachers who shaped me: Mary Helen King was my first teacher dating back to preschool, and I have always carried her teaching and wisdom with me, including one of the first poems she taught me, which said, "I know I am Somebody Cause God Don't Make No Junk." I want to thank my second-grade teachers and the special space they created for us to think and dream with books: Mrs. Hildetary (Jane Hildebrand and Lee Singletary) and Mrs. Karen Smith. Karen Milton, Karen Redhead, Betty Lamb, Alix Davis Williams, Leland Thompson, Coach Milton, Coach Thompson, Mrs. Walters,

Ms. Diliaglou, and Sharon Wheeler have been instrumental in my educational journey throughout elementary, middle, and high school.

I first became an anthropologist at Millsaps College. I never intended for this to be my life's work but thank you to Elise Smith who encouraged me to take an introductory class—I am so glad that sociology was full. It was my college professors who first made me want to be a professor, and a special shoutout goes to Darby Ray, Raymond Clothier, George Bey, Ming Tsu, Catherine Freis, Amy Forbes, Brit Katz, and Lisa Garvin. A big thank you to Iren Omobare for inspiring me to explore my interests beyond required courses—may you rest in peace. My anthropological career would not have been possible without the amazing support of the Millsaps College SOAN Department, especially Julian Murchison and Mike Galaty. Julian was my first anthropology professor and graciously read my first paper, which was supposed to be six to eight pages but ended up being twenty-six. I first told Julian that I wanted to travel abroad, and shortly thereafter Mike invited me to join his summer project in Albania. Thank you, Mike and Julian, for guiding me through so many life seasons, from travel to eastern Europe or East Africa, to reading countless drafts, to writing recommendation letters, to helping me carry the infamous giant yellow travel bag. Thank you, Mike, for convincing my parents to let me travel to Albania, for guiding me my first time out of the US, and for recognizing that perhaps my strengths were in sociocultural anthropology and not archaeology. I am deeply indebted to you for your mentorship.

I had the pleasure of working with and learning from an incredible group of scholars during graduate school at the University of Texas at Austin. I remain deeply grateful to Katie Stewart for her keen insight, care, and encouragement. Thank you for helping me find my ethnographic voice. Mary Neuburger, Kamran Ali, Craig Campbell, and John Hartigan provided invaluable feedback and direction. Thank you, Mary, for everything you have taught me about the Balkans, and thank you, Kamran, for all our conversations about Enver Hoxha. Thank you, Craig, for asking about images at my dissertation defense—this book definitely includes more. Jemima Pierre also has continued to mentor me in my career. Thank you, Jemima, for always pushing me in my analysis, particularly how to historicize race. Nita Luci, I want to thank you for pushing me to think critically about anthropology and the Balkans. I want to also thank you for your friendship.

UT Austin has served as my intellectual home for many years, both as a graduate student and now as a faculty member. I want to thank professors and mentors, many of whom have now become colleagues: Christen Smith, Joao Vargas, Ted Gordon, Kamala Visweswaran, John Hoberman, Lok Siu, Circe Sturm, Maria Franklin, Pauline Turner Strong, and James Brow and James Denbow, may they rest in peace. Thank you to Meta DuEwa Jones, who made me feel like I could be a writer. I was fortunate to become friends with some of the brightest and fiercest scholars during my time in graduate school. Many of these friends played a role in helping me finish this book. Thanks goes to Sade Anderson, Gio Batz, Jenny Carlson, Abdul Haque Chang, Haile Eshe Cole, Bisola Falola, Ayana Omilade Flewellen, Sarah Ihmoud, Maryam Kashani, Jenny Kelly, Adam Mehis, Omer Ozcan, Naomi Reed, Tathagatan Ravindran, Luciane O. Rocha, Jodi Skipper, Raja Swamy, Heather Teague, and Elizabeth Velasquez. Thank you, Maya Berry and drea brown, my circle of Black Brilliance. Thank you to my "cousin" Nedra Lee for your friendship and endless laughs. Liz Lewis has a remained a close friend, always ready to be a listening ear, share an inside joke, or grab a drink whenever I need. Thanks also goes to my dear friend Gwen Kirk who, over fifteen years ago, invited me to join her for a glass of sweet tea, and the rest is now history. And to Traci-Ann Wint, my Black feminist-sister-anthropology-friend: we have shared so many late-night writing sessions, joys, tears, and tacos. Thank you for your support, feedback, and insight through it all.

Several of my UT colleagues have played a role in shaping this book and I want to especially thank Mary Neuburger, as well as Agnes Sekowski, Sonia Seeman, Sam Pinto, Joan Neuberger, Tom Garza, Karma Chavez, Vladislav Beronja, Kiril Avramov, Maria Sidorkina, Degi Uvsh, Steven Seegel, Marina Alexndrova, Jason Roberts, Nidhi Trehan, Caroline Faria, Eric Tang, Celina de Sa, and Abena Osseo-Asare. Thanks to our amazing department administrative staff who keep all the balls rolling, and special thanks to Cara Keirstead who has listened to me talk through this book for the past five years. Volodymyr Kulikov organized an excellent department writing workshop series, and I am thankful for the feedback from him, Degi Uvsh, Nicholas Pierce, and Mary Neuburger on chapter 4. I would like to also thank colleagues from the UT Dell Medical School who provided tremendous support during my postdoctoral fellowship, chief among them Alex Garcia, Julie Zuniga, Virginia Brown, and Carmen Valdez. I want to also thank Christina Jarvis, Kacey Hanson, Ricardo Garay, Tasha Banks, Nitakuwa Barrett, Denise Dodd, Brigid Keenan, Rene Salazar, Tracee Hall, Courtney Bailey, Carrie Barron, Bill Tierney, William Lawson, and many others. Additional thanks to Vox Jo Hsu and Lina Chunn. Thank you to Nessette Falu for constant encouragement and our many conversations about anthropology, race, and health.

I am so fortunate to be connected to an amazing group of UT colleagues who have become friends. Thank you to my crew of colleagues and friends: Ashley Farmer, Ashley Coleman Taylor, Ade Adamson, Mónica Jiminez, Ana Schwartz, Khytie Brown, Amira Rose Davis, Ashanté Reese, Bedour Alagraa, Roger Reeves, Pavithra Vasudevan, Nicole Burrowes, and Snehal Patel. I immediately connected with Ashley Coleman Taylor during our faculty orientation at UT and she has been a light in my life since—thank you, sis. A huge thanks goes to my fellow ethnographer and friend Ashanté Reese who read early drafts of fellowship proposals, scrutinized sections of the book with so much care, and routinely reminded me that sometimes it is just time to let it go. I really do not think that this book would have been written without Pavithra Vasudevan and Annette Rodriguez. I was not sure what would unfold when Pavi first approached me about forming a No Bad News writing group, and now here we are, more than three years later, having spent countless hours and days writing collectively, always building each other up and pushing one another forward. You two have read every chapter of this book, some chapters twice, and I want to express my deepest appreciation. Every time I thought I could not finish, you two have reminded me that I could. Pavithra, I am grateful that we get to do this life of scholar motherhood together, collectively planning out camps, playdates, and retreats, and dreaming about possibilities.

Several colleagues have enriched my research and life and for this I am thankful. A very special thank you to Lori Amy and all the conversations, adventures, and journeys we have shared, whether in Tirana, Moscow, or New York. Thank you, Lori, for pushing me to work through challenges and teaching me how to value growth. Thank you to Deborah Thomas for serving as my Ford postdoctoral fellowship mentor. Thank you for encouraging me to reapply when I did and for providing insightful support and feedback on the book. Thank you, Sunnie Rucker-Chang, for our collaborative work to expand Black studies in Slavic studies. Thank you, Elana Resnick, for all our extended conversations, whether they be at conferences in the United States, during workshops in Europe, or via long text threads. Thank you to Piro Rexhepi for being a listening ear and for sharing insight about race and the Balkans. Additional colleagues I would like to thank include Smoki Musaraj, Eli Krasniqi, Ian Hancock, Ioanida Costache, Margareta Matache, Enkelejda Sula-Raxhimi, Miglena Todorova, Bolaji Balogun, Catherine Baker, Aniko Imre, James Mark, Bogdan Iacob, Ivan Kalmar, Riché Barnes, Nessette Falu, John L. Jackson, Terrell Starr, Kimberly St. Julian Varnon, Amarillis Lugo de Fabritz, Alexa Kumanov, Nana Osei-Opare, Eric Prendergast, Inis Shkreli, and Antonia Young. In Albania I want to thank Ornela Gjergji, Rubin Zemon, the late Marcel Courthiade, Ols Lafe, Anisa Brano, Mirela Çupi, Armanda Hysa, Blerta Bodinaku, Ilir Kalemaj, Vasilika Laçi, Jonida Laçi, Brisilda Taço, Olsi Sherifi, Bredi Xhavara, Xhekson Cela, Briselda Reme, Hadroj Rami, Marcella and Greg Dill, and my landlords Albert and Majlinda. Thank you to the staff at the National Archives of Albania. I want to also thank friends that I have made in Albania over the years, including Camille Nuamah, Keelah Rose Calloway, Alasha Black, Peter and Kim Hakkenberg, and Mindy Michaels. I extend my sincerest thanks to Artan Hoxha for all your help over the years, whether that has been obtaining documents, confirming citations, or sharing a laugh over coffee. Thank you to Elidor Mëhilli for reading a draft of chapter 1 and providing feedback. Enxhi Beka has been a fantastic research assistant in Tirana, and I am truly grateful for your help and expertise. I want to thank Davijola Ndoja for her friendship and her translation expertise, and for invitations to read poetry at Hemingway bar. Thank you, Matthias Bickert, for your friendship and research collaboration. A huge thanks also to Rebecca Barrett Fox and the Any Good Thing writing community. For all those I may have missed, please charge it to my head and not my heart.

I also want to thank a very special group of students. I enjoy all of the classes that I teach, and one special class in particular helped shape this book in its final stages. Thank you to my graduate students in my spring 2024 Global Race and Racism course for your thoughtful engagement, your keen questions, your witty humor, and your incredible final papers and projects.

Jim Lance at Cornell University Press was excited about this book from the beginning. Thank you, Jim, for that enthusiasm and all the support that you, Bethany Wasik, Jennifer Dana Savran Kelly, and the Cornell UP staff have provided throughout this process. I want to extend a big thank you to two anonymous readers and their feedback, which really strengthened the manuscript. Ajkuna Tafa graciously edited the Albanian writing in this book and gave very helpful feedback—I keep singing her praises! Sections of chapter 3 were previously published in an edited volume, *Off White: Central and Eastern Europe and the Global History of Race* (Baker et al. 2024) from Manchester University Press and reproduced with permission of the publisher.

This research was made possible by numerous funding entities that have supported my ethnographic fieldwork, language study, tuition, and writing over the years. I have had the privilege of support from the US Fulbright program, the National Science Foundation, the Foreign Language and Area Studies program (FLAS), the International Research and Exchanges Board (IREX), the University of Texas at Austin College of Liberal Arts, the School for Advanced Research, the Ford Foundation, and the Center for Russian, East European and Eurasian Studies (CREEES) at UT Austin. So much of this book came alive through a residential writing fellowship at the School for Advanced Research in Santa Fe, New Mexico. What a special time I enjoyed as SAR welcomed me and my family for an academic year that allowed me to complete so much of this book project. Special thanks to Michael Brown, Paul Ryer, Kat Bernhardt, Mary Madigan, Ashley Flores, Leslie Shipman, and the staff there, and so much love and appreciation to members of my cohort for all their feedback and support: Benjamin Junge, Adriana Linares-Palma, Andy Aguilera, Dmitri Brown, and Klint Burgio-Ericson. Thank you to Deborah Winslow and Carol Ann MacLennan for participating in my scholar workshop and providing generous feedback. I want to thank friends in New Mexico that helped in so many ways, including Terry Stofocik, Sarah Guzman, Abby Feldman, and Tiffany Florvil. A very special thank you to Meghan Mercer who became not only a friend but also an ongoing source of support, encouragement, and laughter.

This book would not have been possible without childcare and my kids' many teachers and caregivers. I am truly indebted to numerous daycares, preschools, babysitters, and after-school programs that made this possible, particularly in seasons of intensive travel and solo parenting. Special shout to Deja Bean, Vanesa Fulcher, Mari Hernandez, Ms. Stella, and Ms. Sam, who were teachers that became babysitters, even giving of their evenings and weekends so that I could squeeze in writing time. I am so very grateful. Coffee also made this book possible, and there are some very special coffee shops and baristas that I need to thank. My friend Berta in Albania makes some of the best homemade Turkish coffee, and many of her coffees have sustained me over the years. I am also grateful for spots like Friends Book House, E Per7shme, and Radio in Tirana, and of course the original Bennu Coffee in Austin, where I have made a writing home dating back to grad school. Many thanks to my favorite baristas there and their readiness with my favorite coffees in my favorite mugs. Thanks also goes to Nina Simone, Erykah Badu, Beyoncé, and Sia for providing numerous soundtracks in these writing spaces.

I cannot begin to express my thanks to members of my church family and community who have prayed for and with me throughout this process. A special thank you to Morgan Stephens, Rosalynn Smith, Nicole Cummings Lewis, and Cori Sullivan. Melissa Williams has walked this mama-scholar journey with me, and I am truly grateful. Thank you to my EP gal pals, Ashley Behnke, Amelia Bowie, and Brittany Clay, for always having the right words, prayers, memes, or jokes to make my day and to keep encouraging me to get it done. My family has been blessed by the friendship of Brandelyn and Terrance Green: thanks to you both for your encouragement, advice, and listening ears over the years. Thanks also goes to my therapist—I am grateful for your open ears, wise words, and constant reminders that I can do hard things.

The following friends have long supported me in various life endeavors, and I want to express thanks to Mrs. Ora Frazier, Sister Isabelle Evans, Mary Helen, Theophilus, Margaree, and the entire King family, my homie David Dennis, my roommate for life Rachael "Jimmie" Joe, my "aunt" Christina Lee, my "sister" Allilia Price, as well as dear friends who have been there for me since childhood, through college, and now in adulthood, including Mallarie McCune, Elizabeth Ofem Kline, Sylvia Holmes, Arlene Nicks, and Maggie Neff. I am indebted to Ace Madjlesi, who has listened to me dream about this book for more than fifteen years, has read drafts of my writing since college, and still sometimes gets inundated with long voice texts as I try to work through ideas. Sylvia Deskaj and I have had numerous adventures through the Balkans, and wherever we meet up in the world, we just pick up right where we left off—thank you, shoqe. To my CAKE sisters Amber and KeNosha: thank you for being such loyal friends who surround me with grace, compassion, check-ins, prayer call, emails, texts, and video messages—thank you for helping carry me when I could not carry myself. Courtney Robinson Thompson, one of my oldest friends, has always kept me connected to books, from when we were younger and used to mail books to one another and trade books on road trips, or now in our extended catchups about life—thank you for your support. Natalie King Powell and I love to tell the story about how we met in fifth grade and became fast enemies, each of us getting so upset when people would compare us. Nat, thank you for being my best friend, for always talking me over hurdles when I hit a wall, for looking over contracts and documents, and for even offering to read my texts even though I know you do not always want to do so. *Ti je shumë e bukur.*

Writing a book has proven to be harder than I imagined but truly a rewarding experience. Part of this is due to my family. Through it all my family has served as my rock, my retreat, my home. Carmen and Hal Dockins have cheered me on from the beginning, eagerly reading everything I write, proudly hanging postcards on their fridge, and putting Albanian souvenirs on their desks. Thirty-eight years ago, my grandmother Pearlie Mae Robinson West chose my godparents—or rather, she told my parents who my godparents were going to be. Turns out she knew exactly what she was doing as Jackie and Ronald Hawkins and Richard and Debra Graves have been the ultimate cheerleaders and supported me every step of the way. I am indebted to my Auntie Bee for sustaining me with her prayers, her care, and her calm. You are a gem. My cousin Tiffany was the first person to tell me that I had to leave Mississippi and travel somewhere else in the world. I do not know if she meant Albania, but she is the reason I took the chance. In recent months I have enjoyed chats with my Uncle Roy about world history and trivia, and it has brought warm memories of doing the same with my dad—thank you, Uncle Roy. My Natchez cousins have continued to be beacons of encouragement and inspiration throughout my research and writing: thank you to Joy, Leon, Briana, Eboni, Corliss, and William. Special thank you to my cousin Ronnie, who has read every blog post, watched multiple talks, and framed pictures for my office walls. Thanks to my in-laws, Clifford, Ardella, Jonathan, and Adamma, for welcoming me and supporting me with so much enthusiasm. Thank you to my extended Bacon, Robinson, and West families, and thank you to the Darden family for your unwavering love and prayers.

My brother Alex enjoys cracking jokes, some at my expense, but he is always there for me when it counts, no matter what. Thank you, brother. Thank you to my cousin Jason for instilling a love for adventure in me from an early age. Thank you to my sister-in-love Alisha for being a reminder of hope. My uncle Harold has unceasingly told me to always "Go Hard" in everything I do—thank you, Uncle, for being an inspiration for me. To my grandmother Lillie Mae: as Millie says, you are the queen. The lily flower, which I associate with you, symbolizes renewal, and your love does just that for me, helping me keep going in the face of adversity. I am so grateful for you, for our hugs, our talks, our laughs, and our inside jokes about Greece.

This book and the road leading here have been such an endeavor, and I find it incredibly difficult to sufficiently thank my mother. My mama made every single list, checked every box, packed every single medicine bag for international travel, joined me in Albania in 2008, and talked to numerous friends over the phone even though she does not speak Albanian; she has been my editor, my coach, my protector, and my friend. My mother's support for this book and for everything that I do has remained unwavering. I love you so much, Mama, truly I do.

This book is dedicated to my three: my husband, Jaustin, and our daughters, Westlynn and Amelia Brielle. This book has been a long time coming, and I thank you all for not giving up on me; for supporting my fieldwork travels to Albania and at times accompanying me there; for understanding when I needed to write extra late or attend a writing retreat; for being up for adventures during my residential writing fellowship in Santa Fe. Thank you, girls, for all your hugs, kisses, and back rubs. One of my greatest joys is watching your love of books unfold and awaiting the stories that you two will someday share with the world. Jaustin, my beloved, thank you. Thank you for your enduring care, love, and persistence. You have buoyed me in more ways than one, always reassuring me that it will all work out in the end. You are such a gift to my life, illustrating what the book of James tells us, that every good and perfect gift is from above.

In June 2008 I received a brown envelope in the mail stating that I had been awarded a Fulbright fellowship to Albania for a year, and as he heard my screams of excitement, my dad rushed to the mail slot as we celebrated with jubilation. Shortly thereafter my best friend Micki was at the house helping me plan a massive packing list, and when it was time to leave, my incredible cousin Linda made the trek to Jackson from Natchez to help me fit all my things into my infamous giant yellow bag. When I started my blog, they were often the first ones to comment and ask questions, always serving as huge sources of hope and belief that one day I could complete this book. They traveled to Austin to help in so many seasons of graduate school. They attended talks, read drafts, and excitedly shared my work with the world. My dad was my muse, my Micki was my hype woman and confidant, and my cousin Linda was an angel on earth. That none of them survived to see this book published feels hugely unfair and hurts in ways that I often fail to adequately capture with words, yet I am comforted in knowing that it was their faith in me that helped get this book to the finish line.

A Note on Language and Terminology

This book includes written Albanian text. I translate all the Albanian expressions and statements into English, but I choose to include Albanian writing and expressions as part of my commitment to ethnographically capture local socialities.

I use the capitalized form of Black when referring to African diasporic peoples, whereas the term "blackness" is written with a lowercase B. I use the lowercase form when discussing how groups such as Albanians and Roma make claims to being "black."

I use the Albanian spelling of Kosova throughout the text.

The term "Egyptian" in this book does not refer to Egyptian nationals but rather is the name of a group in the Balkan region that is often considered Roma but in fact asserts a non-Romani identity. For this reason, I use "Balkan Egyptian" throughout this text. Egyptians do not speak Romani and most often speak Albanian as their first language, and unlike Roma, they claim an Egyptian origin, as opposed to an Indian origin. The book's introduction and chapter 4 include extended discussion of Egyptian groups in the Balkans.

The term "g*psy" is a slur and misnomer and is denoted throughout the book as "g----."

Except where noted, translations are my own. Additionally, all mistakes are my own.

INTRODUCTION

Alba was a Romani woman who, in 2014, lived in a small shack in the Selitë neighborhood not far from the building affectionately known as the *pallati me shigjeta* (building with arrows). At that time, many of Alba's neighbors had been forced out of their community due to the expansion of the Ring Road (Unaza e Re), but Alba and her daughter had managed to hang on to their dwelling, at least for a moment. They sat along Rruga e Kavajës each morning, selling whatever household objects they could scrounge together from collections and other vendors. On one of the days that I visited, they were selling small kitchen sponges and dishrags. I asked Alba if she wanted to have a coffee, and soon we found ourselves at a nearby café. Alba was very vocal about her experiences with Albanians, or *dorë e bardh*ë (white people), as she referred to them. We chatted back and forth, Alba drinking an espresso, me a macchiato. At some point an Albanian *furgon* (minivan) driver pulled up and approached us.[1] "Mirëdita" (Good morning), he said, his tall physique briefly towering over us as we sat. He waved to the waiter and ordered a coffee, then took a seat, seemingly inviting himself into our conversation. Snickering to myself, I continued talking to Alba, trying to pick up where I had left off, but then the driver interjected, offering unsolicited commentary. "I will tell you the truth about Albania," he began. "In Albania there is no racism between groups like us," he said, moving his hand in a circle around Alba and himself. Alba frowned and clicked her tongue several times, expressing her disagreement. "What about the ways that the majority [*mazhoranca*] mistreat Roma and Egyptians?" she asked. "What about this neighborhood, about this street that is segregated between *dorë e bardhë* and *dorë e zezë* [black people]?" The *furgon* driver looked up, smiled, and retorted, "Well, coffee is black, and we all drink that, so clearly there is not an issue with color in Albania."

I Found Race in a Raceless Place

This is a book about race in Albania, but as the above ethnographic illustration demonstrates, I am often told that there is no race or racism in Albania. Or, when I explain to some that I am an anthropologist conducting research in Albania, I am regularly asked, what does race have to do with it? Famed singer Tina Turner once asked a similar question about love, even naming love as an old-fashioned notion. I too have been told that race is old-fashioned—an outdated concept that died with the Nazis, vanished with the end of apartheid, evaporated after the 1960s US civil rights movement—or simply that race does not exist. So when I tell people about my research on race in Albania, many express immediate surprise and ask two questions: why Albania and what's race got to do with it?

This book is my attempt to answer these questions. It is an ethnographic study of race in Albania, one in which race itself is the ethnographic object. I explore racialization as an ongoing and enduring but still evolving social process (Alim, Kroskrity, and Reyes 2020). With this lens, Albania becomes an ethnographic case study that illustrates how race works, even within a population at times understood to be homogeneously "white" and therefore "lacking" race. While numerous scholars have addressed related concepts of nationalism, ethnicity, and religion in southeastern Europe, this book is the first to interrogate and analyze race in Albania in what I term the "communist afterlife." The significance of race in the Balkans, how racialization emerges, and how people understand and negotiate racial assemblages have been left out of larger discussions of global racialization. One aim of this book, therefore, is to illuminate how everyday local formations are shaped by global ones and in turn inform the global. It is a book in which I ask what a contextualized analysis of Albania can reveal about race and belonging broadly.

Albania in the Communist Afterlife

Located in southeastern Europe, in a region commonly referred to as the Balkans, Albania is a relatively small country often known for its infamously high mountains, its coastal riviera along the Adriatic, and the history of its "exceptionally repressive" (Pojani 2010) communist regime led mostly by Enver Hoxha.

FIGURE 1. Map of Albania. Since the printing of this map, the country of Macedonia has officially been named the Republic of North Macedonia according to the Prespa Accord. United States Central Intelligence Agency, Albania map, 2008. https://www.loc.gov/item/2009575118/.

"Lenin changed Russia, but Stalin changed the world" (Ypi 2022). This is how Albanian writer Lea Ypi recounts a lesson from a childhood teacher. These words poignantly capture Hoxha's relationship to Stalinist rule and the ways that glorification of Stalin permeated everyday Albanian society, in what was arguably the most extreme form of totalitarian control and isolation in Central and Eastern Europe. The Communist Party came into power in 1946, and Hoxha would remain at the helm until his death in 1985. The regime was restrictive and coercive, bolstered by terror, paranoia, and an allegiance to Stalinism even after Stalin's death and Albania's subsequent break with the Soviet Union. In the 1960s Albania aligned with Mao's communist China, but the late 1970s witnessed the Sino-Albanian split, with Hoxha increasingly implementing isolationist policies. Student anti-communist protests began in late 1990, and 1991 may mark the year that the regime was formally dissolved, but communism is not absent in the contemporary landscape. The sociopolitical and economic effects of communist dictatorship are ongoing; they dwell, linger, inhabit, persist, and remain. Scholarship on the broader region of Central and Eastern Europe has long focused on the notions of *post*-socialist or *post*-communist (Berdahl 1999; Burawoy and Verdery 1999; Humphrey 2002; Hann 2002; Shevchenko 2008; Verdery 1996). This research on political economy, marketization, and material culture has informed my work, but the frameworks of post-socialism and post-communism do not adequately capture how people dwell in the space of communist afterlives, the registers, remembrances, and remnants that shape daily life. Moreover, since the fall of the Berlin Wall, many scholars and experts have told the story of Eastern Europe as one of triumph—the triumph of capitalism and free-market democracies. As anthropologist Katherine Verdery (1996) has cautioned, however, there is a particular danger in presuming triumph and a need to analyze the fabrics of societies more critically as they have exited extended periods of state socialist rule. Like anthropologist Kristen Ghodsee (2010), I use ethnography to explore the ways that ordinary people are living in the present moment.

The communist afterlife is a period of entanglement.[2] It speaks to the multiple, overlapping, and wide-ranging sociopolitical and economic transformations in Albania since the 1990s. This framing of the afterlife tries to capture the aftermath of reforms that were chaotically interrupted by the 1997 Ponzi schemes that engendered economic collapse and a near civil war. It addresses the aftermath of the Greek and later international economic crises of the early 2000s and highlights what anthropologist Smoki Musaraj calls a persistent "nervous uncertainty" of the contemporary moment, marked by unemployment and economic insecurity (2021, 159). The communist afterlife is a mode that continues to affect time, shaping how people imagine the past, present, and future.

Achille Mbembe's conceptualization of entanglement draws attention to the layering of temporalities that creates "an interlocking of presents, pasts, and futures that retain their depths of other presents, pasts, and futures, each age bearing, altering, and maintaining the previous ones" (2001, 19). Unlike the framework of *post*, I do not assume a linear progression but instead explore how the present is interlocked with the past and future. The field of quantum mechanics offers an additional way to consider entanglement. As a physics subfield, quantum mechanics speaks to matter, energy, and the momentums of everyday life. Whereas Mbembe's notion of entanglement focuses on the interlocking, quantum entanglement focuses on the simultaneous actions of two forces at once, two forces that are separated but still affect one another (Bengtsson and Życzkowski 2017). Michelle Wright has written about race and history in relation to quantum mechanics, arguing that physics and humanistic inquiry can provide an interdisciplinary lens to study phenomena that do not operate linearly but rather through what she calls a "spacetime" (2015, 16). Wright challenges the use of the *post* to indicate linear cause and effect, or to presume that *post* equates advancement. Her approach to spacetime is one that asks what it would look like to examine histories not just through a straight line or arrow but perhaps as a circle with multiple arrows (20). In a way similar to Wright, this book ethnographically traces those particles that shape the entangled temporalities of the communist afterlife as a way to think outside of a more linear before and after. The forces of the communist afterlife represent an entangled system, whereby pastness (Trouillot 1995) continually intersects with and shapes the contemporary landscape.

My use of the afterlife as a framework calls attention to other conceptualizations of afterlives. Writer and scholar Saidiya Hartman has defined the afterlife of slavery as entrenchment, how slavery itself "established a measure of man and a ranking of human life and worth that has yet to be undone" (2007, 6). Similarly, Nadine Attewell's conceptualization of the afterlife of empire and its remains demonstrates the "multiple and varied ways that empire lives on" (2014, 6). For Attewell, empire is ongoing, haunting its afterlife. Hartman's framework of the afterlife is about the non-break, and Attewell emphasizes empire that does not end. In this book I argue that communism may not remain active as a sociopolitical and economic system, but it is still a force that animates in this interconnected and globalized world.

Communism reconfigured Albania's social landscape, and its afterlife provides the ethnographic backdrop for tracing race and racialization. Racial analyses must be historically and contextually situated, and while I am not a historian, and this book addresses more modern history from the twentieth century, historical contextualization is necessary to understand how race takes shape in the present.[3] Later sections of the book include more in-depth analyses of Albania's history and geopolitics, but here I want to briefly introduce the ethnographic setting. Though I have conducted research throughout Albania, and my first summers in the country were spent in the high northern mountains of the Shala Valley, the bulk of the research for this book was conducted in Tirana and Central Albania. Since 1991 Tirana has witnessed dramatic social, political, and economic shifts. Whereas Hoxha's regime imposed centralized control over city infrastructure and population control, Albania has more recently experienced widespread growth, particularly the Tirana-Durrës corridor in Central Albania. Of Albania's population of nearly three million, close to one million live in Tirana. Within Tirana I conducted a significant part of my research on the margins of the city, where rapid expansion and development continue to segregate Roma and Balkan Egyptians on the edges and outskirts of the city.

This book focuses on the social process of racialization, primarily with Albanians, Roma, and Balkan Egyptians. The names of these three groups speak to multiple social, racial, ethnic, and national formations, and the boundaries of group belonging are often reconfigured and contested, as later chapters will demonstrate. Because of this, I am often asked by scholars such as political scientists and demographers to define in- and out-groups, and to highlight numbers and figures regarding population counts. It is important to note that there have been very few in-depth, countrywide counts of Albanian social groups. This situation is shaped by many factors, including the controversies that have arisen in contested areas of Southern Albania, whereby Albanian and Greek communities have resisted population counts that would measure ethnicity (Likmeta 2011c). The 2011 census, taken by INSTAT (Albanian Institute of Statistics), was the first Albanian census to allow respondents to select an ethnic category outside of "Albanian" or "Greek."[4] The collected census data from 2011 listed 8,300 people who identified as Roma, 3,368 who identified as Egyptian, 2,644 who marked "other," and more than 300,000 who stated that they preferred not to answer. Many Romani and Egyptian groups contest these figures, and other scholars and organizations do believe the number of Roma in Albania is closer to 120,000 (Qejvanaj 2021). Due to the COVID-19 pandemic, the census scheduled for 2020 was delayed until 2023, although as of September 2024, INSTAT has yet to release those figures. Critics have continued to question the population count of Roma and Egyptians, which they believe is drastically underrepresented. So instead of me trying to concretely demarcate the demographic characteristics of each of these groups, I allow the ethnography to reveal the ways that race is made and remade, and how the categorizations of race, nation, ethnicity, and religion play a role in these processes. Scholars like Marcel Courthiade (also written as Kurtiade), one of the leading researchers about Roma in Albania, have stressed that relationships between Roma and Albanians may be antagonistic but do not necessarily reflect racism. This book is an effort to think through racial assemblages and all the deeply imbricated layers that extend beyond *who* is racist or not, and whether racism is present or not. Ethnography provides an opening to trace the multiple complexities that give race its meaning and shape. I position race as my object of ethnographic inquiry, and Albania's marginal positioning within Europe makes it an ideal location to conduct research on this subject.

Conceptualizing Race, Racelessness, and Racialization

Race is an imagined and invented construct that hierarchizes people along axes of superiority and inferiority. Though race is socially and politically constructed, it continues to register as biological (Roberts 2011). That race is invented and imagined does not imply that race is not *real*, as the effects of race are tangible, measurable, material, and evident; rather, the emphasis on imagination reveals race's shifting meanings and chameleon nature (Stoler 1997; Turda 2021). This book is an exploration of race-making and racialization, that is, the ways that race itself operates and is made, remade, produced, and reproduced over time.

In most cases, race immediately registers as singularly epidermal, as simply phenotype and hue, with varying skin tones, hair textures, and facial shapes serving as immediate markers that denote racial difference. These are common understandings of race, and numerous scholars have long studied skin color as a key marker of race and modernity (Gates and Curran 2022; Painter 2010; Mills 1997; Roediger 2005; Smedley 1998; Zakharov and Law 2017). In this book I do examine the role of the body and how the body indexes race. Yet race is not simply skin color, and it is not just about bodies. I demonstrate this throughout the book while challenging the assumed racelessness of Albania and southeastern Europe. Such notions of racelessness are not unique to this region, as racial discrimination and race are frequently disavowed worldwide. But when it comes to modern conceptualizations of race, it was indeed Europe that exported this calamitous ideology all over the world (El-Tayeb 2011).

Lay understandings in contemporary Europe often reflect a belief of race as a remnant of an imperial past despite its very active presence. Changing migration patterns, sociopolitical conflicts, forced evictions, human rights violations, and Russia's invasion of Ukraine (and the subsequent displacements) have prompted questions and conversations about who is white, who is Western, who gets to be a citizen, who belongs. But too often race is denied, or discussions of race quickly devolve into questions of *who* is racist, as illustrated by my ethnographic exchange with Alba and the *furgon* driver. Ever since my first fieldwork experiences in Albania in 2006, I have been told by a wide range of people (interlocutors in Northern and Central Albania, fellow scholars in fields such as Eastern European studies, diplomats, and Albanians in the wider diaspora) that there is no race in Albania. It is not here, but there, or elsewhere. Or race is not anywhere. A nonfactor, nonexistent, nonsense. Nationalism may be present—ethnicity too. Ethnic conflict, ethnic groups, ethnic cleansing, ethnic strife, ethnic unrest, ethnic hostility, ethnic feuds, ancient ethnic hatreds, ethnic tension, nationalist tension, tribal conflict, xenophobia, sectarianism—but not race; race is over *there*. At the same time, I, a Black woman, was experiencing multiple encounters about race; over time these encounters shaped longer conversations and discussions. Race and racial logics were in fact very present (and are still present) in Albania, but perhaps many people were trying to articulate that Albania's racial landscape was not the same as that of the United States or the West broadly. With this in mind I have set out to study race in terms of what Ruth Wilson Gilmore argues are distinct yet densely interconnected social and political geographies (Card 2020). I do not ask what American or Western frameworks of race tell us about Albania but rather, what can an ethnographic and locally situated study of Albania tell us about race?

At times race can function as ethnicity, or ethnicity and nation can become race. Many sociological texts distinguish race and ethnicity in terms of ascription. Whereas ethnicity is thought of as self-ascribed, race is assigned, and while race is rigid and speaks to a valuation on merit, ability, or worth, ethnicity may be considered more flexible and typically celebrated (Cornell and Hartmann 2007). Yet race, to invoke Stuart Hall (2021), is a sliding signifier. The productions, meanings, articulations, and delineations of race are constantly shifting. When it comes to Eastern Europe and Eurasia in particular, the production and reproduction of global and local racial grammars and logics has meant that ethnicity is at times "imbued with racial connotations" (Zakharov and Law 2017, 12). In the field of East and Southeast European studies, race is often hidden in articulations of nationhood (Baker 2018). As anthropologist Damani Partridge writes, "Nationalism is a reassertion of 'the natural' in terms of both its racial and gendered articulations" (2012, 41), and while not as common today, historically, conceptualizations of race have been intimately tied with nations, for example, the German race or the Nordic race (Roland 2013). Later chapters will illustrate how contemporary articulations of identity in Albania continue to couple nation with race. To argue, therefore, that the Balkans is outside of race and can only be studied through the lens of ethnicity and nation implies distinct boundaries between these concepts—boundaries that are in fact much more fluid, intersecting, and imbricated. These are not benign social categories but overlapping constructs that play hide-and-seek with one another (Hall 2017). While I emphasize race's importance, I do not mean to imply that it is deterministic (Winant 2001) but rather to highlight how race has and continues to hierarchize societies along imagined axes of whiteness, blackness, and otherness.

Humans have long recognized differences between people, but most scholars of race have argued that it was not until the age of European Enlightenment that such differences were racially categorized (Winant 2000; Smedley 1998; Omi and Winant 1994; Goldberg 2002). Scholars such as Geraldine Heng (2018) have traced race's invention to the Middle Ages, whereby religion operated socially and biologically to shape a hierarchy of humanness with varying access to power and resources. Others such as Sonia T. Seeman (2023) have considered the ways that non-Western entities such as the Ottoman Empire relied on racialized constructions of black g-----s to constitute Turkishness.[5] The conversation of race and the origins of racial thinking will continue to expand, but we do know that the eighteenth- and nineteenth-century understandings of race, as shaped by European exploration, colonialism, and the quest for scientific rationality, profoundly shaped new ideas about humanness, power, and worth (Turda and Quine 2018). There is much utility in the concept for studying those hierarchal orderings that often silently structure the globe (Wekker 2016).

Eighteenth-century naturalists like Carl Linnaeus, often called "the Father of Taxonomy," created systems to classify the natural world. About his research, Linnaeus is thought to have said, "God created, Linnaeus classified" (Blunt and Stearn 1971). His 1758 publication of *Systema naturae* divided humans into four varieties: *Europaeus albus* (those from Europe), *Americanus rubescens* (those from the Americas), *Asiaticus fuscus* (those from Asia), and *Africanus niger* (those from Africa). These classifications included phenotypic features such as skin color, hair texture, and body posture, but also personality traits, clothing, and form of government. The variety of *Europaeus*, for example, was classified as "white and sanguine, with plenty of yellow hair and blue eyes, wise, inventor, protected by tight clothing, and governed by rites." *Africanus*, by contrast, was categorized as "black, phlegmatic, and lazy, flat nose, swollen lips, women with breasts lactating profusely, sluggish, neglectful, and governed by choice" (Linné 1964). In subsequent work he would even refer to a classification of *Homo troglodytes*, a beastly species thought to be separate from humans. Such categorizations would have lasting impacts, including the ways that scientific thinkers in the Balkans would later use the term "Troglodytes" to refer to Albanians (Jezernik 2004). Ideas of human groups or varieties (Blumenbach 1795) would develop over time, giving race its malleable form.[6] Later figures such as French thinker Joseph-Arthur, Count de Gobineau (1915) would go on to define certain races as inherently superior and others as naturally inferior.

The resulting races and racial logics derive from what Sylvia Wynter (2003) considers an Enlightenment representation of the human, a construct that would go on to deeply shape our global understandings of humanness, including anthropological inquiry. Some scholars have argued that during his lifetime, the naturalist Johann Blumenbach, who coined the term "Caucasian," was a vocal opponent of slavery and racism, and in his work he often questioned whether race was biological at all (Junker 2018). Yet, as framed by these Enlightenment-era works, combined with later surges in social Darwinist beliefs, increasing global imperialism, and eugenics movements, the idea of race itself would continually be cemented as biological fact. Though the twentieth century would later also witness a rejection of scientific racism, these imagined taxonomies of human varieties morphed into the racial thinking that continues to animate global society today. Race remains stealthy and enduring, sustained by deeply embedded racial logics that are difficult to reimagine (Turda and Quine 2018; Winant 2001).

As aforementioned, the Balkan region has been more commonly theorized in terms of how ethnicity and nation have organized social relations (Baker 2018; Bjelić 2018, 2021). This tendency has shaped an assumed racelessness that emerges in two ways: an understanding of race as an inapplicable concept, and racelessness as an invocation to refute an idea of malice or hate. This denial of race is not limited to the Balkans or Eastern Europe, as race is disavowed across Europe, particularly in the post–World War II landscape. If, as anthropologist Matti Bunzl (2005) once theorized, the European Union envisions itself as a project that is the antithesis of Nazism and the Holocaust, then it might be expected that the majority of European countries might see themselves as outside of race (Goldberg 2006). As a US-based scholar of race I have been questioned about epistemological hegemony (Khan 2019) when it comes to studying race in Europe. However, to reiterate Fatima El-Tayeb, race finds many of its origins in Europe, and contrary to commonly held beliefs, race did not dissipate with the Nazis. This disavowal of race, or "antiracialism," as David Theo Goldberg (2009b) terms it, illustrates the intensity with which many want to get over or forget race.

A key argument of this book is that scholars can analyze racialization and racial logics as they manifest globally yet emerge in varying local ways. Race is not a constant variable but rather an epistemological tool (Khan 2019) that speaks to complex exchanges, shared logics of sense-making, and structures of power that facilitate and maintain societal hierarchies (Khan 2019; Lemon 2019; Chang and Rucker-Chang 2020; Goldberg 2009a; Pierre 2013; Wekker 2016). The Balkans have often been overlooked or excluded from scholarly conversations about race, but they should not be (Rexhepi 2023; Baker 2018). Recent work by Piro Rexhepi (2023) illuminates the forms of global raciality that have marked and continue to shape Balkan landscapes, even when race is denied or dismissed. When we turn attention away from a singular focus of measuring degrees of racism and notions of racial division, and toward a consideration of processes that give race its meanings, we can see that even these claims to racelessness are actually shaped by racial logics that continually shape who is white, marginally white, *off* white (Mills 1997; Baker et al. 2024), and how Eastern Europeans become more or less white over time (Böröcz 2021; Kalmar 2022).

Tied to these assertions of racelessness are local rejections of race, as for many, race is immediately associated with malice. I elaborate this topic further in the book's second chapter, but many of my Albanian interlocutors sincerely believe that Albanians are incapable of expressing racism because they are naturally respectful and welcoming, particularly of foreigners and guests. Whether in my research with my neighbors in Tirana or Shkodra, or with strangers at a *byrek* shop in the Bronx,[7] I often promptly hear, "Why are you writing about race? Albanians are not racist." The immediate mention of race implies a fear about racism and therefore an assumption of malice or even hatred. This is counter to their deeply held Albanian values of hospitality and respect. The conversation elicits a particular discomfort, especially in post–World War II Europe. And for many of my Albanian interlocutors, their own experiences of marginalization within both Western and Eastern Europe produce common understandings that they experience racism as always outside others, but there is no such notion of race in Albania.

Albania provides an ideal setting to probe the dynamics and discourses of race in relationship to hospitality, respect, and the treatment of foreigners. In this book I include the ways that I myself am positioned as a guest and foreigner, and how my feelings and what it means to be welcome and well received are prioritized. The ethnographic research in this book traces these cultural forms as tied to racialization and race-making as beliefs and understandings about respect and hospitality lead many to assert that any negative experiences reflect presumed demographic homogeneity and the lack of multiculturalism, purported ignorance, or a particular *mentalitet* (mentality)—but not race. At the end of World War II, Albania, for instance, was the only European country where the number of Jewish people was higher than at the outset of the war. It is also a country where many cling tightly to religious tolerance and social harmony, particularly in relation to neighboring former Yugoslavia. For many of my interlocutors there is an attachment to racelessness as further shaped by Albania's communist past, a past that for many symbolized anti-imperialism and anti-racism, and one that has shaped a raceless place. As such, and as will be shown in later chapters, for many of my interlocutors, even the mention of race speaks to their conceptions of not only what it means to be racist but also what it means to be Albanian.

Race cannot be understood simply in terms of interpersonal hostility but more broadly as the racial logics that shape social relationships. These logics of race are present even amid practices of hospitality and articulations of racelessness.

One-dimensional conceptual frameworks do not attend to processes of racialization, and in fact I argue that the adamant proclamations of racelessness shed light on the ways that racialization is entrenched through denial. The effects of racialization have been consequential beyond measure, shaping empires, enslavement, genocide, structurally and institutionally embedded as it continuously demarcates power and the parameters of inclusion and exclusion. Race is quotidian, and racial logics are ordinary. Race continues to shape livelihoods and lifeworlds, still tied to power, still writing contracts (Mills 1997), still molding spaces of belonging and nonbelonging. Taking race as the ethnographic object and Albania as the ethnographic site of analysis, I ask, what are the actions, doings, and mechanisms by which people are racializing and being racialized—how does race happen? Why do people employ certain categories (i.e., race, whiteness, or blackness) and what are the historical situations that have shaped these belief formations (Zakharov and Law 2017, 10)?

Racial analyses give scholars windows and tools to study history and social formations, but racialization is not uniform—it involves many uneven processes (Heng 2018). Even as scholars trace these uneven processes, the discourse surrounding race is often fixed. Ethnography becomes a way to work through these tensions—to explore the sites, modes, and practices of race-making. Racialization and racial assemblages speak to the relationships between peoples, between bodies, and not necessarily defined oppositions or ancient enemies. Bodies are interrogated and become sites of racial formation (Fassin 2011; Lemon 2002), as "the body," writes Fassin, "is precisely where the dimensions of reality, experience, and expression are articulated.... Racialization is exerted, experienced, and performed through the body" (2011, 428). Similarly, Alaina Lemon asserts that like nation and gender, race too is about bodies but emphasizes that race speaks to the ways that people index connection *among* bodies (2002, 58). Racialization is about citizen bodies, noncitizen bodies (Partridge 2012), desired bodies, religious bodies, and migrant bodies—blackened bodies, browned bodies, and whitened bodies. Racialization speaks to how certain bodies are organized, read, named, recognized, or not—what it means to be Albanian, to be Greek, to be Serbian, to be European. In today's global age of migration and relocation, bodies transverse multiple planes, yet many forms of racialized identities continue to be imagined as concrete. This is demonstrated by the ways that the European body is imagined, the Muslim body, the Roma body, the invader body, the bodies that are *of* Europe as opposed to those *in* Europe (Goldberg 2006).

Racialization is about relationality, making it an apt analytical lens for exploring social relationships in Europe, with Europe situated as both a geographic referent and geopolitical concept (Boatcă 2010). Albania occupies a marginal space in Europe, and many Albanians articulate a longing for Europe or lament about not being *real* Europeans. My interlocutors regularly express their frustrations about the country's social and economic landscape and the normalization of political corruption: "it is inescapable," my friend Mira frequently tells me. Europe, in this case Western Europe, is a place to escape to, and European belonging is intensely sought after—Europe is imagined as less corrupt, more modern, more superior, more developed (Boatcă 2010). Race is about imagination, and the racialization of the Balkans has been constitutive of the formation of Europe as superior and of European whiteness. A study of race in Albania, therefore, can illuminate who is imagined as European and who is not—a window to understanding who is imagined as inferior, as primitive, as backward, as those with "lesser whiteness" (Boatcă 2006), the not *quite* white (Kalmar 2022), and therefore those who are not "authentically" European.

Peripheral Whiteness and the So-called N*iggers of Europe

The afternoon was sleepy. A man sat on a small chair at a coffee shop near Tirana's city center. When I first walked by, he gave me a glance then turned away. But then he called out to me with sort of a wave and asked why I was in Albania. I smiled and explained that I was a researcher writing an ethnography about race. "Oh, you are writing about race," he asked, with an expression somewhere between intrigue and appreciation. "Well, look at us!" he continued. "Albanians are the n*ggers of Europe! Do you know how they treat us in England? In Greece? In Italy? We are *the n*ggers*!" His voice grew shakier at this point as he yelled with greater intensity. I listened. As he returned to his chair he said, "Make sure you write about that."

This exchange in the fall of 2013 was not the first time I had an Albanian person express an equivalence between Albanians and Black people. In fact, by this point I had heard variations of this assertion multiple times, from conversations around dinner tables to watching hip-hop videos where music artists like Noizy portray Albanians as gangstas coming straight out of the ghetto. Such sentiments commonly circulate, both within Albania as well as its broader diasporic community in the Balkans and Europe, and reflect how Albanians are racialized and imagined outside of Europe or Europeanness. This book follows racialization, not only because this is one way that people are made different but also because these racialization processes shape logics, livelihoods, and lines that delineate inclusion and marginality. Europe and Europeanness are continually demarcated and negotiated, and Albania continues to find itself Eastern, Southeastern, Balkan, and now Western Balkan, which does not even have an eastern correlate.

Albanians are rendered outside of European whiteness, but as I argue in this book, this rendering is partial, what I refer to as peripheral whiteness.

Peripheral whiteness calls attention to the ways that global racial orders shape paradoxical local landscapes, such that white European belonging is not fully conferred to Albanians, and at the same time, Albanians enact whiteness in relationship to those locally racialized as "black," particularly Roma and Balkan Egyptians. Sociologist Eduardo Bonilla-Silva (2018) asserts that race works in most societies without having a discursive space, but my research reveals the ways that racial discourse is present in Tirana's everyday vernacular. The racial discourse includes the ways that Albanians are racialized outside of European whiteness and the language of *dorë e bardhë* ("white hands" or "white side") and *dorë e zezë* ("black hands" or "black side"), whereby Albanians are racialized as white while Roma and Balkan Egyptians are racialized as black. Peripheral whiteness attends to race's shifting nature, as Albanians are simultaneously racialized in and outside of whiteness, and how understandings of blackness for Roma and Egyptians may shift yet they remain outside of the boundaries of whiteness. This concept additionally takes into consideration what it means to long for European belonging as shaped by Albania's particular histories of imperialism and state socialism, and contemporary aspirations for European Union membership. It highlights the angst produced by the longing for what people consider to be full inclusion within Europe, revealing what it means to *feel* and *not feel* white (Essed and Trienekens 2008). Europe is imagined as superior, as first-rate, as a promise to get to, as a whiteness to attain. In chapters 3 and 4 I ask what it means for Albanians, Roma, and Egyptians to assert whiteness or blackness, and under what conditions do people employ this racialized language? What does this tell us about race as assigned categories but also the language of race as a means of empowerment?

This analytic of peripheral whiteness is further informed by Cedric Robinson's notion of racial capitalism, calling attention to the genesis of race and racialization *within* Europe; the terms of whiteness were largely constructed outside of East Europe and those othered as Eastern/Muslim/Slavic/Roma were the first to be racialized outside of whiteness, with terms such as "slav," "g----," and "Muslim" having long served as racial markers (Robinson 2000; see also Mark 2022). The expansion of Western capitalism, Robinson argues, was itself racialized, and social hierarchization of so-called racial groups was thought to be natural. Albania's position within racial capitalism must be nuanced, as Albania occupies a place of peripheral whiteness in relationship to Western Europe, yet contemporary understandings of racial capitalism produce local racial logics within Albania that demarcate the value of humanity as shaped by capitalist structures (Jodi 2015). Such structures shape the livelihoods of Albanians, Roma, and Egyptians and their proximities to whiteness and blackness. In the case of Albanians, peripheral whiteness speaks to the paradoxes of the space of the margin, where Albanians are racialized outside of some boundaries of the white world and simultaneously have historically performed whiteness for Western audiences, as well as performing whiteness locally.

Peripheral whiteness further attends to the lived experiences of Albanians outside of Albania, in Kosova[8] and in the Albanian diaspora throughout Europe. Russell King and Nicola Mai have produced multiple studies of Albanian migration in Italy; in one of their texts they interview an Albanian migrant who says that "*Albanian* is the adjective Italian people use when they show contempt for something" (2008, 188). As I further demonstrate in chapter 3, my Albanian interlocutors share similar sentiments about their experiences in Greece and the United Kingdom, in which they feel that "Albanian" is equated with "outsider," "intruder," or "criminal." The recent discourse surrounding Albanian migration to the UK has further illustrated the ways that Albanians have been perceived and named. In 2022 Albanians accounted for the highest number of asylum seekers entering the UK through the English Channel. Britain's interior minister, Home Secretary Suella Braverman, questioned the legitimacy of Albanian asylum claims, referring to the migration crisis as an "invasion" and to Albanian migrants as "criminals" who pretend to be refugees in distress (Casciani 2022). Braverman's comments reflect the increasing global anti-migrant sentiment, but they also illuminate the racial logics that shape Europeanness and Albanianness, whereby Albanians are not thought to be authentically European and therefore not white.

Such logics additionally exist in the Balkan region, where Albanians are relegated to a realm of otherness, particularly in relationship to Slavic groups. Writing about the former Yugoslavia in the late 1990s, author Slavenka Drakulić (1999) maintained that many Albanians lived under an apartheid system: "The Albanians were never integrated into the country's social, political, and cultural life. They existed separately from us, barely visible people on the margins of our society, with their strange language that nobody understood, their tribal organization, blood feuds, different habits and dress. . . . It was clear that they belonged to a different category from Serbs, Croats, Macedonians, Montenegrins or Slovenes." Chapters 3 and 5 of this book include further elaboration on this subject, but I share Drakulić's reflection here as a means of illustrating the interconnectedness of the constructions of Albanianness, whereby both Western and Eastern Europe locate Albanians as outsiders and outcasts. Returning to the fieldwork encounter, this articulation of the n*ggers of Europe speaks to the ways Albanians are marginalized within southeastern Europe, as shaped by linguistic, religious, and, I add, racialized othering. These claims to blackness illustrate the ways that group dynamics take shape and how people might articulate what it means to feel black, but the articulation of blackness also draws attention to the ways that borders, resources, and social inclusion are racialized as shaped by logics of hierarchy and exclusion.

Race is about imagination, and many narratives of race, ethnicity, and nation in the Balkans have focused on national narratives of people groups and who make claims to certain identities. Some of the more popular narratives might sound familiar; for example, Bulgarians might make claims about Macedonians *really* being Bulgarian, Serbians might make claims about Bosnians *really* being Serbian, but rarely is this the case with Albanians or Roma in the Balkans. Kosova, for example, might be proclaimed as Serbia in terms of geopolitical territory, but Kosovar Albanians are not claimed as Serbian. Roma are regularly relegated to realms of perpetual strangers. The rhetoric of ancient enemies or ethnic hatred is also not new to this region, as these are some of the more common frameworks for studying nation and ethnicity. With this book I am trying to disrupt the idea of natural ethnic or racial hatreds, to complicate the discussion of race in the Balkan region and also situate the Balkans, and Albania in particular, into broader studies of race. Identity politics and narratives of difference and xenophobia are not new to this Balkan region, but I am arguing for an attenuated ethnographic lens that examines racialization in a particular way. The local constructions, articulations, and assemblages of race carry multiple significations, and ethnography allows me to trace them. Such an approach, I believe, enables a relational analysis of race, where the emphasis is not solely on comparative study but rather parallel and interlocking racialization processes.

On Conducting Ethnography of Race in the Communist Afterlife

Sometimes even the mention of the word "fieldwork" gives me a slight chuckle as I am always questioning what it means to be in "the field." My family and many of my interlocutors certainly find it odd that I refer to my research as *field*work. I regularly get asked, "What are you doing in Albania?" and "Why are you *here*?" "Why are you *there*?" There is a level of puzzlement as well as an understandable suspicion about my research. Am I an intruder? Am I a spy? Why would someone get funding to study in Albania? For some the idea is obscure, and for others it is absurd.

This was the case for my neighbor, Lindita, who owned a bread shop near the apartment where I stayed in 2013 and 2014. I often purchased bread from her, and our exchanges usually involved *muhabet* (chitchat) about my day, my family, my seemingly odd "research." Lindita and her son were very friendly, always checking to make sure I had everything I needed. They would show special concern when I walked to my apartment alone in the evenings, as it is atypical for women to live alone in Albania. One day when I visited Lindita, she was deep in conversation with another customer ahead of me. This customer had curly black hair and a beauty mark above her right eyebrow. "Mirëdita" (Good afternoon), I said, as I waited my turn. Lindita popped her head around and smiled as I said, "Ç'kemi?" (What's up?). "She is a foreigner, an American," Lindita said to the customer. "Oh, okay," the customer replied, "because I was wondering who she was." Her facial response was a combination of hesitation and bemusement that I had grown accustomed to seeing. "Do you miss your husband?" Lindita asked me, a frequent inquiry I received. "Yes, of course, a lot," I said. She smiled. "Why, where is her husband? Is he not here?" the customer asked, directing her question to Lindita and not me. "Oh no, he is in the US," I told her. "Why?" she demanded. "He has to work," Lindita interjected, demonstrating her familiarity with my life story. "He works for the government," I further explained, "so he is in the States while I live in Tirana." The customer looked at me somewhat disappointedly. "He will be here in March," I added, "to visit me for a while." "And is he like you?" she asked. "Or is he white?" "He is like me," I told her. "What is the word for your people—how are you called?" she asked. I settled on "people of color" (*njerëz me ngjyrë*), not feeling in the mood to have a longer conversation about the use of words like *zezakë*[9] or even *Amerikane-Afrikane*, which is loaded with assumptions about whether I am *really* from Africa, because in the Balkans it is commonly assumed that only white Americans are the *real* Americans.

Turning away from me and back to Lindita, the customer asked, "But why is she here? What is she doing here?" Lindita told her that I am in Tirana to conduct research for a book about Albania, her face beaming proudly as she knew information about me. "Well, *kismet zotit* [if God gives the chance] to write a book," I added, a common expression hoping for good fate. "Well, how long are you going to stay in Albania?" "She is going to stay eight years," Lindita answered. I quickly interjected that at that time I had traveled back and forth in Albania over the past eight years, but my current duration was only for one year. The conversation continued with questions about my hair, and how I could keep my locs together. "Is it fake hair?" the customer asked Lindita, to which Lindita responded with the quintessential facial response that said, "Why the hell would I know?" They still looked puzzled even once I said that my hair was my actual hair and not fake.

The customer changed the subject. "So where do you live here in Albania?" "Nearby," I told her. "In a rented apartment." "You live alone?" As she awaited my response, she looked appalled that I might just say yes. "Yes," I responded. She gasped as they were both taken aback. I am not sure why Lindita reacted this way because she already knew this, yet she still gasped as though this were new information. "And how much do you pay in rent?" Lindita asked me. "Two hundred and fifty euros," I told them. They did not think that it was necessary that I should pay that much to live alone, and my ability to do so certainly reflected a level of privilege inaccessible for most Albanian families. They were even more flabbergasted when I explained that I had a research fellowship that paid for my expenses. "Someone pays for you to live here, eh? And to write about Albania?" the customer asked. I nodded in affirmation, and not the American up-and-down nod but the Albanian quick side-to-side nod. Their faces seemed frozen in perplexity. "I can understand this, though," the customer began. "Americans come here because we are warm, nice, friendly people. Americans are really cold, right?" she asked, her face searching mine for confirmation. I hesitated but then realized that what she really wanted me to do was to acknowledge how nice Albanians are. "Well, Albanians are very warm and hospitable," I told her.

"So, all you do every day is write, just write about Albania?" the customer asked. "Yes," I told her, which garnered further strange looks. "Where did you learn Albanian? Did you take a course or something?" I told her that I took a course in Tirana at the university and another at a language center. "And you are going to write a book about Albania?" "Yes, ultimately a book about Albanian culture and society," which was my concise way to describe the book. "Eh, culture, so Albanians have culture, huh?" Lindita asked, and the two of us laughed. "So will all of this be available in Albania when you are done?" the customer asked me. I assured her that I would do my best to make it available. "Well, just make sure you only write good stuff," Lindita remarked. "How old are you?" the customer asked me. "Twenty-seven." "Do you have any kids?" she pressed. "No, not yet." "Will you have kids?" she asked. I told them I hoped to do so someday but at that time it was important to finish my research. "Important, to write about Albania?" the customer asked, as she snickered. "You need to have a child now," Lindita added. "She is young," the customer retorted, but Lindita's face showed that she was not convinced.

I share this story to highlight my own positionality and relationship to my research—to explore what it means to do anthropology, to do ethnography in Albania. I first took Introduction to Cultural Anthropology my first year of college, and one of the books assigned for that course was Collin Turnbull's *The Forest People* (1962). Set in what was then known as the Belgian Congo, Turnbull documents his experiences with the Indigenous Mbuti people over a period of three years. The book is framed as a study of "pygmy" people or the "forest people." The term "pygmy" was used by white anthropologists in the late nineteenth and early twentieth centuries to denote a group of people who were darker-skinned and of a shorter stature. The term itself emerges from the idea of encounter: what happened when white people, white anthropologists, encountered persons who did not look like them, subsequently named them, studied, and analyzed them? Years before Turnbull's study, Mbuti people were regularly captured and forced into zoos (Newkirk 2015). *The Forest People*, set decades later, is an in-depth account of the cultural and ritualistic practices of the Mbuti, and Turnbull attempts to write about them in a more complex and humanizing way, one that contrasts with the human zoos. At the same time, it is impossible to separate Turnbull's book from the broader facets of colonialism and exoticism that have shaped the field of anthropology.

I initially assumed that all ethnographic research was like Turnbull's, particularly the idea that an individual, often Western, anthropologist traveled somewhere far away and studied a distinct people group and their culture, especially those most unlike *us*. In my early days as an anthropology student, I did not have the tools to adequately critique these ideas or to probe deeper questions about what it means to *do* ethnography. I did not get much exposure to ethnographies written by people of color, and as such, many of the ethnographic texts I read were largely by white outside observers who studied, labeled, and named people of color and Indigenous groups. I did not yet grasp that when authors wrote about what it meant to study those most unlike *us*, the *us* in those ethnographies did not necessarily include *me*.

Turnbull's text reflects what may be considered a more classical example of how to do ethnography, and the field of anthropology has long since taken more reflexive, engaged, and experimental turns. Texts such as *Women Writing Culture* (Behar and Gordon 1995) and *Black Feminist Anthropology* (McClaurin 2001) have shaped the way that I, a Black woman ethnographer, approach my research, which necessitates attentiveness to the relationship between the ethnographer, that is, the ethnographic self, and her interlocutors (Abu-Lughod 1991; Berdahl 1999; Ebron 2001; Visweswaran 1994). This relationship shapes processes of knowledge production as well as the circulation of that knowledge.

I first traveled to Albania in 2006 as part of an ethnoarchaeological project in the Shala Valley. I had never left the United States. Not only was Albania the first country that I visited, within two days of landing I found myself in a remote village where most of the people had never met a Black person. At that time most of the residents of the valley rarely traveled outside of Northern Albania, and because the Shala region at that time was not very accessible by car, few foreigners had ever visited. Stares and followings became the norm as people tried to make sense of my presence in Theth and Shala. I did not speak Albanian in the summers of 2006 and 2007, but I knew from my immediate interactions with people that they had lots of questions, and whenever I was with Albanian-speaking members of our archaeological team, they would be inundated with inquiries about me and why I was in Albania. People would touch my skin to see if it rubbed off, would grab my hair to feel its texture, and occasionally ask for a picture when we visited the closest largest city.

This curiosity is what initially spurred my interests in cultural anthropology and the study of race in a global context, but as an anthropologist researching race in a space often thought to be raceless, many challenges have arisen as I negotiate my positionality as a woman, a Black woman, and a Black woman anthropologist, as well as the impact that my ethnographic research has on those around me. Rather than positioning myself as "the knower" and Albanians, Roma, or Balkan Egyptians as objects of inquiry to be known, this book takes race as its ethnographic object as I follow, trace, and map racialization and race-making. In doing so, the book also asks what it means to produce an ethnography about race in Albania as a Black woman. What do my encounters reveal about the ways that race is understood? What responsibility do I, as an ethnographer, have to my interlocutors, particularly considering the ways that Albanians and Eastern Europeans are constantly responding to what people think about them, especially Americans? Conversations like the one at the bakery initially seemed to be interruptions in the research process or minutiae at best. Over time, however, I have come to see how such encounters and interactions are key for mapping how both race and ethnography operate.

As I ethnographically trace race, I highlight the ways that my Black female body is questioned, read, harassed, categorized, and labeled. I also draw attention to the ways that some Roma and Egyptians express a shared racialized position with me, that we are all "black" folks. It has not been uncommon for interlocutors to discuss a connectedness and at times fictionalized kinship, for example, with my Egyptian interlocutor Shpresa, who often refers to me as her sister. Such moments are a part of the ethnographic research process as they further highlight how race is named and understood. Paulla Ebron (2001) elucidates various ways to appreciate cultural tensions in the field, arguing that an autoethnographic approach must situate personal senses and memory of events alongside our analysis of sociocultural practices; these frameworks must include this intersection. While my experience is not necessarily autoethnographic, I argue that this type of critical reflexive ethnography is important for thinking about methodological and theoretical inquiry, as well as how we communicate and share situated knowledge (Haraway 1988; Collins 2000). Anthropologist Ida Susser once had this to say about ethnography: "Ethnography puts the self in the equation. . . . The self can be called into question in the process and in many cases is never quite the same afterwards. . . . A good ethnographer combines theoretical rigor with the continuing interpretation and rethinking of chance circumstance, everyday dynamics, historical events, and passing conversations. Such observations are not necessarily representative but rather indicative of larger conceptions" (2009, xi). Similarly, Jemima Pierre has noted the following about the positionality of the ethnographer: "The affirmation of personal narrative and experiences as legitimate sources of knowledge and the recognition that positionality (i.e., 'standpoint') is an important aspect of all knowledge production have endowed us with key theoretical and methodological insights. Further, the possibilities available for the insertion of the racialized female at the center of both research and analysis have opened up a space for nuanced critiques and innovative praxis" (2008, 128).

As a graduate student, I was at times warned about being ethnocentric when it came to how I responded to my own racialization in the field—that somehow I could be misreading what was going on around me, especially if my experiences with race were thought to be negative. With time I have also come to recognize the ways that others' scholarly anxiety about race (and ultimately, worry about racism and who is racist) can limit the opportunities to study it. Indeed, some of my ethnographic encounters have been painful, distressing, and at times difficult to name. My position as an anthropologist has often required a critical distancing, which has entailed periods of repression or deferral of emotional response to fieldwork encounters. The process of writing this book has given me the chance to think through these encounters as they relate to processes of race-making as well as my own standpoint. While this type of ethnographic sensitivity to the self could be termed "navel-gazing," I instead think of this approach as a way to recalibrate the ethnographic approach, to broaden the ways that anthropologists engage with inquiry surrounding positionality and the ethnographic stories, happenings, and encounters that make up fieldwork, and to engage Black feminist epistemology.

This book draws from detailed fieldnotes, observations, interviews, life histories, and archival research. The storytelling and writing feature key friends and interlocutors whom I have known for several years, but this is not necessarily meant to be a representation of all Albanian, Roma, or Egyptian people as much as it is designed to be a sociocultural analysis of racialization and race-making. Agreeing with anthropologists Kristen Ghodsee (2010), John Jackson (2005), and Kathleen Stewart (1996) that stories are not just products but are themselves productive, this book maps and highlights various scenes and stories of socioracial manifestations. Many of these stories were captured through *muhabet* and *bashkëbisedim*, which can be translated from Albanian as "table talk," "confabulation," and "conversation." These interactions have occurred over years, at café tables, lunch tables, dinner tables, and makeshift tables; on the side of the road, in cars, on *furgons*, and in living rooms; at birthday parties, New Year's parties, and street protests; while drinking coffee, wine, and raki;[10] during times of celebration and mourning. The manifestations I have captured are precarious, kinetic, vulnerable, defensive, and reactive, composed of forms and affects that produce racial assemblages, and speak to global racial formations, emplacement, and cultural forms of belonging. The present-day sociopolitical and economic landscape of Albania is riven with friction. It speaks to location, relocation, and dislocation. I explore forms of race-making through what I am calling a slowed ethnography of the everyday, a method that tries to capture the textures of the ethnographic present and those configurations that are not always immediately legible. This methodological attunement enables me to grapple with how racialized configurations emerge in a moment replete with intensity and precarity in Tirana.

Book Overview

This book's first chapter is a continued discussion of the communist afterlife. The chapter is divided into two parts. Part 1 is a semi-chronological overview that serves as a historical backdrop for the book. Part 2 of the chapter introduces the readers to the lives of three people whom I have followed over ten years: Mimoza, Shpresa, and Besa. Taken together, these ethnographic narratives trace histories, memories, anticipations, traumas, frustrations, and longings that animate the communist afterlife, revealing the ways that people are living out the contemporary moment. I ultimately argue that the story of the afterlife underscores the lingering forms of trauma, nostalgia, and longing that permeate the social landscape and shape how racialization is enacted.

As a Black woman anthropologist, I at times "live my anthropology" (Mwaria 2001, 204) as I experience racialization while I document it. In chapter 2 I engage with some of these questions of living this anthropology and set the stage for the reader to understand how particular racial encounters themselves serve as entry points for studying race-making in Tirana. The chapter begins with the retelling of my experience on a national Albanian TV show in 2013. What was initially planned as a conversation about my research quickly morphed into a vivid exchange with the show's host and a local psychologist about racism versus ignorance, during which I was frequently asked why I thought Albanians were racist. I use the events of the television recording to frame my ethnographic exploration of what I term "the Hunger Games," which speaks to the ways that hospitality, respect, and shame are enacted and how they are related to race. In doing so I am able to analyze sociracial identities in terms of authenticity and sincerity (Jackson 2005), examining claims of what it means to be authentically Albanian but also the ways that practices of honor and respect are thought to demonstrate what it means to sincerely be Albanian.

Chapters 3 and 4 focus on the variegated notions of whiteness and blackness in Albania as shaped by global racial orders. Chapter 3 includes an expanded analysis of peripheral whiteness through an examination of the history and historiography of race, as well as contemporary manifestations. This chapter additionally includes ethnographic accounts from Albanian return migrants from Greece and how they have navigated this peripheral whiteness. Examples like this one highlight what it means to long for whiteness as shaped by Albania's particular histories with Ottoman imperialisms, communism, and contemporary aspirations, and the subsequent angst over the desire to belong in Europe.

In Chapter 4 I turn attention to blackness and the racialization of Roma and Balkan Egyptians in Albania.[11] The story of blackness is complex and imbricated, involving multiple names, but the construction of these naming practices yields insight into historical and ongoing processes that have racialized Roma and Egyptians outside of whiteness, Europeanness, and Albanianness. In this chapter I historically and ethnographically trace race through six connected key terms of "black" subjectivities: *arixhi* (bear tamer), *gabel* (stranger), *Roma* ("man" or "person" in Romani language), *jevg* (deriving from the term *jevgjit*, a variation of "Egypt"), *Egjiptian* (Egyptian), and finally *dorë e zezë* ("black hands" or "black side"). By exploring these terms, I reveal what local racialization processes can illustrate about the ways that race travels and shapes social worlds.

As I explore throughout the book, discussions of race oftentimes collapse into the question of *who* is racist. In chapter 5 I explore what *counts* as racist or not and ask what these logics reveal about race-making in the Balkans and Europe. To ask another way, how is racism imagined, named, disguised, ignored, and what does this tell us about race? This chapter is divided into three acts. Act 1 examines a 2014 football match between Albania and Serbia that ended in a major brawl.[12] Act 2 is an exploration of blackface and brownface on an Albanian variety television show. Act 3 focuses on forced evictions and displacement of Roma and Balkan Egyptian communities in Tirana. Together, these three areas speak to the multiscalar nature of race and racism in multiple arenas through the modes of sport and geopolitics, representation and performance, and the structural and spatial.

A final note as you read this text. One of my favorite Albanian expressions is "Sa do rrojmë, do mësojmë," meaning, "As long as we live, we will learn."[13] I have often clung to this saying as I have carried out this research about race. This book in many ways is about layered racializations, and ethnography enables me to explore these layers. This work has emerged over numerous years through many friendships and relationships, over innumerable coffees and meals, with people who have graciously invited me into their homes and their lives. I am grateful to these friends and interlocutors who have helped me as I examine, analyze, and map, to help me see that as we live, we learn. Long-term ethnographic engagement has provided me the chance to build relationships with people, recognizing that people are not just racial objects but rather occupy various racial subject positions (Jackson 2005). I noted earlier that race itself is deeply entrenched within our social fabrics and is also difficult to reimagine. This difficulty, however, does not mean that it is impossible. I return then to the saying "Sa do rrojmë, do mësojmë."

1

THE COMMUNIST AFTERLIFE

I could tell that Mimoza was a bit taken aback when she asked what I was doing later that day. I told her that I was going to have a coffee with a friend who was helping me find a new place to stay in Tirana because my current landlords were selling their place. Mimoza, a woman I sometimes affectionately refer to as my Albanian auntie, was hosting me and a friend of hers for lunch that day. I knew right after I mentioned my need for a new apartment that I probably should not have said anything because she would wonder why I had not simply asked to rent the spare room at her house. Mimoza and I first met the previous year, in 2008, and at that time I was looking for an apartment and a friend introduced us. Mimoza had recently lost her husband and had a room to rent, ideally to a young woman. During our first interaction, though, Mimoza eagerly explained that if I lived with her, she would provide a space and cook, clean, and do laundry for me. "She says that she will take care of everything, especially since you are a young woman alone in Tirana," my friend translated. "She wants to be like your grandmother. And she makes some of the best food in Tirana," he added with a lively smile. I did not speak much Albanian at the time, and I asked my friend how Mimoza would react to my schedule, which often involved significant time outside the house, writing and thinking alone in cafés, having coffees with multiple new people, including sometimes men, and traveling to other Albanian towns, sometimes on my own. They discussed this and Mimoza grew concerned. She told my friend that she would want me to follow more of a schedule and to be home at certain times, especially for meals. To the extent possible, she wanted to know where I would be at all times. She did not like the idea of me traveling anywhere alone, even on a bus. I ultimately chose a different apartment, but since I had heard that Mimoza was such a great cook, and since I was still learning Albanian, my friend suggested that I could visit her weekly for cooking and Albanian lessons. Now many months later I found myself in her kitchen telling her that I needed a new place to live. "I know!" she announced. "You should have a coffee with my niece. She has an older vacant apartment and I think it will work well for you. I will give her a call now. The apartment is in December 21st [21 Dhjetori]." "Wait, what did you say?" I asked, confused as to why she said a date. "The apartment," she said, "it is in December 21st."

Ish 21 Dhjetori. The area that used to be the 21st of December, named for Stalin's birthday. Though at that time the communist regime had fallen nearly twenty years prior, most people in Tirana still referred to the neighborhood by the name of what it *used to be*. The same would happen with directions, when someone would tell you to get off the bus at *ish stacioni i fundit* ("what used to be the last bus stop"). The first time someone told me this, I asked whether it was the current last stop, and he replied, "Well, of course not, but it used to be." Statues of Enver, Stalin, and Lenin once stood prominently in Tirana's city center, keeping watch over the city's residents. Those statues were torn down, and streets and schools were renamed, but even some high schoolers today refer to their schools by the names they used to have, such as the school that *used* to be called January 11th, the date that marked the official proclamation of the People's Republic of Albania with Enver Hohxa as its head in 1946. I lived near that school for almost a year, and I still do not know its current official name. On my walks home from my friend Mira's house I would walk past an area called *ish ekspozita* (the location that used to be called Exposition). Ekspozita Shqipëria Sot, or Ekspozita as it was commonly known, had been the site of numerous shows, recordings, and concerts during the communist period, often heralded as a model of what Albania was building for the future—the future as it was imagined *në kohën e Enverit* (in Enver's time).

Contemporary Albania, in the time beyond Enver's time, is rife with reordering and restructuring. As I noted in the introduction, I do not argue that Albania's communist past is inescapable; rather, I want to draw attention to how the reverberations and echoes of communism shape the contemporary moment and its sociopolitical landscape. Some ethnographies include a distinct chapter contextualizing a particular place through a historical account. In this chapter I do offer historical writing that situates Albania's communist afterlife, one that does not necessarily speak to or represent every person's experience during the reign of the regime. I provide a broader overview of historical moments and then highlight the stories of particular people that I believe ethnographically illustrate some of the ways that people are living out the contemporary moment.

Throughout my fieldwork, many individuals have expressed sentiments of a lingering in-betweenness—between a communist past and a precarious future. The tightly embraced desires, opportunities, and anticipation that seemed possible at an earlier date had at some point become elusive. For some this has begun to engender fears of returning to a communist past. At the same time, others have expressed a longing to retreat to that same past, dismayed by unfulfilled promises of what Albania was to become. This chapter tries to contextualize and situate this in-betweenness.

These arrangements of the communist afterlife highlight the ways that race is configured and reconfigured. Racialization is textured; it involves attachments, affinities, and frictions. It speaks to the desires for Europe and the idea of being European. The doings and undoings of communism have shaped race-making processes that are not always acknowledged or immediately legible. The historical accounts and ethnography included in this chapter are key for setting the scene to explore race as Albania lingers between Hoxha's communist vision and capitalist democracy's promises of Europe. Part 1 broadly focuses on those doings of communism, where I delineate sections with keywords, many of which are terms that people have used in fieldwork to describe a particular season of the regime. Part 2 ethnographically chronicles aspects of the undoings. The communist afterlife has illuminated multilayered and imbricated borders, and in this chapter I reveal the folds, strands, sediments, and particles that shape the materiality of borders, the embodiment of borders, and the voices from the inside looking out as well as the outside looking in. I locate the fragments of longing and angst that tell the story of the present moment, particularly those that help us examine the racial logics that shape belonging.

The ethnographic stories in part 2 highlight how people are living through the contemporary moment as shaped by the residues and registers of the afterlife. The first story is about Mimoza, mentioned at the opening of this chapter. Mimoza's story provides an opportunity to explore larger questions through routine and regular interactions with one person, with a focus on how cruel optimism (Berlant 2011) animates the communist afterlife. The second story, the story of an event, similarly explores unmet expectations by chronicling the story of Shpresa and her daughter's fifth birthday party. Though chapters 4 and 5 of this book include closer analyses of Roma and Egyptian communities in Tirana, I include Shpresa's account in this chapter to illustrate some of the particularities of the afterlife for these socioracial groups. The third ethnographic story of this chapter is longer than the first two and focuses on the life of my friend Besa. I have closely followed Besa's life for more than twelve years. Her story offers a longer arc, across years, to think through some of the textures of the communist afterlife through one family.

Part 1
Plastic Flowers

The orange bus to Kombinat slowly made its way to the final stop. Passengers nonchalantly disembarked into the grinding summer heat. We made our way to Sharrë and eventually to the cemetery where we trekked up the hill to see the unassuming headstone marked Hoxha. The sun was particularly hot that day, but the plastic flowers did not melt. His grave was covered in them. Many people regularly make the journey to Varrezat e Popullit (the People's Cemetery) to visit the burial site of the former dictator. Once buried with an elaborate memorial

FIGURE 2. Grave of Enver Hoxha. Photo by author.

at the Cemetery of the Martyrs of the Nation, Hoxha's remains were relocated to the People's Cemetery in 1992. We watched for a while as people walked through the area, some specifically visiting the cemetery, others cutting through on their journey to the other side of the hill. We saw multiple people stop near Hoxha's grave site. For some, their visit was brief, a short encounter. Others dwelled a bit longer, perhaps searching for something, perhaps just passing the time. The plastic flowers clustered, gathering one by one, remaining, not fading.

One thing you should know about Enver Hoxha is that he believed he was a liberator. As leader of the newly formed Communist Party of Albania and the National Liberation Movement, Hoxha emerged onto the political scene at a time when Albanians had experienced numerous years of foreign occupation, by first Italy and later Nazi Germany during World War II. The group known as the National Liberation Movement, led by Hoxha, established the Democratic Government of Albania, a provisional government that would later give way to the People's Republic of Albania.

FIGURE 3. Enver Hoxha, Congress of Përmet, 1944. Photographer unknown. Wikimedia Commons.

In Hoxha's 1944 speech at the Democratic Government's arrival in Tirana, Hoxha proclaimed:

> People of Albania,
>
> Today another page is being opened in our history, a page which it is in our power to write, and which we shall make as glorious as our war against the occupiers: this is the battle to reconstruct Albania, restore the economy, raise the culture and education of our people, and raise their social, economic and political level. At the critical moment, our movement undertook that gigantic and unequal war and emerged victorious because our people were united as one around the National Liberation Front. Our national liberation movement will undertake this second struggle too, and will emerge victorious, because that is the dying wish of those who fell on the field of honour, because that is the entire life of the people and their future.[1]

This speech was strategically delivered on November 28, 1944, the anniversary of Albania's independence from the Ottoman Empire in 1912. Albania was the last Balkan country to achieve independence after nearly five hundred years of rule. When Hoxha portrayed himself as liberator and emancipator, it was thought that he was freeing Albania, not just from fascists during the Second World War but from all foreign enemies. The liberation of the country from fascism eventually became inseparable from the communist cause, as the wartime motto gained traction: "Death to fascism—freedom to the people!" (Mëhilli 2017). In the wake of the war there were nearly thirty thousand people dead in Albania and many villages destroyed. At the time of Hoxha's ascension to power, poverty and illiteracy were widespread throughout the country. The Italian occupation was viewed as a type of colonial occupation, and as such, the notion of social revolution carried much appeal (Mëhilli 2017). The initial airs of aspiration and possibility flowed throughout the country. As the Communist Party made its way to Tirana, members were joyously welcomed and celebrated, with people cheering and laying flowers at Hoxha's feet. Albanian historian Elidor Mëhilli maintains that the socialist future represented a new horizon across Eastern Europe, and while different people in the region had different relationships to it, the horizon existed nevertheless, "enforced by rules, extolled by propaganda, and made part of everyday life" (2017, 55).

Urbanization was a major theme of the regime's early years. Prior to the beginning of the communist period, the majority of the Albanian society lived in rural regions. The first decade of the regime witnessed a rural exodus (Sula-Raxhimi 2021), with more than a quarter of the population living in urban areas, a number that doubled by the 1960s. This increase in movement was tightly regulated by the state and directly shaped by industrialization and rapid economic changes as Hoxha worked to build factories and create jobs. Hoxha remained steadfast in his mission to create an independent country and a united Albanian people.

The purges began early. A significant number of the country's elite had already been forced into exile by the war's end and many of those that remained were killed or detained by the regime. Historian Isa Blumi remarks that during the early years, "Coercive labor was also a key element to producing an atmosphere conducive to state power. Often forced labor was used to sanitize Albania of its dissidents while 'developing' a 'modern' society" (1997, 386). Blumi argues that those dissidents were often from Northern Albania. Whereas prior to the war many of the country's leaders hailed from the North, Hoxha favored those like himself who were from the South. This shift in political control and overall southern disposition and superiority would have lasting impacts on the country, especially as it pertains to racialization and identity formation. This is not to suggest that Hoxha did not also target people from Southern Albania. Hoxha was known to make use of violent and deadly tactics even against those close to him. An example derives from the case of Abaz Omari, Hoxha's own cousin and schoolmate. Towards the end of WWII Omari sided with the nationalists and not the communists, and because of this, he was executed once Hoxha came to power (Fevziu et al. 2016).

There is a reason that an entire neighborhood area of Tirana was named after Stalin's birthday. Hoxha's regime was closely aligned with the Soviet Union, and while they resisted a close relationship with the former Yugoslavia, Hoxha's allegiance to Stalin seemed at times impenetrable. One of the more marked ways that Stalinism manifested in Albania was through labor. As Mëhilli notes, the Soviets did not invade Albania with people but rather with machinery and work styles, as evident through such projects as Kombinat, the first factory to be built from scratch under the Hoxha regime (Mëhilli 2017). Land was confiscated from wealthier people and divided into collective farms. Many families were relocated to control and restrict movement, as well as through the regime's plan to promote brotherhood and unity among all Albanians. Hoxha implemented compulsory education and led efforts to eradicate illiteracy. Women and men both worked in various industries, and the regime emphasized marriage and childbearing as dutiful practices of Albanian nationhood.

Repression and terror were woven into the everyday societal fabric. Even after the death of Stalin, Hoxha remained Stalinist, executing those branded as party enemies (*armiq*) and charging people with imaginary crimes (Mëhilli 2017). Labor camps and prisons for party and national enemies continued to expand. Those families with people who openly expressed dissent were unfortunately familiar with trauma and torture. For those few who somehow managed to escape the country, for example, those who fled from prisons and made it to the former Yugoslavia, their families were stigmatized and often experienced community isolation, and at times they were even imprisoned. One interlocutor told me that because of having a family member who fled the country, his family was always looked at *me një sytë tjetër*, meaning "a different kind of eye." They had what was commonly referred to as a bad biography. Many of those considered national traitors were interned at the most notorious labor camp in Tepelenë, nicknamed "the Albanian Auschwitz" (Mernacaj 2021). Barbed wire surrounded the entirety of the camp where entire families were imprisoned; numerous people died from malnutrition and starvation. This camp, along with the prison in Burrel, was reserved for the most sworn enemies of the state, often those who were members of the elite and more educated classes prior to communism (Mernacaj 2021).

Albania slowly broke all ties with the Soviet Union after the death of Stalin. Hoxha did not believe that Nikita Khrushchev's policies were aligned with Stalin, and further, during the larger Sino-Soviet split, Albania decided to align with China. As the fifties turned into the sixties, the Soviets gradually suspended their economic support for Albania and China increased theirs. Inspired by Mao's cultural revolution, Hoxha began a series of purges, specifically targeting those religious leaders who remained in the country, as well as officials in the military and Politburo. Religion was formally outlawed, and Albania declared an official national religion of atheism, the only country to this day to have ever done so. "Feja e Shqiptarit është Shqiptaria" (The religion of Albanians is Albanianism) goes the saying from late nineteenth-century poet Pashko Vasa during the country's national awakening. And such sentiments seemingly animated Hoxha's actions as nearly two thousand religious institutions and buildings were physically destroyed. Religious leaders like Catholic bishops from the North were forced to clean streets and bathrooms, at times having to dress up like clowns and wear signs that said, "I have sinned against the people" (Blumi 1997). Apart from high-ranking party officials, personal car ownership was banned. Hoxha increasingly employed fear tactics to cement control. Afraid that the country would someday be invaded by outsiders, Hoxha began a nationwide security program, which eventually led to the erection of nearly 700,000 concrete bunkers, of which many remain intact due to their weight and size.

Though Hoxha's regime had the support of China, and despite its insistence on self-sufficiency, the government struggled to ensure adequate wages and food security. Yet the party maintained an outward appearance as "revolutionary activist" (Mëhilli 2017). Both externally and internally the Albanian government

FIGURE 4. Bunker in Albania near Macedonian border. Photo credit Dennis Jarvis.

proclaimed a commitment to unity in the worldwide proletariat revolution, which renounced discrimination and racism. For Roma and Egyptians in Albania, this stance translated into greater access to housing and jobs, even though they were often still seen as the bottom of the social hierarchy (Woodcock 2016; Chang and Rucker-Chang 2020). Discrimination, in the official sense, was illegal, yet there were no high-ranking Roma or Egyptian officials in the party at any point. Very often Roma and Egyptian students faced barriers when they tried to continue school beyond grade eight, and it was not uncommon for Roma and Egyptian families to have housing but still occupy the most dilapidated portions of buildings or neighborhoods (Woodcock 2016). Many others remained without homes at all.[2]

Albania split with China at the end of the 1970s as the country became more detached and isolated. By 1978 China cut all economic and military aid. It is not uncommon today to hear someone say that Albania in the 1970s and 1980s was the equivalent of contemporary North Korea. Very few people had knowledge of what was going on inside the country. Hoxha's regime promoted more and more self-reliance, though in reality there were widespread food shortages, and the country lacked the infrastructure for greater production. In many cities, workers earned around 100 lekë a day (just over US$1) but bread was 50 lekë for one kilogram, half a day's earnings (Woodcock 2016). The regime's secret police, the Sigurimi, relentlessly maintained a close watch on people, with family members often forced to reveal secrets about one another under intense interrogation and scrutiny. Television and radio programming were led by the state and correspondence was severely restricted, with most people only allowed to send one letter per month. All mail was censored. There were public executions for those who were caught trying to flee the country, with some being arrested and shot within hours.

Leeks

There are many local expressions in Albania involving leeks (*presh*). One of my favorites says, "Mos fluturo me presh në bythë!" (Do not fly with leeks up your butt!). In this instance the expression is used to tell someone to not get too carried away. I once asked a friend why so many sayings are about leeks; she shrugged, speculating that maybe it is because in the 1980s, that is all they had to eat.

Hoxha died in 1985 after four decades of ruling the country with what some have called an iron fist (Fevziu et al. 2016). He was still beloved by many, and his death cast even greater uncertainty on Albania's trajectory. Many foods were scarce, and indeed the only readily available vegetable was leeks, which eventually became a symbol of Albania's despair (Abrahams 2015). The regime had modernized the country, painting a vision of life, work, and Albanian nationalism, while Enver presented himself as Albania's protector (Bejko 2021). Now, in the wake of his death, Ramiz Alia was next in line, but not everyone was confident in his capabilities at the helm. Many questioned whether he could lead in the way Enver did; further, a few political leaders wondered how he would bring Albania out of its dire economic state. This wonderment was soon met with confirmation only a few years later, in 1989, as many parts of the world celebrated the fall of the Berlin Wall. That year, however, found many Albanians going about their day-to-day lives, with few having access to broadcast news outside of state-sponsored television. But soon after the fall of the wall, anti-communist movements began to gain more traction in the country, with many college students and young adults demanding change. In 1990 Alia was eventually forced to give a public speech in which he acknowledged that there would need to be substantial changes made to Albania's government, but he maintained that even with changes, Albania would continue to be led by its Party of Labor.

The Arrival of Democracy

Only one year later, democracy was ushered in through waves of vigorous and feverish anticipation. The seemingly impenetrable walls of the regime eventually fell as Albania became the last country in Eastern Europe to end its period of communist rule. In the first democratic elections in March 1991, however, the Party of Labor, led by Alia, won the majority of votes. Some interlocutors have expressed to me that at that time they felt like Albania was finally free, but the Party of Labor was still so familiar to them, and as such, many cast ballots in the party's favor. The aftermath of the election triggered collective opposition and a strike, and ultimately a transitory government was created that included communists and noncommunists for the first time in nearly fifty years. Growing prodemocratic student movements demanded an end to communist rule, and eventually a mass group gathered in Tirana's center and toppled the large statue of Enver Hoxha that had towered over the city for years. Though not completely destroyed, the statues of Stalin and Lenin were similarly torn down. During elections in early 1992 the newly formed Democratic Party secured its first victory.

Amid the celebrations, however, the socioeconomic and political landscape was suspended in crisis. Many people remained impoverished; others were now without homes as people fought to reclaim land seized by the regime. There were numerous searches organized to find missing loved ones who had been either imprisoned or killed by the regime. At the time of the regime's fall there was a single stoplight in the country, a result of Hoxha's ban on car ownership outside of party members. While many Albanians viewed the regime as paternalistic, as Julian Bejko (2021) highlights, "[The party's] ideology and class struggle were used to foster division, conflict, fear, and insecurity as a means to control the social flux and to strengthen state hegemony. On the one hand, individuals felt protected in terms of labor, health, and physical security, insofar the state assured life; on the other—especially after the regime's collapse in 1991—the lack of rule of law and democratic institutions reintroduced insecurity in physical, psychological, and social terms" (Bejko 241).

State-run factories and cooperatives closed en masse as hundreds of thousands of people found themselves without jobs. Many people turned to temporary jobs, borrowed money, or increasingly began to rely on remittances from those who migrated out of Albania (Musaraj 2021). Migration out of Albania was occurring at unprecedented levels; in fact, the out-migration of Albanians in the early 1990s was at that time the largest internal migration in Europe since the end of World War II. After his inaugural speech as prime minister in 1992, Sali Berisha proclaimed, "The greatest dream of every Albanian is the integration of Albania

FIGURE 5. Albanian migrants on ship from Vlorë. Wikimedia Commons.

into Europe" (Kajsiu 2011). Europe in this context carried multiple meanings, calling attention to a past temporality where Albania belonged to Europe but also to a future European belonging and inclusivity that was tarnished by the Ottoman regime and forbidden during communism. The dream of Europe has been a hallmark since the early 1990s, at times configured as a dream of hope, hopelessness, and haunt. About the immediate years following the regime's collapse, politician and writer Eglantina Gjermeni once wrote, "We did not know what 'democracy' meant, but we threw away everything from the past in order to chase it" (Gjermeni and Amy 2016).

'97

At times people speak of this period with only two numbers: Ninety-seven, or Nëntëdhjetëeshtata, as it is commonly known, was a momentous and chaotic time for the newly pronounced democratic country. In 1995 the International Monetary Fund (IMF) declared that among formerly communist countries in Eastern Europe, Albania was heralded as a success story of market reforms (Bezemer 2001). But even as reform was taking place, pyramid firms were growing in number, with many people understanding them as a type of homegrown capitalism (Musaraj 2021). Albania was not unique in having pyramid schemes, or more aptly Ponzi schemes, as Smoki Musaraj (2021) terms them,[3] but the scope and breadth of the schemes in Albania, relative to other countries in the region, were unprecedented. The 1990s seemed to swell with an atmosphere of exhilaration as the firms expanded, and by 1996 the firms had accumulated 50 percent of the country's GDP, or roughly $1.2 billion USD (Bezemer 2001). According to Musaraj (2021), at one point the IMF actually inquired into the growth of the pyramid companies, raising concern about their legitimacy. But in a later response, then-president Sali Berisha renounced any notion of money laundering, proclaiming, "The money of Albanians is honest!" (Musaraj 2021, 9).

Many people invested all their personal belongings and even their houses in hopes of getting wealthy. In fact, housing was one of the biggest areas affected by the Ponzi schemes. With the fall of the regime, state-owned apartments were privatized as Albania's real estate market emerged for the first time. This market, notes Musaraj (2021), was one of the most dramatic changes of Albania in the 1990s. As people sold their houses, family farms, livestock, and heirlooms to invest in the firms, they were promised they would see returns of 30 to even 100 percent. Albania at that time had very few commercial banks, and those that did exist did not give many loans for purchases, but the firms promised to provide cash; Musaraj argues that with these investments, Albanians were not just motivated by exuberance or greed but desire for European modernity (2021). People throughout the country were galvanized by desires for increase: increased housing, increased space, increased wealth, increased status, all envisioned as attainable with the now-broken shackles of the regime's restraints.

It was late December 1996 when the first major firm collapsed (Musaraj 2021) and the next soon followed. At that time, it is believed that nearly two-thirds of the country's population had invested in the widespread schemes (Bezemer 2001; Musaraj 2021). The year 1997 was marked by anarchy and violence as people flooded the streets in anger and rage. Weapons once possessed by Hoxha's regime were stolen from government offices (Jarvis 2000) as both political and geographic divisions from the North and South were inflamed in response to the collapse. The government soon fell and nearly two thousand people were killed in mass rioting and violence. Calamity ensued as the country nearly erupted into a civil war. Albanian migration to nearby Greece and Italy increased significantly, and many foreign nationals were evacuated from the country. The value of the Albanian currency, the lekë, plummeted as the social landscape of Nëntdhteshtata was increasingly animated by despondency, melancholy, trauma, and desperation, from which many of my interlocutors as late as 2014 said they had not yet fully recovered. It was not until 1998 that a newly formed parliament, assisted by outside international entities, was able to secure control of the firms and begin to stabilize the economy.

"Ç'farë do të bëjmë?"

The events of '97 were incredibly profound, and the years that followed the calamity witnessed efforts to rebuild and restore. Albania still had to navigate other sociopolitical and economic challenges as people worked to rebound from the Ponzi schemes. These included the 1999 Kosova-Serbia war in which Albania served as host to several thousand displaced Kosovar Albanians fleeing violence. The subsequent global economic crisis circa 2008, particularly Greece's economic downturn, had a significant impact on Albania. This eventually led to greater political infighting, particularly between the two leading parties, the Socialists and the Democrats. In 2013 political protests turned violent when leaders from the two parties clashed in downtown Tirana and at least five people were killed. I conducted most of the fieldwork for this book between 2008 and 2018, and in the aftermath of the communist fall, many of my interlocutors still found themselves trying to make sense of the contemporary moment and its cruel optimism (Berlant 2011).

Coined by Lauren Berlant, cruel optimism is regarded as "a relation of attachment to compromised conditions of possibility whose realization is discovered either to be impossible, sheer fantasy, or *too* possible, and toxic" (2011, 24). Thinking with the notion of cruel optimism opens a window to analyze sense-making, the apprehensions, desires, disappointments, conditions, and questions that contour the communist afterlife. The concept further draws attention to those forces that shape collective attachment to and emotional investment in Europe and European belonging. Cruel optimism, I believe, is one way to explore the ever-present angst of the current moment, one infused with a simultaneous optimism and pessimism, as well as forms of longing and trauma. As an analytic it could perhaps offer insight into the ways that fantasies of the past manifest and how those fantasies shape ongoing contemporary forms of precarity. "Por, çfarë do të bëjmë?"[4] ("But what can we do?" or "But what are we going to do?"). It is a question frequently posed, whether over coffee, during an interview, or while discussing current events. It is a question that can be both rhetorical and have an expected response. As you will see in part 2 of this chapter, it is a question asked by Mimoza when she is fed up with national politics. It is a question asked out of exasperation. For Shpresa, who is also featured in part 2, it is more of a statement than a question, not to ask what will happen but rather to assert that things happen because that is just the way things are. Others, like my friend Mira's mom, who asks me the question often, may inquire as to whether I know of any job opportunities for her adult children in the US or Canada because she does not see a financial future in Albania. In this way it also becomes a question of desperation. Yet the afterlife of communism is still shaped by eagerness and anticipation and marked by a particular futurity and disposition of expectation. It is an afterlife of entanglement.

Unlike neighboring countries, Albania, in the thirty years since the fall of the regime, has not had a truth and reconciliation committee to address the wrongs of the communist regime. In addition, a significant number of members of the former Party of Labor and the Sigurimi have made careers in the current public administration. Many streets and symbols in public squares are still marked with names of people deemed communist heroes who are considered by others to be persecutors whose names should be buried and not beloved. Others remember the communists as national heroes, particularly heroes of the anti-fascist war (Papa-Pandelejmoni 2021). A survey of Albanians from 2016 found that 56 percent of respondents saw communism as positive. These tensions and debates surrounding the histories and memories of communism have been ongoing since the fall of the regime, but they recently emerged in the public sphere in a more sensational fashion. In 2018 the Institute for the Studies of Communist Crimes and Its Consequences (ISKK), founded to address the violence and terror of the regime, and at the time led by Agron Tufa, produced a documentary about the former prisoner camp in Tepelenë. This film caused an uproar about the historical account of the regime. The documentary, which included testimony from survivors about their experiences, was among the first to showcase the brutality of the camp. Today there are still numerous families searching for the graves of their loved ones at the site of the Tepelenë camp. At the same time, these viewpoints have been publicly challenged by historians such as Pëllumb Xhufi, who has argued that the conditions of the camps were not as bad as they have been made out to be. In 2019, during the seventy-fifth anniversary commemoration of Albania's liberation from Nazi occupation, members of the former communist regime were openly celebrated as heroes, and ISKK leader Agron Tufa made public comments in opposition to the celebrations. The ISKK then received a governmental cease-and-desist notice, and Tufa, claiming to have received multiple death threats, sought asylum in Switzerland.

As I previously noted, I have not configured this chapter as a chronological historical account but rather as a broader overview of people, events, sentiments, and happenings that hopefully help situate and contextualize the communist afterlife. The next section, part 2, will introduce you to the lives of three people, Mimoza, Shpresa, and Besa. With each of the stories we will trace histories, memories, anticipations, traumas, frustrations, and longings. It is my hope that taken together, these ethnographic narratives will further reveal the textures of the communist afterlife and draw attention to the ways that people are living out this moment.

Part 2

Mimoza

> You are here to write about Albania? It must be a book about politics, right?
> There are only three men that one needs to know to understand everything in Albania! Mbreti Zog i Pari [King Zog I], Enver Hoxha, and Sali Berisha. Zog was the king after we were freed from the Turks, Enver made sure everyone had jobs and went to school, but then Sali destroyed us. Today Albania is a catastrophe thanks to Sali!
>
> —Thoughts from my neighbor, spring 2014

Mimoza was still in a deep state of grief when we first met. She had begun to reincorporate colored clothing into her wardrobe and had retired most of her solid black dresses to her closet, but she remained very tender after the loss of her husband. She still had trouble even saying his name. The night we were supposed to begin our cooking and eating lessons, I actually got lost trying to find her house. Eventually a young girl who spoke English saw me wandering the neighborhood and was able to lead me to Mimoza, who was incredibly flustered by the time I arrived because I was more than thirty minutes late. Once I was finally inside it dawned on the both of us that even though I was supposed to practice speaking Albanian with Mimoza, she did not speak English, so we had to just start communicating one word at a time. She picked up a wooden spoon and shoved it in my face saying, "Lugë!" Mimoza's food was in fact delectable, and as we finished eating, she gestured toward tea to ask if I would like any. I said yes, and after she got the tea brewing, she stepped into her bedroom and returned with a shoebox. She put a finger over her mouth as she opened the box, her eyes paranoid, her actions deliberate. I looked around confused as I knew no one else was in the room, and I was not sure why I needed to be quiet. But I did as I was told and peered into the box to see letters as well as magazine clippings and a couple of pens. "Fshehur," she said. I wrote the word down in my notebook. Later at home I checked my dictionary: "hidden." I then understood Mimoza shared items with me that she likely was not supposed to have in her possession. I later learned that her family had acquired many of them illegally, during Enver's time.

"Sa mbrapa jemi, sa mbrapa!"[5] Mimoza and I had finished lunch, and she was watching the news, her posture weighted by shame as she kept yelling about backwardness. Our visits had become routine at this point, though we no longer cooked together. Around the third week Mimoza had grown impatient with my cooking skills, which were no match to hers, only complicated by our inability to communicate well. Eventually Mimoza decided that her job was to make food and mine was to eat it. She liked having me over, she told me. It helped her feel less alone. Over time I became more proficient in Albanian, and we were eventually able to have fuller, longer conversations. On this day she continued to yell about how backward Albania was as the news channel showed footage from a recent parliamentary session. Leaders from the two main parties, the Democratic Party and the Socialist Party, were fighting once again, unleashing unpleasantries from the parliamentary floor, and Mimoza was upset. "We do not have to be like this," she said. "Democracy is here now; life is better. We are democratic. *We* are in Europe too! . . . But look at this," as she gestured to the television. "Look at these animals!" Minutes later she questioned aloud why Albania could not be more refined like the United States. "Oh believe me, there are many problems with politics in the US," I began, but she waved me off, fed up and disinterested in whatever I had to offer.

Mimoza had known since our first exchange that I was studying Albanian, but it took a while for me to explain why I was learning the language. I once tried to describe my anthropological research interests in "livelihoods" in Tirana, but instead of communicating that exactly, I used the Albanian word *jeta*, which means "life." Mimoza seemed initially unsure of how I was going to study that, but she let me know that she would share with me whatever she could. We talked about so many people, about Enver (referencing Hoxha), about Mehmet (Mehmet Shehu, Hoxha's second-in-command until his mysterious death), about Sali (Sali Berisha, former prime minister and then leader of the Democratic Party), about Edi (Edi Rama, former Tirana mayor, leader of the Socialist Party and the country's current prime minister as of August 2024). Mimoza never represented herself as a member of any one political party, but she had thoughts about everyone. The Albanian word *tregoj* can be translated to English as "tell" but also "share," "show," "point out," or "relate," among others. Mimoza did all of these. She shared stories about her family, about her grandmother, about her siblings. She told me about her experiences growing up during the regime, about daily living but also about repression and fear. She showed photos and books. With time she began to share more about her late husband too, a subject chaperoned by both tears and joy.

Mimoza loves talking on the phone. Her daughter lives in Germany and they speak every two to three days. Mimoza has earned a special German visa that allows her to visit her daughter every summer. "I do not like to fly but anyways, I really like taking the bus and seeing all the different landscapes. It is a very long ride, but I believe a person appreciates it so much more if they could not previously see it." I once arrived at her house and Mimoza was giddy, excited that she had just finished a long phone conversation with her son and granddaughter who lived abroad. She had recently received photos of her eight-year-old granddaughter, who wore a purple leotard and matching ribbon, posing in a dance studio. Mimoza beamed with joy as she shared them with me, savoring the images of her loved ones she rarely encountered in person. We never revisited much about that night that she first shared the shoebox, but she expressed how nice it was to receive letters and boxes without fear from the constant surveillance of the Sigurimi. I have heard her and her friends occasionally wonder whether the Sigurimi may still be watching.

The television is often on when I arrive at Mimoza's house. She will lower the volume or mute it when we have conversations during lunch, but like many retired women who spend a lot of time at home, she watches news programs and soap operas. Television is a way to pass the time, especially for those who no longer work outside of the home, but it is also a gateway to world news and events, a conduit for access to international programming that was previously occluded. Mimoza gets frustrated by local and national news, and at times saddened by world events, but she also enjoys the ability to be in the know. One afternoon we watched a local news segment about the construction of a new mosque in Tirana. Mimoza is from an Orthodox family in Southern Albania. "Albanians are a very tolerant people and we always have been," she said to me while we watched. "We all have friends who are Orthodox, Catholic, Muslim." She later reiterated that Albania is tolerant but then expressed suspicion about the mosque, especially when the reporter questioned whether the mosque was being built with Saudi Arabian financial backing. Mimoza got upset. "Women in Albania were emancipated with Enver—we did not have to cover ourselves. I saw a family on the road the other day and the wife had to cover [herself] and walk behind her husband. He was walking far ahead, and she had to stay behind him. Albanians have never practiced Islam this way."

If ever I arrive and there is a French soap opera on TV, I know that Mimoza is agitated. Television under the regime was tightly regulated, but some people eventually found a way to secretly get Italian broadcasts, and as a result, many Albanians like Mimoza learned Italian and continue to speak it fluently. But she neither speaks nor understands French. The French soap operas tend to be on when she does not want to be bothered by local news. So, when I arrived one late afternoon for coffee and heard French as I changed into a pair of *shapka* (house shoes), I knew she was upset. "What kind of government do we have, huh? What kind of government is this?" Mimoza was frustrated by low pension benefits, the lack of jobs, and housing infrastructure that she believed the government needed to address but would not because of corruption. "People only want more money for themselves!" Mimoza was also agitated because the water in her apartment was out again, though the municipality had assured her that they were working to quickly correct the issue. "Democracy arrived—we are supposed to be better now." She continued, "Shqiperia është nuse e bukur por me rrobat pa larë," meaning "Albania is a beautiful bride but with dirty clothes." Mimoza regularly made remarks like this. "Kemi kokën tonë," she said. The literal translation is "We have our own head," but in this case Mimoza was referencing what she considered a particular Albanian mentality (*mentalitet*) that she believes is different from the rest of Europe. "Are we supposed to enter Europe like this?" Mimoza was not the only person that would express such sentiments about a mentality that was seemingly immutable and unable to shift: "Sa gjynah! . . . ç'do bëjmë?" (What a pity/ How awful! . . . What are we going to do?).[6]

The afternoon and evening streets were crowded with people moving to and fro; others just stood still. That is what one man was doing next to a long row of books, the only movement occurring when he subtly brought his hand to his mouth to take another smoke of what seemed to be a never-ending cigarette. I would see him almost every day, and because I always glanced at his books when I saw him, each day he would try to convince me to buy some. His collection of

FIGURE 6. "Friend of the Book." Photo by author.

communist-era books was vast, complete with Hoxha's manifestos as well as children's magazines littered with propaganda.

On one occasion I did purchase a few of the children's magazines when I was first learning Albanian because they were easier to read. One day on the way to Mimoza's house, I looked at a box that was next to the books. This time the salesman had a set of pins and tiny medallions that children were awarded during Enver's time. Some of the medallions were awards for reading, for math, or for being a patriot. I asked him how much he wanted for them, and he chuckled, asking, "You want these?" He sold me three or four for 200 lekë (roughly US$2). I showed them to Mimoza as soon as I got to her house, and the sight of those medallions brought laughter that the pages of my field notebook failed to completely capture. "They used to give these in school. How did you get these?" she asked, her laughter enduring. I told her that I got them from one of the men who sold books in the street. "Wow," she continued. She kept laughing as she went to the kitchen to get our soup for the table.

Merita's Birthday

The afternoon was Merita's birthday, and she was turning four years old. Her mother, Shpresa, had told me that Merita really wanted a toy *motorri* for her birthday, a small replica motorbike that she could ride around like her dad and uncles do on their waste collection routes. All the children in the Kreshtë neighborhood liked to pretend they were riding motorcycles, especially the younger ones, who would press their lips together and make the motor sound as they ran around the informal settlement near the abandoned communist factory. Merita was dancing outside her family's *shanti*[7] when I arrived, wearing a newly washed dress that her mother found in the river. "People around here throw out dresses and shoes all the time," Shpresa said. "So I go down and grab what I can. I have already found three dresses and a pair of sandals that I have washed and made new for her." On this day Merita's dress was sleeveless, bright green and pink, with small ruffles along the bottom.

"Shpresa has been playing music since the very sight of morning," the neighbors said, as they laughed. About seven or eight people had gathered in chairs and on top of plastic stools outside of their tents. Shpresa tried to get a few folks to dance with her, and one of the neighbor's sons, a teenager, eventually joined in for a little *valle* (dance). A conversation erupted about the empty apartment buildings near the neighborhood, apartments that towered over this community of folks living in tents and sheds. "Sa gjynah!" (What a crime!) someone lamented. "Those buildings are there, *kot* [useless], when we are struggling just feet away." Neighbors continued to talk about the municipality, a few choice words trickling through. Shpresa kept dancing.

The music vibrations crept throughout the neighborhood. Wearing a black romper and pair of tights, Shpresa tied a scarf around her waist and hips as she continued to dance. Merita and her friends joined in with her mother. Afërdita, one of the neighbors, sat outside on a cinder block smoking a cigarette. Her young son is the teenage boy that was dancing with Shpresa. Afërdita helped Shpresa serve some glasses of Pit Bull (a drink similar to Red Bull) and candy to neighbors. They forced everyone to take a few pieces, even when people vehemently objected. This is a common practice, the back and forth over food. Many people feel shameful for taking food from someone, while on this day Shpresa was ashamed that she did not have more to offer. Laundry hung from a line just over everyone's heads. After a while Shpresa finally sat down on a cinder block and released a big sigh. The music, still loud, started to go in and out, the beats sounding as though someone was spitting them out one at a time. A neighbor got up to fix the music, but there was a problem with one of the speakers. The kids ran over to try to change the volume. "Mistrec!" (Troublemaker!), yelled one of the adults, as they tried to get the kids to scatter. Afërdita moseyed toward her tent but yelled for Shpresa to turn the music up, as she still wanted to hear it. "It is too hot out here, but I want to enjoy the songs."

Shpresa went inside and returned with a small watermelon that she began offering to neighbors and guests. Her husband, Merita's dad, yelled, "Everyone we know is coming over; we will not have enough watermelon to give everyone a piece!" He went inside but quickly returned with his friend's large drum. He announced that he was heading to the main road and would be back shortly. Shpresa sat down and told the kids to move along, as it was time for a grown-folks conversation. One of the kids stumbled and fell, and Shpresa laughed, saying, "She's drunk," in response to the nonalcoholic Pit Bull. It was half past one. Shpresa said she is *mërzitur*,[8] a complex word whose meaning can range from upset and sad, to bored, annoyed, or frustrated. She was perhaps experiencing a combination of these feelings. She did not have much for Merita's birthday: a few gifts, no decorations, and barely any food for guests. Her husband's grandfather provided a couple of beers and the Pit Bull. Shpresa fished a broken doll stroller out of the river. Aside from a missing wheel, most of the stroller was intact, and she was able to clean it for Merita. But Shpresa did not have a cake. People will likely stop by throughout the day, including her mother and sister-in-law, who will arrive later. Her husband was supposed to walk over with them after he finished playing the drum in the street, which is where he went to try to make a little money for Merita. Playing music in the streets of larger cities is a common way for Roma and Egyptians to earn small amounts of money.

Shpresa would say that she was *mërzitur* most of the days that we spent time together. She would share that she was worn out, upset with her marriage, lamenting her living situation, and feeling hopeless in Tirana. "U lodha, shumë" (I am very tired), she would tell me. Whenever she could find a reason to celebrate, like Merita's birthday, it seemed that she would squeeze as much joy out as she could before retreating to a more disenchanted state.

Someone found a large umbrella that only had one or two small holes. Shpresa set it up on a table to try to provide shade. She put out the remaining candy for some of the guests who were sitting in the sun. Her husband returned, wearing a white baseball cap and button-up shirt, carrying the large drum strapped around his shoulders. He hugged Merita, burying kisses on her face and neck, then gave her a small lace sack that had 100 lekë (about US$1) inside. Merita started dancing and singing to her friends, waving her money above her head. Wearing her sandals from the river, she and the other children made their way down the road, heading to the small *dyqan* (store), more than likely to buy candy. Her dad sat in one of the chairs and took off his hat, revealing the sweat beneath the brim. He got up, repositioned the umbrella, and sat back down. He had played the drum up and down the road for nearly an hour to get that money for Merita. "Turn the music down!" he demanded, as the speaker was once again on the fritz. "It is giving me a headache."

Merita returned and ran to her dad, clasping a blue plastic bag. Inside there were small pieces of candy, a chocolate croissant, and a red powder that she poured inside of a plastic bottle of water to make a sweet drink. Edi, one of the neighbors, walked by and asked Shpresa about the music, which had gone out again. He said that he had a speaker system if she wanted to use his. Some of the neighborhood boys switched out the systems and got the music going again, as more neighbors resumed dancing. "You have to really shake your ass to dance well," Shpresa said to me, as she swayed and smiled, the women nearby laughing at this. Another neighbor came over to greet Merita. "Edhe një qind zemër!" (And another hundred years, my love!), she said, kissing her cheek. Shpresa offered this neighbor some of the candy and one of the remaining pieces of watermelon. Her husband interjected, "Well, the whole damn neighborhood cannot come over—we do not have enough watermelon for that! And quit giving all of that candy to the kids—we do not have enough candy! How are we supposed to welcome guests like this? I am ashamed that people see us like this!" He struck the top of their barrack as he went inside. Shpresa yelled after him, "Për zotin, ti më mërzit jetën!" (I swear to God, you ruin my life!).

"Jam shumë e lodhur" (I am very tired), Shpresa lamented. She sat back down on a cinder block, the music once again sputtering in and out. Merita danced with her friends, waving what remained of the chocolate croissant.

Shiu i Tiranës (Tirana Rain)

We met early on a Friday morning at Zogu i Zi to head to the village. Besa had invited me to visit her parents and brother for the weekend, and I gladly accepted. She finally had a day off from work and needed to see her family, to help her parents with housework and take care of the farm. We could not take just any *furgon* from Tirana—we had to wait for Fredi, the same *furgon* driver that Besa had used all her life to travel from the big city to the village. When Fredi came out from the nearby café, he waved at Besa to let her know that we would start loading. He was a jovial fellow and playfully slapped my back as I climbed inside, as if we had been old pals for years. We encountered the typical traffic as we made our way out of Tirana, sitting side by side with other frustrated drivers leaning on their horns. Drivers may rarely use their turn signals, but they certainly know how to use a horn. Tall buildings and busy streets faded into the countryside, and we continued to climb our way north. We picked up additional passengers from the road, and soon Tirana was in our rearview.

The water of the Mati River reflected a blue-green hue. We followed its path, zig-zagging through the mountainous bends. The tops of the mountains still had snow from the previous winter. "Si mal me borë, si fushë me lule" (Like mountains with snow, like fields with flowers), wrote Albanian poet Pashko Vasa. In his poem about Albania in the late nineteenth century, the next line chastised, "You used to be clothed; today you are in tatters." Besa first taught me the poem and often sighs at that line, expressing that the same could be said of Albania today.

FIGURE 7. Tirana, 2018. Photo by author.

I was lost in my thoughts when I felt a woman near me tugging at my shoulder. She looked at me with kind eyes as she offered me a soft biscuit (cookie) from a plastic bag. She smiled with relief as I accepted it.

At some point on our journey, we made a stop for coffee and pilaf. Besa told me that Fredi always stopped at that same restaurant. We were close to her village. As we entered, Besa immediately recognized people at the café. Some asked about her family and brothers. Besa is one of six children, and most of her siblings live abroad and cannot afford to make frequent visits to Albania. Two of her siblings fled the country in the late 1990s as refugees and still lacked sufficient documentation to travel to Albania. As usual, the same folks who asked about her family made sure to wish everyone well and good health, and Besa thanked each one of them as she made her way to the table to quickly eat pilaf. The pilaf was fresh, topped with just enough gravy. I also ordered a macchiato, which we finished drinking outside. It was a bright day, the sun casting down its vibrant rays. I tried to take a picture on my camera but was not able to quite capture the view. A cute little girl came next to me and stared for a bit. I asked her if she wanted to see the photo that I just took, and she indicated that she did. "Oh, *vogëlushe* [little one]," Besa said to her, as she grabbed my camera and snapped a shot of the girl's sweet smile.

Besa abruptly switched to speaking English with me when we were back on the *furgon*. Puzzled, I asked her why she suddenly made the change, and she told me that people from her village were very nosy and that she did not want them to know all her business. As such, from that point on we only spoke English until we got to her house. I told her that she should not be so presumptuous, that maybe some of the people around us may know English, but this only made her laugh. "We are not in Tirana anymore," she said.

Fredi started honking the horn as we entered Besa's village, and almost as soon as he did, Besa instructed me to get my purse and notebook. We pulled up to a hill, and Fredi parked the car and turned off the engine. I was used to being dropped off at destinations, but Fredi got out to get our bags and escort us to the house. I crawled out, surprisingly only stepping on one person's foot, as by this point several of us were crammed inside. Once outside, I saw Besa's dad, Ahmet, slowly walking toward us, his jacket on his shoulders but his arms not in the sleeves. He grinned as Besa yelled, "O ba," and ran to greet him. She did not kiss him twice as I had been accustomed to seeing but rather leaned her head to each side of his head then hugged him tightly. I followed suit when I greeted him, immediately taking note that Besa has his eyes. Ahmet shook Fredi's hand and thanked him for getting us there. Soon the engine revved as Fredi bid us adieu and began his trek up the mountain to drop off others. I looked up to see Besa's mom, Fatjeta, peering down. She was wearing a black headscarf and yelled something in our direction, but I did not understand her. She continued to mutter as we walked to the top of the hill. Besa explained that because of her mom's thick accent and frequent use of Turkish words, I would likely not understand a thing she said. I laughed. I approached Fatjeta to greet her, and she grabbed my arm, gripping me tightly. She pulled back, still touching my arm, and said something to Besa. Beni, Besa's youngest brother, and her cousin Lumi came downstairs to greet us, and once again we touched our heads on each side rather than hug or kiss.

"I sent her to Tirana to become a millionaire." This is what Ahmet said to me when I asked why he wanted Besa to attend high school in Tirana, the first child in her family to be educated outside of their small village. He followed his response with a slight, childlike snicker, his cigarette hanging slightly out of his mouth. Besa and Beni laughed loudly. Besa first arrived in Tirana at the end of 1996, shortly before the events of '97. I continued to ask Ahmet questions about their family and his family history. He said his name is Turkish, and many aspects of daily life in this village, the mosque, the spoken dialect, the landscape, displayed the remnants of the long period of Ottoman rule in Albania, more so than areas like Tirana. Whenever I asked Ahmet questions about seemingly mundane things, such as how many cigarettes he smoked daily or how often he visited the mosque, he gave me that same chuckle as if to say, "Why in the hell do you want to know all of this?" He joked that I might be a member of the CIA. Besa and Beni began to walk around the fields as I continued my conversation with their father. Soon Fatjeta called all of us back up to the house, yelling that it was time to eat. When we made it to the top of the hill, she said something to Besa along the lines of, "I hope your friend actually eats something this time," in regard to the "little" that I had eaten the previous night. All throughout dinner and afterward, Fatjeta was concerned because I only ate two bowls of soup, chicken, spaghetti, bread, and salad. She complained that it was embarrassing how little they had fed me.

Besa was the fifth of six children born to her parents in this small village. When she was born, Ahmet was walking nearly fifteen kilometers one way each day to teach school in a different village, reflecting Hoxha's attempt to increase interaction and brotherhood between citizens. He said his joints and body parts showed the impact of the everyday journey through rugged mountainous terrain. Besa and her siblings, however, were able to attend school in their local village. Most of their classmates were cousins and distant relatives. Fatjeta spent most of her time in the home and managing the family's land. She and Ahmet had married when she was young, only seventeen, and though Besa says she was strict like a military commander, she had a soft spot for her children, especially Beni, the baby of the family. When the family suffered from widespread food shortages, Fatjeta always found a way to stretch meals, often going without food so that all her children could eat.

Ahmet joked that Enver was not that bad of a guy and that in fact he was good for Albania. Other older family members in the village who had joined in our conversations agreed with him. While cities like Tirana witnessed protests and marches after the regime collapse, Ahmet believes that many aspects of daily life in his small village remained the same. They incurred some problems about land and animal ownership with neighbors but fortunately these were quickly resolved, aided by the fact that most of the family's neighbors were relatives. Beni added that the division of property was not necessarily easy but that it was smoother compared to what occurred in other areas of the country. Ahmet said that one of the biggest changes he observed was the decline in education. He felt that the village schools were stronger under communist rule and that in the early 1990s he became increasingly frustrated. That is when he said he made the decision to send Besa to Tirana to complete high school at a residential school. Besa's oldest sister had already married a man from their village, and her other sister was soon to marry as well. At this point Besa chimed in to say that they sent her to Tirana because she was the smart one and then flashed a sly, cunning smile.

Tirana was wet, soaked with rain, when Besa first arrived. Not cold in temperature, like her mountainous village with its crisp air. Tirana seemed cold and gray. Capricious. Hostile, even. During the period of unrest in '97 she was forced to temporarily return to her village. Another young girl from a nearby town was also attending school in Tirana, and this friend's father was able to get the girls out of Tirana and back to their homes to await the end of the crisis. In the village Besa spent time with Fatjeta and Ahmet, helping them in the fields and cleaning the house. She was nurtured by the scent and feel of home. When it was time to return to Tirana, she pleaded with her father to stay in the village, but he insisted that she had to go back. "I told her that she had to become a millionaire." Besa always smiled when Ahmet said this. During Besa's second year of high school she became friends with three other girls who were also staying in the residential dormitories, and they formed a close circle. They began to regularly meet for coffee after class and always ate dinner together at the cafeterias. Besa said that this made her feel more at ease in Tirana.

In 1999 Besa's two older brothers fled Albania in search of a new life. They both desired to relocate to Greece soon after the fall of the regime, but their parents felt they were too young to migrate, so they remained in the village. The oldest brother eventually moved to Tirana to look for better work. But neither time nor the country's newfound democracy had been kind to the family's financial position, so Besa's brothers sought the chance to get out. Leaving the majority of their possessions behind, they joined a group of men on rubber boats, the only plan being to get somewhere else. Besa said that neither of her brothers had considered steps beyond getting out; they just knew that they longed for something better and did not see a path for betterment in Albania.

Back in Tirana, Besa finished high school and began college with the same set of friends. Her change in dialect became more noticeable. The hard-sounding "a" became softer. She pronounced words differently and used more Tironse verbiage, the dialect spoken in Tirana and the surrounding region. When she traveled back to the village, always with Fredi's *furgon*, she switched her speech, learning to turn off and on the village speak. Her older sister had permanently relocated to Italy with her husband, and her eldest sister was expecting her first child. Fatjeta asked Besa about getting married, but Besa wanted to finish college first. Her mother mentioned a young man from their village who was in search of a wife, but Besa could not see herself married to him nor could she imagine herself back in the village. She wanted to live, to work, to stay in Tirana.

Besa completed her degree at the university, the first in her family to do so. She landed a reputable job with a decent salary, but her parents increasingly worried about her being a woman who lived alone. They eventually sent Beni, her youngest brother, to live with her. He enrolled in the university and went to school during the day while Besa worked. Over the course of a few years Besa managed to save enough money to buy an apartment in a new development in a more affordable area of Tirana. At this point Tirana's population had swelled as more people relocated there from smaller cities and villages. Sections of the city had become stigmatized as the areas where villagers and newcomers from the North resided, and this was the case with Besa's new neighborhood. Still, she was extremely proud of herself and her accomplishments. When Besa would travel home to the village, her mother would show her pictures of her sisters' children. She pestered Besa about finding a husband. She did not show much enthusiasm about Besa's new apartment. Back in Tirana, Besa slowly furnished her place, buying home goods and accessories as money allowed. At night she watched everything from her balcony: people meandering to the café, sunsets, and Tirana rain.

Beni finished school and decided to remain with Besa in Tirana. But he was unable to find a job, and unemployment rates were high. So he stayed at Besa's house all day. She regularly asked her parents what she should do about the situation, as she referred to it; she told them that she was not Beni's babysitter, but Fatjeta chastised Besa for not supporting her family during difficult times. Every month Besa still traveled back to the village to help her parents wash the floors and clean the walls. Fatjeta's body was getting frail, but her determination and stubbornness did not wilt. She often inspected Besa's cleaning efforts, at times offering more critique than praise. She asked Besa about a husband. Besa asked how much longer Beni would be in Tirana.

In 2011 the family received a dismal phone call. Erjon, the younger of Besa's two brothers who lived abroad, had been diagnosed with cancer and needed immediate surgery. Besa's face was sullen as she shared the news with me, her eyes red and stained from Tirana rain. She smoked a pack of cigarettes in two hours. "How could he have cancer?" she kept wondering aloud. "He never, ever smoked, not even once." Erjon had the surgery a couple of days later, but the doctors informed their family that he would need continuous care and assistance to recover. At this point Besa's oldest brother had obtained citizenship abroad, but Erjon was still under refugee status and could not travel home to Albania; moreover, his doctors did not think he was healthy enough to do so. The family did not believe that Ahmet and Fatjeta were in a position to make the long journey, and since Besa's older sisters had husbands and children, it was decided that she would go and stay with Erjon for three months and help him recover. Besa worried about her job. She was convinced she would not even qualify for a visa to leave Albania—she had previously been denied twice. Istanbul was the only place she had visited outside of the country because Turkey did not require visas for Albanians. They say that the third time's the charm, and in Besa's case it was. She obtained the visa and secured a leave of absence from work, but she still felt that she did not have enough money for the trip. We met for a beer one night before she left, and as usual she would not let me pay for the drinks. Toward the end of the night, though, I put a small envelope with cash in her hands. She threw the money back in my face and yelled at me for even thinking that she would accept it. She cried of shame, horrified at the thought that I would feel obligated to help her. I picked up the money and gently placed it back in her hands. She sank lower in her chair and cried even more, a steady stream of tears. She vowed that she would repay me every single cent.

Besa stayed with Erjon just over three months. He needed so much care that she rarely left the house. I had to travel back home for a while, but I wrote to her from the United States, and she often talked about being too busy for anything except for helping her brother. The doctors were able to fully remove the tumor, but Erjon needed significant rehabilitation and time to heal. There was a strong likelihood that he would never again regain some of his faculties, like the ability to speak. Besa knew that she had to return to Tirana soon for work, yet her mind and heart were torn. She felt a duty and obligation to her brother and family, yet she did not want to lose her job. She missed Tirana. She missed her apartment and her life there. When she did decide to return to Tirana, however, she missed being away from Albania. She said she liked being somewhere else and now she found herself making more frequent trips to the village to help her parents. At times Beni joined her, and on one occasion he decided to spend an extended time in the village. For the first time in a long time, Besa felt a morsel of relief and independence, but it was short-lived when later that year her mother fell ill. Fatjeta was just as stubborn as before, believing that she only needed rest and tea to get better, but she was feeble, and her body felt unfamiliar; she no longer recognized it. There was no clinic or hospital in their village, and the closest city lacked the proper medical specialists, so the family traveled to Tirana in search of answers.

It was 2014. The illness seemed to quickly manifest but slowly infected Fatjeta's body. Her doctors in Tirana said that life in the village was not suitable and recommended that she stay in the city. The family moved Fatjeta into Besa's apartment, into Besa's bedroom. Besa felt that her mother's care was adequate, but she was dissatisfied and wished that they had access to health care outside of Albania. If they wanted a greater quality of care, then they would have to seek help from a private hospital, but no one had the money for private care. Besa was grateful that her cousin, a nurse, was able to set up an IV in the apartment and visited each evening to administer medicine and fluids. Besa slept on the couch while Beni and Ahmet traveled back and forth on Fredi's *furgon* between Tirana and the village. Some days Fatjeta moved around, asking Besa when she would find a husband and complaining about the way Besa made soup. Other days Fatjeta refused to eat and only left the room to use the bathroom. Soon she did not feel like getting up at all.

I was not aware of the seriousness of Fatjeta's health when I arrived in Tirana later that year. Besa had only written to me to say that her mother was sick but that all was well. When I finally visited Besa at her house she cried inconsolably, unable to even whisper the word "cancer." In fact, she never actually said it but talked around it. Fatjeta talked to herself a lot at night. Besa said most of it was incoherent, though she could make out the names of relatives who had already passed. Fatjeta vomited often. She moaned. Most nights Besa lied awake at night, unable to sleep, feeling suspended in time and space. The nights were warm, heavy with moisture from the recent rains, yet Besa confessed that she could not shake a frigid chill. She prayed that the days would both speed up and slow down. She was not even sure to whom she prayed.

One day in November it happened. Fatjeta was gone. I arrived at Besa's apartment and saw lines and lines of people in the courtyard below. Nearly everyone was dressed in black, most people quietly lingering, waiting. I looked to see a group of men surrounding Ahmet. He wore his suit jacket around his shoulders, his arms folded across his chest, a loose cigarette hanging out of the side of his mouth. Besa greeted me, firmly gripping my shoulder with her arm. She kept telling, "O Chels, mos u mërzit" (do not worry or get upset). She was trying to maintain composure and order. I told her that I would stay outside, but she insisted that I go upstairs with her sisters. It was crowded in the apartment. Besa's cousin from the village greeted me. I ducked into the kitchen and tried to stay out of the way. Few words were spoken as lament loudly announced its presence. At some point Besa's two older brothers burst into the room wearing jeans and leather jackets. Her oldest brother wailed as family members grasped him and one woman gently rocked him, the way a mother would a small child. Minutes later those of us who were not immediate family were ushered outside to give them time alone. It was the first time in over fifteen years that all the siblings were in the same place at the same time.

Outside the large crowd began to gather as Besa, her siblings, and other family members came down the stairs. Her oldest sister was pregnant at the time, and family members said she could not visit the cemetery, so Besa's youngest sister stayed back with her. I stood farther away from the family and could not hear very well, but there was a man who led a prayer and short song. We were then ushered onto a bus to go to the burial site.

It was twilight when we arrived at the cemetery. I could only see men gathered behind Ahmet when I stepped off the bus. They stood near the large plot where the body was to be buried, and two men wearing T-shirts and jeans were close by with shovels. Most of the women stood farther back, though Besa was closer to the casket, somewhere in between. Some of the men bent down and said prayers. One man sang a song of lamentation as the body was lowered into the ground. Besa's brothers used the shovels to help cover the body. They both wept but tried to push away their tears. I saw Besa run close to the plot as they shoveled, as the rain fell from her eyes and my own. She tried to get even closer, but her oldest brother grabbed her and pulled her to his chest, her sobs joining his in unison. Besa's cousin comforted Beni as he wept. I watched as Besa slowly began to walk away with her brothers, but she soon fell over into a relative's arms, her body surrendering to the weight of heartbreak. It was darker now and more difficult to see. There were faint glows from cigarettes. Soon I felt Besa's cousin tugging my arm to tell me it was time to leave. We trekked through the mud and climbed back onto the bus.

In this section I have presented three different kinds of ethnographic narratives: the story of what emerges from ordinary lunch encounters, the story of a particular event, and the story of a friend and her family over time. All three of these ethnographic illustrations speak to the assemblages of the communist afterlife in distinct yet overlapping ways. I do not share these stories as a means of direct comparison, and as has been shown, all three women occupy different sociopolitical, economic, geographic, and temporal positionalities. I share their stories here to illustrate how the communist afterlife is animated by certain rhythms of anticipation and expectation, questions of belonging, practices of sense-making, and deeply embedded forms of longing and frustration, all of which shape how people like Mimoza, Shpresa, and Besa are living out the current moment. If we return to the idea of the communist afterlife as entanglement, we can see through these stories the ways that past, present, and future are all interlocked and interconnected.

Though I chronicle difficulty and anguish in the lives of all three women, I do not tell these stories to only highlight misery. In fact, I highlight things that bring them joy and also try to highlight areas of personal agency, reclamation, and resistance. At the same time, I also call attention to the idea of fading. The pace of the 1990s in Albania, and Tirana in particular, is often discussed in terms of speediness and acceleration, as numerous changes occurred quickly and acutely with the rupture of the regime. Fading, though, speaks to processes that are more gradual, taking place over and across time, and can provide a lens for understanding disillusionment and its accompanying waning hope. This is not to suggest that these three women or all my interlocutors are antidemocracy, or hopeless about the contemporary moment, or that any of them would say that they want to retreat to a communist past. Rather, I use this framework of fading to consider the proliferation of cruel optimism that shapes their lives. With this approach, I attune my ethnographic analytic lens to studying how race unfolds in the communist afterlife.

Historical and Local Contextualization

In the beginning of this book, I said that race is about imagination, and with this first chapter I have situated the exploration of the racial imaginary within a broader context of imagination as it relates to the communist afterlife. Imagination played a huge role in Hoxha's regime, including the imagination of a different future and the reimagination of everyday life. Communism remains an active register in Tirana and in Albania and speaks to the reordering and restructuring of daily life in local and global contexts. Approaching the contemporary moment as a communist afterlife helps us understand the lingering presence of Albania's past and analyze processes of race-making that are not always acknowledged nor immediately legible. These include ideas of backwardness, mentality, national prosperity and well-being, and what it means to become authentically European.[9] This chapter has also illustrated the ways that for many, Tirana has become both a dreamland and opportunity, a step closer to Europe for some, and yet also a place of deep disparity and desperation for others. In the following chapters I continue to probe these ideas, drawing attention to how race in the communist afterlife is shaped by growing inequality, dispossession, and ultimately the ways that capitalism functions in the everyday livelihoods of people in Tirana.

Throughout the book I invite you to consider how histories, shifts, rifts, expectations, and memories captured in this chapter have shaped the idea of what Albania was, is, and was to become, and who Albanians are or are not; what constitutes Europe and who is or gets to be European. All of these are explored to shed light on the particularities of racialization in local and global contexts. There are other helpful things to keep in mind as this chapter transitions to the next. As I argued in this book's introduction, the communist afterlife calls attention to the abrupt shifts and openings as generated by the fall of Hoxha's regime. The resulting global connectedness produced various engagements with media and technologies, and as such, we must return to the work of Arjun Appadurai (1996) and ask how notions of Albanianness, Europeanness, whiteness, and blackness are shaped by the convergences of mediascapes, technoscapes, and ethnoscapes. That is to ask, how do the flows and movements of people, technology, and media shape race-making in the communist afterlife? These globalization frameworks remain very relevant for examining racialization. Additionally, the themes of shame (as *turp*) and frustration (as *mërzitur*) highlighted here will reappear in the continued discussion of race in relationship to customary practices of hospitality. The next chapter will include more attention to the ways that many of my interlocutors go to great lengths to ensure the well-being of guests, and what this may tell us about configurations of nation and race.

Chapter 1 has historically contextualized the analysis of race, and in the next chapter I provide local contextualization for understanding racialization as I chronicle my experiences on an Albanian national television show. What initially began as an invitation to discuss my research turned into a much different experience involving questions of race. As I recount the experiences from the television show and other ethnographic encounters, I further explore how my interlocutors make sense of, negotiate, and articulate what race is and what race is not.

2
THE TRIAL OF THE ANTHROPOLOGIST

"Racism in Albania?" I overheard Blerta ask through the phone, aghast. "But I did not know that Albanians could be racist."

I sighed.

An hour earlier I was telling my friend Mira and her sister a story about serving as a translator for a friend who was going to be on Albanian national television. As I was talking Mira appeared somewhat preoccupied as she casually lit her cigarette and blew the first puffs of smoke in my face. "You know, Chelsi, *you* should go on television," she said. Amused, I asked, "Why should I go on TV? What would I talk about?" "About your research, about racism," she said. "And about the things that go on here in Albania. People need to know these issues and need to hear about your work." "Well, I do not just study racism, I study racialization . . .," I began, but as Mira does, she was already making moves before I had the time to finish or contemplate her proposition.

As such, I now found myself sitting against her couch while she spoke with Blerta, her friend and colleague who knew the host and producers of the nationally syndicated morning show *Wake Up Tirana*. I listened to their conversation as Blerta requested more evidence about racism in Albania. I started to slightly panic and tugged Mira's arm to end the phone call, to let Blerta know that I was not accusing anyone or generalizing an entire group as racist. Mira, however, continued chatting. When she ended the call, she said, "Blerta is phoning her friend now, the one who hosts the morning show." "Well, what did she say?" I pleaded. "Oh yeah," Mira said, shaking her head in a way that she does when she is very proud of an accomplishment. "They are *definitely* going to want to talk to you." "Really?" I asked, somewhere between question and doubt. Mira's phone promptly rang. "Okay, next Tuesday?" I overheard. She leaned over to me. "Can you go down to the station next week on Tuesday to meet the host? After that they want to have you on for a live taping the following Thursday." "Yes, I can do that," I said. "Good," she said, seemingly to both Blerta and me. "I will go with you."

The Pretrial: Weighing the Evidence

I met Mira that following Tuesday morning outside the Pyramid, a building that was designed and commissioned in the late 1980s by Enver Hoxha's daughter to honor his legacy in Albania. There are numerous ongoing conversations about what should now be done with the Pyramid, but at that time, in the fall of 2013, it was covered with graffiti, and during the day many young children would climb to the top and use it as a giant slide.

A couple of television and radio stations occupied the inside of the building, including the one that broadcast *Wake Up Tirana*. Mira informed the guard about our meeting, and he directed us to the second floor. On our arrival we found Enon, the show's host, waiting for us, along with five other people. I was initially caught off-guard as I thought we were only meeting Enon, but I quickly learned that several members of the production staff would join us. After brief introductions Enon immediately began with opening questions. He started by asking me to detail my experiences in Albania because, as he said, "I did not

FIGURE 8. The Pyramid in Tirana. Photo by Diego Delso, http://delso.photo/.

know there was racism here in Albania." Mira interjected to explain that I am a social anthropologist and there are several issues that I study pertaining to race, but Enon wanted concrete evidence about racism and racist people. I initially fumbled a lot of my words as I began to talk about my interests in Albania, but I stressed that while yes, I had experienced many racist encounters, my research was not about measuring racial animus or discrimination per se. The conversation was initially slow and difficult. I had trouble summarizing all my thoughts in a matter of minutes. My body was tense, and the group's presence was somewhat overwhelming.

They wanted to know how I knew that Albanians even knew about race. I began by sharing about my initial research interests, how many people think about the region as disconnected from race but even a cursory look at media or public discourse revealed that race was presently active. I could eventually tell that they wanted to hear more about me personally as opposed to my larger research aims, so I offered a few stories about encounters. I talked about many people regularly assume that I do not speak Albanian, so while I frequently hear them call me "n*gger," I also know they call me darkie, black ass, strange, ugly, questioning my hair, my hygiene, or my body. Enon interrupted to ask, "Well would we call this racism or curiosity?" I told him that this was the exact kind of question that I explore in my research to understand how people think about race, how they interpret what they say and do, and how people are racialized. I shared with them another story in which I was once on a plane to Tirana, the only non-Albanian onboard out of about 20 total passengers. At one point an older woman boarded the plane and loudly exclaimed, "N*gger, n*gger!" when she saw me. She then ran toward me and began pinching and touching my cheeks and hair. I remained in my seat, jaw tight, eyes bulging, in a state of shock, really, as I was unsure how to react to this Fanon-like rupture (Fanon 1967). She turned to her husband behind her and pointed at me and shouted, "N*gger!" As I finished sharing this story in the studio, most of the group immediately shared comments like, "No, she was not racist . . . she was just curious." Someone referred to it as *clean* racism. This led Albana, one of the production assistants, to suggest that maybe I cannot differentiate between curiosity and racism. "Albania is now democratic and tolerant—I do not think this woman meant any harm by her actions." I explained to the group that the incident itself was very telling about how people respond to race, and blackness specifically, but that I also was not necessarily trying to debate whether the woman meant any harm. At the same time, I took note of their collective response to this story as it shed light on their desire to justify the woman's actions as *just* curiosity.

Enon and his crew wanted more evidence. I reiterated that it was not my intention to call anyone racist as much as I wanted to understand how race worked. They demanded more stories. I described the ways that some people used offensive Albanian slurs with me, the ways that people casually referred to people of African descent as inferior, the times where people would grab me in the street, throw rocks at me, or even follow and chase me home in the evenings. I tried to convey that amid the difficulty these encounters produced, I was still trying to ask what they revealed about race and otherness. Enon wanted to know more about the meaning behind the actions of people, inquiring as to whether I could explain why people might behave this way. I could tell that he was getting somewhat defensive as he talked. He asked me if I thought these actions were intentional, to which I gave a rather textbook human rights response about impact being greater than intention. I also reminded him that I was interested in the broader question of how race shapes interactions, even if people think that it does not. In the studio I began to feel that scholars regularly talked about these types of subjects among themselves, but it played out differently with a more general audience. The show's representatives began to question whether I *really* understood Albanian culture. They reasoned that if I could better understand where people were coming from, I would *know* better, and there would be no reason to study race in Albania. At the time I found it difficult to say that these exact meaning-making processes are also a component of my research interests.

At this point the show's staff was still concerned that I was unclear about Albanian culture, and that while I was trying to understand race, the consensus seemed to be that it was me who *mis*understood. Mira then spoke up, saying that she had personally witnessed some of the encounters I had mentioned. Up to this point my evidence had seemed weak, but once Mira entered the conversation, it was as if she validated my stories. "I have been there," she said. "Trust me, I have seen these things." Once she said this, many of the producers' demeanors changed. I reiterated that I was not just researching racist incidents or moments, but Enon interrupted me to ask, "Well, where are these things happening? I know none of this happens in Tirana." "Actually," I responded, "yes, I mostly conduct research in Tirana." He and the sound engineer both snorted as Enon remarked, "Well, then, it is not the people who are *really* from Tirana." Here Enon was calling attention to a sentiment I hear often, that those from rural areas are uneducated or uncultured, and therefore more likely to offend people. The same thing was said to me when I once had my wallet stolen on the bus. "Must have been one of the villagers," my friend said. "They always give Tirana a bad reputation."

Other staff in the studio began to ask more questions, especially about how Albanians respond or react to Black people. In addition to my encounters, I began to share about subjects like blackface on Albanian TV, specifically the nationally syndicated variety show *Portokalli*. One of the popular sketches featured the blackface character of Drumba. Chapter 5 of this book features a more in-depth conversation about Drumba, but as it pertains to the conversation in the studio, I started to give the production staff a brief history of blackface and caricatures, but as I did, Enon unfolded his arms and interrupted me, saying, "The personality that you are referencing on *Portokalli* is something that has occurred in a specific Albanian context—let me explain the history to you." He said the sketch was easy to understand as *simple* humor about African football players who are recruited to play for Albanian teams. He did not address why Drumba dances wildly and makes monkey sounds. He did not explain why the character of Drumba is missing teeth or why the audience is encouraged to laugh at him and his supposedly natural incompetence. Instead Enon reiterated, "It is *only* a joke." I tried to extend the conversation, including my own interviews with African football players, but Enon abruptly halted the conversation by saying that Drumba was a completely different matter not at all linked to race. "In Tirana," he later added, "you can see that we treat Black footballers very well, with respect."

Enon mentioned the fact that I am from the United States, which, compared to Albania, had a different history and context with race, and as a result, I could not try to study race or racism in Albania in the same way. "I should remind you," he said, "that Albania was very isolated. We have been isolated from the whole world for a very long time, and maybe people are, I do not know . . . afraid of newcomers." I nodded in agreement and informed him that I situate my research questions with similar things in mind. Enon followed with an example of relationships between Albanians and Greeks, arguing that from his perspective, Albanians have been the victims of racism from Greeks for a very long time. Albana, one of the show's producers, added that to her, racism in Albania had a different *tone*, one that did not necessarily deal with skin color, illustrated by what she also considered racism between Albanians and Greeks. I told them that I was not trying to compare Albania to the United States but rather attempting to understand how Albania can inform scholars about race, including the study of Albanian-Greek relationships. This seemed to somewhat delight and intrigue Enon.

But once we began our discussion about relationships between local social groups, I also added that I research how Roma and Egyptians are racialized in Albania. "The Roma community is marginalized," Albana began, "but I do not know if they experience racism . . . During the time of Enver the Roma were treated better than everyone else. They were prioritized!" Her comments echoed broader sentiments that I have regularly heard: that because Hoxha's regime worked to ensure housing and employment for all, whether that was fully realized for all Roma and Egyptians, it seemed to many Albanians that they were not privileged in the same way. I used this opportunity with Albania to clarify that such a history also factored into my research, how social categories like Roma,

Egyptian, and Albanian were created and what it meant for marginalization to fall along those lines. "I am not writing that all Albanians are necessarily racist," I began. "I am saying . . ." "They are ignorant," Enon interrupted, completing a sentence I was not trying to make. Enon sighed as though he were ashamed. I added that I was not thinking in terms of this dichotomy, that people could either be racist or ignorant—this was a misunderstanding of my research.

As I continued with what soon felt like repetitive rambling, Enon said to me, "Well, we want to have you on the show." The producers affirmed this, with one adding that viewers would enjoy the conversation. "You are an anthropologist," Enon began, "and you can speak to these subjects, but we will have a local Albanian psychologist that can talk about the *reality* and explain the things that have happened to you." I was skeptical of this format, but the trial began to take shape before my eyes, and now they had even identified an expert witness. They announced that Blerta, Mira's friend who made the initial introduction, would come on the show with me and speak about Albanian society. It also seemed that she might, in some sense, evaluate me. Albana then said that the show would also provide the opportunity for viewers to participate, such as an option to call into the show. "People will absolutely have questions," she said, "because Albanians do not see things the way you see them." It seemed then that the viewers would serve as jurors who would soon deliver a verdict.

The Trial

On the morning of the live television airing, I met Mira and Blerta outside of the studio. We arrived several minutes early so that I could chat with Blerta about last-minute questions and discuss how the dialogue would hopefully unfold. A production assistant greeted us and escorted us to makeup, where the makeup artist was eagerly waiting. She was very excited that I was going to be on the show because she actually had dark brown foundation in her collection and had never been able to use it. Her excitement quickly diminished when I told her that I very rarely wore makeup due to very sensitive skin and a small allergy to most cosmetic products. We settled on a shiny pink gloss for my lips.

As we approached the start time, Blerta and I entered the studio where Enon greeted us behind the cameras. He let us know how glad he was that we were going to be on the show. The lights in the studio were intensely bright, magnifying the small beads of sweat gathering on my hands. Blerta and I fastened our earpieces and stood behind our respective microphones at the table. At the bottom of the television monitor I saw "Racism or Ignorance?" written as the title of the show. I immediately looked to the producers for a chance to change the title, but I had very little time to think about this as the music started and we received the signal that we were live. Enon introduced the segment: "Today, we are going to feature an argument that I believe will speak to everyone, one that we will discuss with serious attention. I want to introduce Chelsi West. She is a social anthropologist. She is an American. And she has come to Albania to study aspects of our society and our behaviors here." He continued, "Chelsi has seen with her own eyes and critically studied the way that Albanians mistreat people of color, for instance, people like herself." This is not the direction I had in mind for the conversation, but once Enon allowed me the opportunity to introduce myself, I said that while studying race I also research things like the aftermath of communism and cultural aspects of daily life. I felt that I needed to quickly reassure viewers, so I added that I very much enjoyed doing research in Albania. My fear of being misunderstood was so great that I stumbled through this introduction and delivered a very vague description of my research.

Enon continued the conversation, noting that perhaps a particular type of racism, which he denoted with air quotes, may exist in Albania, but in his opinion this was a result of the country's history of isolation and lack of exposure to foreigners. I wanted to respond directly to this, but he first offered Blerta the opportunity to speak. "When I first talked to Chelsi and learned of her experiences, I was shocked," Blerta began. "We were all shocked," Enon added. Blerta resumed, "I was shocked because here in Albania we have not had much contact with people with color [*njerëz me ngjyrë*]; we do not have a history of racism or conflict." After this, we began discussing different types of social phenomena, racism, prejudice, and nationalism. Enon acknowledged that people in Albania use epithets and racist terminology, and that there are differences between groups like Albanians and Roma, but then he turned the attention to me, to ask more about acts of racism against me. I wanted to return to the discussion of racist terminology and how race travels through words, for example, but I once again felt the need to reiterate that I very much enjoyed Albania and that my research is not necessarily about interpersonal racism but instead a broader discussion about racialization. It was at this exact moment in the studio that I again realized how often I list, discuss, critique, and grapple with questions about race in academic circles, but it was more difficult to use this same language and approach in a television studio during a live taping. This was made even more challenging as I also felt as if I were defending myself and even the idea that I could explore race in a place like Albania.

I responded to Enon's questions by acknowledging that I try to analyze what I call encounters and events as shaped by race—that I try to study how race is made and how it is produced and produced. I offered examples about racial categories and the concept of race in Europe broadly. He followed by asking me to share evidence and to recount experiences of racism in Albania. I then shared on-air the previous stories that I had offered during the pretrial interview. I discussed comments that I would hear about Black people, about myself, especially when people assumed that I could not speak Albanian. Though I wanted to elaborate about the construction of othering and difference, I hesitated. I was not sure where the conversation was moving. I felt frustrated and sensed a familiar tension whereby I had grown accustomed to practicing a critical distance from interactions and encounters so that I could analyze racialization from a particular angle. Such a stance had produced a delayed emotional response. At the same time, it was those encounters that had first shone light on the ideas of race versus racelessness in the Balkans, drawing attention to how despite the presence of racial logics and racial grammar in everyday life, they remained vastly understudied. I was flooded with thoughts that I could not completely process in a short period of time.

Enon focused on what he called behaviors and attitudes, and he asked Blerta whether she thought such acts could be explained by Albania's long period of isolation. Blerta said that she could not easily say that was the case—that this type of thing needed to be studied and that it was not simply "part of a trait of Albanian behavior." She added that when discussing issues such as prejudice or racism, it was important to note that these phenomena exist in multiple forms, to which I agreed, as I hoped that we could continue talking along these lines. I especially wanted to steer the conversation away from any discussion of supposed traits tied to nationality or race. Enon, however, began to talk about what he called other people of color, specifically Black football players in Albania. In his opinion, he felt that many of the players were treated well in restaurants and clubs and noted that he knew one or two were married to Albanian women. He also acknowledged that I have interviewed some of these players, who also have shared stories of racist experiences. Enon wanted me to explain to the audience *who* exactly was responsible for racist acts against me. I once again hesitated before answering and eventually said that my experiences have been varied and have occurred in multiple places and contexts. I did, however, offer that I have had numerous negative encounters with people in public spaces of Tirana, including many with men. In hindsight this would have been an excellent opportunity to try to talk about intersectionality and my experiences as a Black woman, but I felt rushed and once again felt compelled to remind viewers that I was speaking in a general sense.

It was at this point that the "jury" had the chance to speak. The night before the show began, I had been very concerned about possible telephone calls, but I was completely caught off-guard when Enon announced, "We are now going to go live to people on the street that we have questioned about this issue." The telecast then switched to a street view of Skanderbeg Square in the city center, where a reporter asked various people, "What do you think, are Albanians racist?" I panicked once more because the entire time I had argued that this was not the way that I framed my research, and yet this type of questioning obfuscated this. We adjusted our headsets inside the studio to hear answers from the respondents, and as the first woman spoke, I overheard a producer utter, "She is a Roma woman." She was racialized before she even finished her answer to the question, and I should note that none of the other respondents were racialized in this way. The first viewer shared the following: "Shumë racistë janë" (They are very racist). She continued, "Albanians do not accept people of my color, those of *us* that are *dorë e zezë* [black]. And Roma and Egyptians cannot find jobs."

This woman's statements were quickly followed by more responses to the same question: "Are Albanians racist?" Other reactions included:

> There could be racist people but only a *small* amount . . . When we have such great harmony between religions, how could we have racism here in Albania?
>
> Albanians are very racist.
>
> I do not think so, because I have seen white children [*të bardhë*] and children of dark color [*të zinj*] cry and they cry the same tears.
>
> We are extremely racist, more racist than we should be.
>
> Albanians are not racist! We are a people of respect.
>
> It varies from individual . . . It is a subjective question. You cannot generalize everyone.
>
> Albanians are not racist. We respect whites and blacks.
>
> We are not racist . . . The [people] who are racist are the Greeks!
>
> Yes, Albanians are racist, though God made us the same, one race.

As the street commentators shared their responses, I observed how this direct questioning captured much of what I wanted to discuss about the discursive practices of race that shed light on processes of racialization. I was initially terrified of what the street jury would offer, but these live clips began to form a type of dataset of expanded questions for my research about the ways people negotiated race.

When the commentary ended, Enon began to analyze the variety of responses, acknowledging the differing opinions. He then asked Blerta for her professional opinion as to whether racism *or* ignorance played a bigger role in shaping behaviors. Blerta argued that prejudice or racism against people of color occurs rarely in Albania, and that in her opinion, most of the negative behavior could be explained by ignorance, though she felt this ignorance does not justify offensive behavior. "But perhaps Chelsi can speak to this matter," Blerta said, "because she has had experiences that have been more offensive, that have gone beyond curiosity or people trying to learn more about her." I did not necessarily like Blerta's framing, including the binary of racism versus ignorance as well as the idea that Albanians had not had experiences with people of color, but I did recognize that Blerta was opening the conversation for me to talk about experiences like the "n-----" encounter from the airplane. I shared this story for viewers, and as I did so, I wanted to communicate that this experience was both curious and offensive, and it illustrated how racialization takes shape in multiple ways—that a story like that one shed light on the ways that people understand, negotiate, and respond to blackness and difference. Yet, right after I shared about the encounter, Enon asked for the *other* side of racism, a more offensive encounter. His framing was sort of a good versus bad racism, whereby one form seemed more intentional compared to another that was innocuous. I reluctantly shared a couple of stories of people yelling *bythzinj* (dark ass) while trying to push me off the sidewalk or people calling me *majmun* (monkey) when they would see me. I did not want to underline what I felt was a murky juxtaposition of what racism is or is not, but the conversation kept returning to these jumbled definitions, who was responsible for racism, and why. The experience on the show highlighted the difficulties of public dialogue about race and racialization in global and local contexts.

As our segment concluded, Enon mentioned that as a result of the 2008 socioeconomic crisis, numerous Albanians had recently returned from Greece, and as he understood it, many of them had been victims of racism while in Greece. I informed him and the viewers that this too is a part of my research, especially in the broader subject of race in Europe. I could not help but feel that with this remark Enon was reminding me that while I may highlight racist encounters in Albania, Albanians too have experienced racism. As Blerta offered her final thoughts, she informed viewers that it was not my intention to chastise Albanians in any way, and that my goal was to spark more conversations about race. I added once again how much I valued my time in Albania and that I looked forward to more dialogue. Enon closed the show by telling viewers that hopefully after more research and time in Tirana, they would like me to return to the show with updates from my studies.

Deliberation

I am unsure whether the experience on *Wake Up Tirana* turned out the way I had planned, as I am not even sure if I was clear about what would transpire. I do know that the conversation demonstrated the need for more research and discussion about race in Albania and the Balkans, particularly in terms of race and racial consciousness among Roma and Egyptians, the meanings of whiteness and blackness, the relationship between race and nation, and ultimately, local racial formations as shaped by global intersections of identity, geography, and nation. The show generated numerous questions that drive my overall research about what slowed ethnography can reveal about the intricacies of racial grammars, logics, and formations as well as multiple additional questions: How do we publicly dialogue about racialization without the conversation immediately collapsing into *who* is racist? Why do some people have such an emotional attachment to racelessness? How do we think about this idea of curiosity and histories of isolation, and relatedly, how do I study racialization without inscribing or reinscribing the idea that Albanians are stereotypically backward or ignorant? How do our positionalities and situated knowledge shape our inquiry and reflexivity, and what do anthropologists do with things that might be ethnographically confusing? Perhaps one way of understanding the show is a particular moment in which various social, aesthetic, and material registers, as well as the meta discussions of race, all pulled apart and reformulated. The processes and frictions of this unfolding, of coming apart, of assembling, all shape the continued analysis of racialization and racemaking in the remaining chapters of this book. Racialization involves uneven processes (Heng 2018), and ethnography is one way of mapping these processes.

The early to mid-twentieth century featured numerous praises and proclamations about the ways that Eastern Europe significantly contrasted with the deeply embedded color lines of the West, especially when compared to the United States. For Black Americans like Langston Hughes, Paul Robeson, and Esther Cooper Jackson, the Soviet Union in particular presented a vision of society free from class *and* race hierarchies (Baldwin 2002). All three were among those Black intellectuals, thinkers, and performers who traveled to the USSR, including Hughes, who spent a year there in the early 1930s. For Hughes, and others such as W. E. B. Du Bois, their attraction to the Soviet Union focused on racial emancipation (Baldwin 2002), but many of these scholars and activists sought a sense of dignity in the USSR, dignity that was often denied in the US. In one of the very few travelogues about the United States produced by an Eastern European writer, Yugoslav author Vladimir Dejijer (1945) recounted a conversation with Black filmmaker Carlton Moss, who fondly talked about Yugoslavia, as he had read that a Black man could be well received there.

Because race is often framed in terms of interpersonal relationships, these histories of welcomeness and openness to foreigners have contributed to understandings of racelessness in Eastern Europe. For Black leaders and thinkers who traveled east, many of them sought the promises of equal treatment in the Soviet Union, and some spent time analyzing class and racial inequality at structural and societal levels (Baldwin 2002). In the former Eastern Bloc, racism was counter to Marxism, and as such, the region was often framed as a place where race did not exist. Recent years have witnessed an increase in scholarship that has critically interrogated and problematized these ideas (Osei-Opare 2019; Carew 2015; Loyd 2021), yet the personal sentiments about esteem, dignity, and respect continue to animate discussions about race in Eastern Europe and contribute to narratives about racelessness in the region. Race is frequently understood as a proxy for racism, and for many people in Eastern Europe, race therefore seems incongruent with cultural and societal emphases on hospitality and welcomeness. The experiences of Black Americans, then, become a type of evidence as race and respect have become mutually exclusive.

I have said that this type of ethnographic research is slowed; it is attentive to multiple and overlapping happenings, doings, goings, and beings. When it comes to conducting ethnographic research in Albania, whatever the research subject might be, the research process will often involve food, and a lot of it. It was early in my research that I began to make note of cultural practices surrounding food, in particular the ways that respect and hospitality are intimately tied to meals.

As I continue to follow race as my ethnographic object, I now turn to an exploration of the cultural forms of respect and hospitality in relation to race in Albania, and the broader region of Eastern Europe. I argue that the exploration of these practices can further illuminate the elements that shape local constructions and formations of race. The conversation from *Wake Up Tirana* serves as one example in which even the mention of race elicits surprise because offensive behavior toward visitors or guests feels antithetical to what it means to be Albanian. In the next section I rely on a slowed ethnographic approach to explore ordinary and everyday practices, performances, and discourses of hospitality in Albania to interrogate how these resonances of respect and esteem take shape through the sharing of food. In doing so I hope to further examine how Albanian collective identity is often understood and articulated as a particular posture toward guests, dispositions thought to be naturally rooted in honor, hospitality, and respect. The practices of hospitality, as shaped by histories of imagined racial utopias, may obscure the ways that racialization has historically operated and continues to operate in local landscapes. Ultimately it is my hope to illuminate the unnamed and unacknowledged racial logics, thereby expanding racialization beyond the racist versus not racist binary.

The Hunger Games

A Party with Pavli's Family

I received a phone call from Pavli on a Monday inviting me to Shkodra the following Thursday. His brother's daughter, his niece, was celebrating her first birthday, and the family wanted me to attend the party. I thanked him and gladly accepted the invitation, telling him that I would be on the first furgon to Shkodra. On Thursday morning I caught my regular red furgon to Shkodra, the one with the nice driver whom I had never witnessed sipping raki between shifts. Pavli was waiting for me near the Rozafa hotel when I arrived in Shkodra's city center. He smiled a big grin, revealing his missing front teeth. "O Çels!" he yelled. We exchanged the typical greetings, and I laughed to myself as I always do, because for the first two summers that I knew him, I only understood a few words in Albanian and he knew no English. Back then we always relied on simple exchanges, the only words we would speak for thirty minutes as we shared chips, drinks, and head nods:

> PAVLI: Chels, u lodhe? (Are you tired?)
> CHELSI: Jo, unë mirë. (No, I am fine.)
> PAVLI: Sot është mirë. Dielli mirë. (Today is nice. The sun is nice.)
> CHELSI: Shumë mirë. (Very nice.)

We walked toward the boulevard and caught the orange bus to the other side of town. Pavli has always acted like a father figure around me, very protective and attentive. He made sure that I got a seat on the bus and stood guard over me the entire ride to his house. His wife, Violeta, was waiting for us at the door when we arrived. She kissed me four times and shed a few tears of joy as she often does when we meet. Their daughter came running around the corner to say hello and welcome me back to Shkodra. I sat down in their living room and Violeta offered me an Ivi soda and a bag of 7 Days baked rolls. I was not that hungry because an older woman on the bus had insisted that I eat cookies from her purse, but still I slowly ate the snacks while Pavli was on the phone. When Pavli finished his call, he encouraged me to eat quickly as we needed to get ready to leave for the village. A friend of theirs soon arrived with a car and we all huddled inside. We began the journey out to the village, in an area somewhere between Shkodra and Koplik. There were at least twenty other people already at Pavli's brother's house when we arrived. Pavli's family embraced one another as though it had been years since their last meeting, though I knew they had probably all visited one another at least once or twice in the past month. I was introduced as Chelsi, their American friend who was visiting Albania for a while. His relatives warmly welcomed me into their home, and two of the young cousins, both high-school age, shyly informed me that they had been studying English and wanted to practice a few words with me.

We congregated in the main room. I caught a glimpse of the birthday baby smiling and giggling in her mother's lap. Soon someone made an announcement to gather around the table. I moved toward a seat near Pavli's daughter, but instead a relative signaled that I should sit at the head of the table next to Pavli's uncle. This uncle was his father's brother, the oldest man at the lunch. They sat me between him and his wife as he opened his second or third beer and lit a fresh cigarette. The uncle looked at me and asked, "Who are you with, Edi Rama or Sali Berisha?" This was in reference to the two main candidates for the upcoming 2013 election for prime minister. Rama and Berisha were longtime leaders of the country's two main political parties, the Socialist Party and the Democratic Party, respectively. "Maybe Edi Rama?" I hesitantly questioned, thinking that at that time his party seemed to have stronger ideas for socioeconomic betterment in Tirana. Pavli's uncle's mouth dropped. "But why? You should be with us, with Sali Berisha! Why Edi Rama?" "Well, Edi did come up with the idea to paint all of the apartment buildings in Tirana, and I love the colors," I slyly answered, after which Pavli's uncle began to laugh hysterically, as he slapped me on the back and roared. He and his wife were both very tickled by my comments, though I honestly had not meant my joke to be that funny. His uncle continued to talk about the elections and on several occasions professed his love for Sali Berisha, though in his heart, he confessed, he was truly a communist. My stomach hungrily rumbled numerous times and I kept looking up from the conversation at everyone else at

FIGURE 9. The author in conversation with Pavli's uncle. Photo courtesy of the author.

the table, but no one seemed to be eating yet. The table was set, complete with fresh salad, soup, olives, onions and pickles, bread, boiled eggs, freshly cut tomatoes with olive oil, and both green and purple cabbage. Soon one of the relatives entered the room with large plates of lamb and placed them in the middle of the table. The smell of the meat made my mouth salivate even more, but still no one started eating. Pavli's uncle, however, continued to talk and tell stories about the history of Albanian politics. Multiple times he mentioned Comrade Enveri (Enver Hoxha). So I sat and listened as he started on a new beer and cigarette.

Some minutes passed, but it seemed like hours. I looked up again to notice, though, that the room had gotten much quieter. Many of the relatives were staring at me while Pavli's uncle continued his chatter. I stopped responding to him and looked around the room as one of the young girls finally said to me, in English, "Excuse me, but can you start eating now because we are all really ready to eat." I looked back somewhat confused, then quickly amused, as I realized that the entire time that I was talking with the uncle, who was still ranting about Enver, everyone else was waiting on me to start eating, as I was simultaneously waiting for them. I thought someone would have made a toast, said, "Ju bëftë mirë" (Bon appetit) or wished the baby another one hundred years, but no, they were patiently waiting for me to start eating because I was the guest. I then took my fork and went for the cabbage, at which point folks began to hurriedly pile food on their plates.

Lunch at Mimoza's House

Last week I went to Mimoza's house for lunch. As I described in chapter 1, Mimoza was a fantastic cook, and while our friendship initially began as Albanian language and cooking lessons, it had quickly turned into a friendship where she cooked and I ate. Mimoza really enjoyed talking about food as she performed in the kitchen. Below is a typical exchange at her house:

> "We Albanians eat fruit after meals, but Chelsi usually does not want it," Mimoza says to her sister-in-law, Eli. We had just finished a midday lunch. I always tell her that in fact I love fruit but when she fills me with *byrek*, peas, salad, soup, and peppers, I do not have any more room for fruit—I am stuffed. "But it is *just* fruit; it is not food," Mimoza adds. A little while later she asked again if I wanted fruit. I told her I would eat a cherry or two. She grabbed two bowls and placed them in front of us, as she began to eat cherries and melon. As I had thought, she probably really wanted fruit but did not want to eat any if I was not going to do so as well. I started eating and remembered how sweet and wonderful fresh cherries were in Albania. Sometimes she would tell people in front of me how far she had walked to get the *good* fruit for me, and when

I would say, "But you did not have to do that," she would always interrupt and say, "No, I do it for you," and smile. "But really, in God's name [për Zotin], this was not easy."

On one occasion at Mimoza's house her niece, Arta, and Arta's toddler son stopped by for a quick visit. Arta insisted that she was not there to eat but only came to say hello. As I sat down at the table, Mimoza instructed Arta to join us. Arta said that she was not hungry. At this point, the hunger games ensued.

> MIMOZA: Arta, *hajde* (come)! Come to the table.
> ARTA: No, *hallë* (auntie), I do not want anything. I am not hungry. We already ate.
> MIMOZA: Please do not be ashamed. Come get food.
> ARTA: No, I swear to God, I have eaten already.
> MIMOZA: We have lots of food. Look at all this food.
> ARTA: No, in God's name, I have eaten. I ate at home.
> MIMOZA: God will give us more food; please, come and eat.
> ARTA: No, thank you, my son and I have both already eaten just now at my mom's house.

At this point, Mimoza sat down and passed me the soup. "Ju bëftë mirë," she said, and we began eating. I have found myself playing this game often when visiting someone's home, but I was surprised at the display that unfolded before me. I had learned that when someone involved God and said something like, "For God's sake, I have eaten," usually people would taper their demands to serve someone food. Over the years I have tried to figure out how to play this game better—how to both extend gratitude for someone's hospitality and kindness but also genuinely and respectfully convey when I am full or not hungry. When I turn down food at my friend Mira's house, for example, her mother frequently tells me not to be ashamed, or not to be anxious around them, that I can feel free to eat anything I want at their house. I always respond that I do feel free, truly, but that I am not always hungry every single time she sees me. This friend's mom has known me for more than fifteen years and she still does not believe me. She is really good at playing the hunger games.

Mimoza and I kept eating. After we finished the soup, we started with the salad.

> MIMOZA: Arta, please, for God's sake, have some salad.
> ARTA: No, no, I do not want any.
> MIMOZA: Look at how beautiful this salad is, how fresh these tomatoes are. I picked out the very special lettuce. I washed all the pieces carefully. Please have some.

ARTA: No, thank you, *hallë*. I already ate. We ate at my mother's right before we came here.
MIMOZA: But the boy, does he not want to eat?
ARTA: (looking at her son): Are you hungry?
TODDLER: No.

Mimoza looked away, feeling rather dejected about Arta's refusal to eat. She started telling me stories about her parents and the Italian invasion of Albania. She recounted memories of her childhood, of Enver, and stories about her late husband, our typical conversation topics. We began eating stuffed peppers.

MIMOZA: Arta, look how beautiful these peppers are. They are so delicious! [She looked to me to help convince Arta to eat. I intentionally looked away, trying not to get involved.]
ARTA: Yes, I see, but I promise, I am not hungry.
MIMOZA: Do not promise in vain; there is no reason for that.
ARTA: I already ate.
MIMOZA: I can make some pasta if you do not want this. How about some spaghetti? Or some potatoes—I can make potatoes!
ARTA: No, I do not want any, but thank you. Do not tire yourself. I am fine.
MIMOZA: But what about this meat? I got this from the butcher and he is the best butcher in Tirana. It is so good and tender.
ARTA: No, really, I am fine.

We finished our meal shortly after this exchange. Arta's son was running around and playing on the house phone while we discussed a recent news story out of the city of Durrës. At this point Mimoza asked me if I wanted *çaj mali* (mountain tea). I told her that I did. She then looked to Arta.

MIMOZA: Arta, do you want tea?
ARTA: *Mirë* (Good).
MIMOZA: *Shyqyr!* (Thank God!). What about a mandarin? Do you want some fruit?
ARTA: No, I do not.
MIMOZA: What about him [motioning to Arta's son]? Does he want any?
TODDLER: [reaches out hand for mandarin]
MIMOZA: *Shyqyr!*

Flora's Birthday Dinner

One day during one of our many conversations along the Boulevard, Flora invited me to her house for dinner. "My birthday is coming up soon," she said, "and we want you to come to our house for dinner. My husband wants to meet you too." I was taken aback by her invitation because up until this point we only ever talked on the road or at a nearby coffee shop. I was also surprised because when I first met Flora's family and inquired about the part of town where they lived, the conversation stalled, and no one wanted to talk further. This was typical during initial conversations with Roma and Egyptian families. I told Flora that I would be happy to come over and marked the date in my calendar.

I met Flora on her birthday evening around half past seven just as the sun was starting to set. She packed up her youngest daughter's stroller and we headed for the bus stop, her five-year-old daughter leading the way. As we walked Flora excitedly chatted about the bottle of red wine her husband was going to purchase and asked me about my beverage of choice. I tried to convince her that water would be fine because I get migraines when I drink red wine, but she began to list every other drink in the world, insisting that I would not come to her house and *only* drink water. This debate continued even on the bus. We got off the bus at the last stop and walked to the small *dyqan* (store) near her house to buy a drink for me. I told Flora that any type of cola would be fine, but she also purchased a Pit Bull drink and a beer. I saw her have a quick and hushed conversation with the store owner, then we made our way out. As we walked away, she informed me that the owner lets her run a tab from time to time, and when her husband has a good day collecting or when they get a good amount of money from window washing, they pay off their debt. I really wished she had not gone out of her way to get me a drink, and I further wished that I had purchased a beverage to bring to the dinner instead of the small cake that was in my backpack.

We got to Flora's house and she showed me into a room that served as the sitting space, as well as living room, and semi-kitchen. The family had a small refrigerator but no oven or stove. Her husband was on the balcony cooking on a portable gas kettle that he had borrowed from a neighbor. Flora poured herself a glass of wine and made me drink Pit Bull, which I found even more unappealing than Red Bull, but I was determined to finish all of it. Flora inspected her birthday cake as phone calls rang in to wish her "edhe një qind." The kids ran in and out of the room, taking off their clothes and putting things in their mouths. The small wooden table in front of us was decorated with what looked like a handmade quilt. After a few minutes, Flora's sister-in-law and two nieces arrived carrying two more large bottles of Pit Bull. We toasted Flora, wishing her long life and health. Beni, Flora's toddler son, could barely pronounce *gëzuar* (cheers), but this did not stop him and his sister from making a thousand cheers as they clanked their plastic cups together. He kept bringing his little pink plastic cup over to touch mine, something like "guzu" coming out of his mouth each time. Every now and then a little of the Pit Bull would spill out of his cup, most of it ending up on his face and shirt.

Flora's husband made delicious chicken and lemon skewers along with *qofte* (meatballs), potatoes, salad, and cheese. He had saved quite a bit of money from the metal he and his brother had collected, and he wanted to cook the first proper meal the family had eaten in a while. As he brought the food to the table, his sister immediately stood up and refused the plate she was offered. She seemed insulted by the idea that her brother invited her to join us for dinner. She and the nieces all turned away from the food and swore to God that they did not need any food. Flora's husband and his sister exchanged more words, their voices getting increasingly louder. Flora said, "Ju bëftë mirë," and encouraged me to start eating. As we ate with the kids, her husband became frustrated as he begged his sister to join us. Flora's oldest daughter was already on her second skewer, and her son yelled, "More meat, more!" As I ate my salad, I heard her husband say once again to his sister, "Please eat, and do not have any shame." For some reason, when he said it this time she and her daughters sat down and ate. I am not sure what triggered a different response, but his sisters and nieces slowly began eating then quickly devoured their meals, indicating that they were in fact hungry. One of the nieces later confessed that they had barely eaten anything that entire day.

Mira's House

As I mentioned previously Mira's mom is really good at playing the hunger games. One evening, while watching our favorite Turkish soap opera, her mother came home and asked what Mira had served me to eat. She told her mom that we had not eaten anything and that we just watched television. "I asked Chelsi if she wanted anything to eat and she said that she was not hungry," to which Mira's mom yelled, "What is wrong with you? How can you do something like that, letting her come over and not giving her any food?" Her mom stuck her head in the refrigerator and began taking out food. "Oh, I am not hungry," I began. "I just had dinner at home . . ." But she interrupted me and said, "Do not worry, you are not a guest here, this is your home . . . Eat as you like." She has said this for more than a decade now. "Yes," I began, "really, I just ate a while ago I am not . . ." She cut me off. "*Mos të vij siklet* [Do not get embarrassed]. Here, eat something. You are at home."

A Visit with Afërdita

Afërdita (Dita for short) was not home when I arrived at the Romani and Egyptian settlement in Kreshtë, but Zamira was inside, along with Dita's youngest daughter. Zamira informed me that Dita would be home soon and told me not to worry (*mos u mërzit*), to just sit down and wait for her to return. I told her that was fine and found an empty stool against a makeshift wall inside their tent. I talked with Dita's daughter about her day and asked whether she had learned any new songs to sing. Zamira stopped what she was doing and came closer to look me in the eye. "Për Zotin," she began, "ne nuk kemi kafe sot" (I swear to God that we do not have any coffee today). She then lowered her face. I tried to assure her that it was okay, that in fact I had already had several coffees that day, which was true, but she refused my words, her ears quickly becoming walls as she continued her chores. We remained in silence until Dita arrived.

I have shared these ethnographic narratives to interrogate forms of hospitality and shame, and what it means to welcome guests. I have known all the aforementioned people for multiple years, some as many as fifteen, and though some of these interactions occurred during a first visit to someone's house, like Flora's birthday, most of my visits to friends' houses at this point had become more routine. My position as an American researcher always shapes my interactions and the ways that people respond to me when I visit their homes, but in many cases in Albania there is widespread emphasis on showing a great deal of reverence for guests in your home, particularly the offering of at least coffee. But whether a host is offering coffee, bread and cheese, cake, fruit, or a full meal, it is frequently not only an invitation to join but more often an insistence. I have named this the hunger games because this insistence rarely considers whether someone may not want to consume anything in that moment. Further, many hosts feel compelled to offer at least *something* to guests, even when that sharing might be expensive or difficult. And as was demonstrated with Zamira in the final story, shame emerges when a family may not have anything to offer, or as was the case with Flora's in-laws, someone may genuinely be hungry and ashamed to look like they are asking for food even when food is offered.

I use the word "game" to call attention to the performances of people like Mimoza or Mira's mom, who are often entertaining in their efforts to make people eat. And in the years since I attended the birthday party with Pavli's family, we have laughed endlessly about my misunderstanding and unintentionally delaying everyone's meal. But I also use the word "game" to highlight rules and structures for hosting and welcoming, ones that shape how hospitality is often thought of as part of the social fabric. Scholars have attributed many Albanian practices of hospitality to the ancient notion of *besa* ("honor" or "oath"). Deriving from the ancient Albanian code of behavior known as the Kanun of Lek Dukagjini, *besa* refers to the sworn practice of honoring and always protecting guests (Luku 2019; Nixon 2009). The *kanun* included directives for how guests were to be welcomed and respected, with strict punishment for those who did not adhere to its laws. While the centuries-old *kanun* no longer dictates social behavior in the same way in most parts of contemporary Albania, its emphasis on customary treatment of guests has continued to shape how people receive guests, as is illustrated with food. The practices of receiving guests and a guest becoming a *mik* or friend remain very rooted in many customary practices when someone is invited into your home.

But the emphasis on welcoming guests does not end with food. Many of my Albanian interlocutors are very concerned with my overall well-being as exhibited by often-heard sayings such as *Mos u mërzit!* (also heard as *mos ke merak* [do not be concerned]). The word *mërzit/mërzitur* has always been among my favorites in the Albanian language, mostly because of the perplexities that happen in my brain when I hear it. *Mos u mërzit* is situational. It could mean "do not worry" or "do not get upset." These might be the most assumed meanings. But it could also be a way to tell someone not to get bored, annoyed, dissatisfied, or disgruntled. It could also be a plea for patience in a difficult moment. The expression is not just a statement or request but can also be an adamant appeal to reassure someone, particularly considering the unanticipated or unexpected event that could change their demeanor. Even for those friends who have known me for many years, there is still a great deal of concern for my well-being, especially during times of waiting, as people want to ensure that I feel welcomed and not upset, bored, bothered, or worried.

Through an analysis of hospitality and what it means to receive guests, the television episode and the hunger games provide ways to explore those local and everyday practices that shape the sociopolitical and economic landscape in ways that may seem counter to the dominant narratives of ethnicity and nation. These acts of hospitality and decorum play into sensibilities about the conceptualization of Albanian identity and, for many, what it means to be Albanian. If race, and by extension racism, is understood to be offensive (*ofendues*), then hospitality, *mikpritja*, is the opposite of that. As such, discussions of race may seem nonsensical for some, as was illustrated by the responses from Enon and the show producers. Many of my interlocutors feel that Albanians are bound by honor to receive guests well, and throughout the country's history there are historical examples that exhibit this oath. As I have previously discussed, race in Europe is often shaped by World War II and its aftermath, and as it pertains to race and welcoming people specifically, Albania was the only European country where the Jewish population after World War II was greater than before the war began. Unlike neighboring Balkan countries, there are multiple examples of Albanian families who harbored Jewish persons and provided refuge. These heroic acts of protection in the face of Nazi Germany have been attributed to the notion of *besa* (Luku 2019), and they are often recalled to refute the idea that any racial logic could be present in Albania. But these practices are more than a refutation—they are also a call to sincerity.

The subject of identity in the Balkans is so often tied to the notion of authenticity: who is *really* a part of one nation or another, which people were *really* first in the region, or who are the *real* Europeans? Race speaks to more than identity and difference, and I do return to such questions throughout the book as I examine how nation and place play a role in race-making. But here I want to draw attention to how the stories of the hunger games is also linked to authenticity and what it means to *really* be Albanian. Returning to anthropologist John Jackson (2005) and his research on *realness*, Jackson argues that what it means to be *real* evokes both authenticity and sincerity. These acts of hospitality and the hunger games demonstrate a kind of realness in terms of what makes someone Albanian, and they also reveal the role that sincerity plays in shaping Albanianness. For Jackson, both authenticity and sincerity offer a lens to understand how people view the self and others, and for measuring what it really means to be or belong, but while authenticity is absolute and delineated by hard lines, sincerity is about ephemerality and partiality. The hunger games provide a way to explore this duality of expressing Albanianness. The acts of showing respect and the insistence on hospitality and sharing become a way to reiterate a genuine collective belief in respecting guests, a shared understanding of what it means to be Albanian. For my Albanian interlocutors, race registers as malice or animus, which, for them, feels antithetical to their understanding of what it means to be sincerely Albanian.

Connected to these forms of hospitality are reverberating social forces of shame. Nicola Nixon (2009) has written about what she terms collective shame in Albania, whereby people can experience the grip of shame and preoccupation with how shame shapes both an individual and their broader family or community. Nixon's research primarily focuses on collective shame as it pertains to gender and the ways that a woman's sexuality could bring shame upon a family, but I think this framework for collective shame could also be applied to the very question of what it means to perform or embody Albanianness. For some of my interlocutors, the very idea of being Albanian involves practices and postures of hospitality as well as deeply held concern with how guests may feel and the potential ramifications if those guests do not feel they are treated well. As such, there is an urgency to serve something to guests in your home, as was the case with Mimoza and her niece Arta, or Mira's mom's outrage when Mira had not offered me anything to eat. Mimoza was committed to getting Arta to eat and would have been ashamed if Arta had left her home without consuming something, even if that was only coffee or tea. In the case of Zamira, who did not have anything to offer me at Dita's house, or Flora's in-laws, who did not have food to offer on Flora's birthday but instead needed to rely on Flora to be fed, collective shame provides a framework for exploring *who* is able to afford to share and the type of house someone has, or whether they have a home at all, as is the case with many of my Romani and Egyptian interlocutors.

Collective shame is one way to think through my experiences on *Wake Up Tirana* and my regular conversations with interlocutors. Whether it is the perplexed reactions to my research about race or the regular cautions to not make Albanians look bad, these sentiments reflect both the obligation to welcomeness and the shame people may feel if that hospitality, and by extension, an authentic and sincere Albanian identity, is in jeopardy. The news and media are rife with depictions of Albanians as backward, villainous, unlawful, and fraudulent, in both the political sphere (as migrant invaders in the UK) and in television and film (i.e., such as the movie *Taken*). In addition to the everyday discrimination they have experienced in Italy or Greece, my interlocutors frequently reference these media depictions as examples for how they feel Albanians are the "n*ggers of Europe." I once visited Athens and while there my bank card stopped working in the airport. An employee tried to help me and asked where I had traveled other than Greece. When I told her that I had been living in Albania, she said this was likely why my card was not working because I had been over *there*, and because Albanians are thieves, the ATM must have recognized that I had been there. She worried that I may not be able to use my debit card at all in Greece because I had been to Albania. It later turned out that the particular machine I was trying to use was not approved by my American bank, and I was able to use a different ATM nearby in the same terminal without any issue. This interaction, while just a small example, is one illustration of the ways that Albanians are collectively imagined not only as thieves or criminals but also as outsiders—as outside of the *real* Europe.

Chapter 1 examined the communist afterlife and configurations of the local landscape in everyday life, with an ethnographic exploration of the lives of three interlocutors. In this second chapter I have used my television experience to interrogate the local discourse surrounding race and Albanian practices of hospitality and shame. These practices are not necessarily shaped by desires to be seen as *not* racist, but I do argue that the cultural forms provide a window into understanding why many of my interlocutors believe Albania and Albanianness to be raceless. Much of this chapter has drawn attention to the meta discussion of race, but this chapter's focus also provides context for the remaining book chapters as I move from the discourse of race to the analysis of the makings and doings of race in local and global contexts.

The next chapter continues this line of inquiry through an in-depth exploration of whiteness. I have already briefly discussed the ways that Albanians are racialized outside of whiteness, which was further captured by Enon's line of questioning on *Wake Up Tirana* as well as viewers who exclaimed, "Albanians are not racist—the Greeks are racist!" How is whiteness relevant for understanding racialization in the Balkans? In what ways does whiteness operate in a region that is often positioned as Europe's Other? What factors shape such articulations of whiteness and blackness, and what do they tell us about the ways that race is locally situated? The next chapter tries to answer these questions through a locally situated historical and ethnographic probing of whiteness. Whiteness, blackness, and otherness are continually reproduced across Europe, and Albania provides an ideal entry point into discussions of European racialization particularly through the framework of what I refer to as peripheral whiteness.

At the same time, as the section on the hunger games illustrates, my Roma and Egyptian interlocutors also perform these sincere forms of Albanianness through acts of hospitality and welcomeness. Yet, as the next two chapters illustrate, they are often racialized outside of Albanianness and whiteness more broadly. This incongruence reiterates the symbiotic relationship between authenticity and sincerity, a relationship that shapes how racial belonging and racial logics operate in the local landscape. Albanians are peripheral to European whiteness, and Roma and Egyptians, locally racialized as Black, are peripheral to Europeanness, marginal to Albanianness, and outside of whiteness.

3

PERIPHERAL WHITENESS

White.[1] In Albanian, *bardhë* (white) means "happiness," "fortune," or "good luck." A person's heart (*zemër*) and face (*faqe/fytyrë*) can both be considered white, signaling generosity or, in the case of a white face, honor or reputation. White as pure, white as color, white as chaste. White snow, white creams, egg whites. Fair white. White skin. White people. Good white, desired white, authentic white. White, *not* black. Whiteness. Whiteness that is elsewhere and out there. Balkans as white, Balkans as in-between, Balkans as almost. Silent white, loud white. Rejected white, proclaimed white. A whiteness longed for; whiteness not fully conferred.

You will recall that this book's introduction includes a conversation in which an interlocutor described Albanians as the "n*ggers of Europe." This articulation speaks to both the ways that Albanians are racialized outside of whiteness and how some may claim blackness. How do we begin to unpack the dynamics that shape the meanings of whiteness and those racialization processes that situate Albanians both in and outside of European whiteness? One way is to think through the nation and national belonging as shaped by racialization. Such an approach enables a locally situated and historicized framework for studying Central and Eastern Europe in particular (Baker et al. 2024; Turda 2021). With current widespread, global conversations about race and white supremacy, and ongoing reckoning with Europe's past and present sociopolitical landscapes, the study of race in Albania can illuminate greater insight into the textures of whiteness and how it continues to shape and animate social relationships and societal structures.

The primary goal of this chapter is to historically and ethnographically explore racialization and race-making through the analytic of peripheral whiteness. Peripheral whiteness calls attention to the ways that global racial orders shape paradoxical local landscapes, such that white European racial belonging is not fully conferred to Albanians, who may believe themselves to be "black" or European outsiders, and at the same time, Albanians enact whiteness in relationship to those locally racialized as "black." This concept additionally considers how longing and national political strategy are shaped by whiteness. In doing so, I explore what it means to long for whiteness as shaped by Albania's particular histories of imperialism and state socialism, and contemporary aspirations for European Union membership, as well as the angst produced by this longing for what people consider to be full inclusion within Europe. Peripheral whiteness is further considers whiteness as strategic, as whiteness itself does what ethnicity cannot do, in terms of demonstrating what it means to be or become European. Europeanness serves as a marker of white racial belonging (Essed and Trienekens 2008). In the case of Albanians, peripheral whiteness speaks to the ambiguity of the space of the margin, where Albanians are both racialized outside of some boundaries of whiteness and simultaneously have historically performed a type of whiteness for Western audiences and, in the local context, continue to perform whiteness in contrast to Roma and Egyptians, who are locally racialized as black.

As some authors have recently illustrated, the analysis of whiteness in Eastern Europe requires historical and local contextualization (Baker et al. 2024; Rucker-Chang and Ohueri 2021; Rexhepi 2023; Kalmar 2022). Like arguments in previous chapters, I do not use this framework of peripheral whiteness to uncritically apply Western constructions of whiteness to the study of Albania or the Balkans. Rather, I use the concept of peripheral whiteness to examine racialization historically and ethnographically in Albania as shaped by global racial orders, paying particular attention to the nuances and subtleties that produce variegated forms of whiteness. While my use of "white" speaks in part to racialized white bodies and how certain bodies are racialized as "white" while others are racialized as "black," I engage whiteness as it is shaped by historical and social processes and practices that produce global racial hierarchies (Pierre 2012). As part of these globalized racial structures, whiteness carries a myriad of meanings as it manifests across various local settings. While analyses of whiteness in the West may not map neatly onto the Balkan region, regional racialization (Goldberg 2006) and marginalization processes underscore how difference and structural advantage are racialized and further emphasize whiteness as a particular standpoint by which those who are racialized white, including those who are peripherally white, view themselves, view others, and articulate attachments to whiteness (Frankenberg 1993). Peripheral whiteness illuminates the shifting nature and fluidity of whiteness and its limits (Maghbouleh 2017), revealing the ways that some become white or gain access to whiteness, while others are excluded and racialized outside of it.

In the first section of the chapter I explore racialized constructions of Albanians as perpetual outsiders, introducing ethnographic examples of what it means to feel and not feel white (Essed and Trienekens 2008). In the second section I examine historical constructions of peripheral whiteness and how Albanians have been othered as nonwhite but at the same time have strived to become "white" through various nation-building projects and promoting claims of authentic Europeanness. I interrogate how national narratives serve as a tool for Albanians to craft a white European racial belonging. I also include ethnographic data captured from interviews with Albanians who at one point had emigrated to Greece and returned to Albania following the 2008 financial crisis. In the final section I explore more recent local manifestations of whiteness as it pertains to the relationships between Albanians, Roma, and Egyptians, whereby Albanians are racialized as "white" while Roma and Egyptians are racialized as "black."

Phone Anxiety

Coffee. Coffee in Albania is a convener, a conduit, a mediator. It is an invitation. Coffee is a sustenance, a nourishment that underpins the to-dos of the day. It is a means of connection, of negotiation, of assembly. Coffee is a therapeutic for relationships. Even if a group gathers and no one drinks coffee, it is still referred to as such. Numerous of my ethnographic exchanges occur over coffee—in a café, at a house, in a bar. A coffee can last five minutes, a quick gathering to complete a specific task. Or one espresso can extend three hours, an opportunity to connect and reconnect continuously.

Albanians have often had to navigate what Isa Blumi refers to as "an anxious self-definition as Europeans" (2018, 40), an anxious self-definition that shapes the social landscape of Europe's margins. On two different occasions, coffee facilitated conversations that yielded initial insight into peripheral whiteness. In one event, the coffee proposition was indeed extended not simply to drink and chat but rather to request assistance for an important matter. In the second, coffee was a means to dialogue and inquire about the *true* identity of Albanians.

I once had a coffee meetup that involved more time and apprehension than I had initially considered. My neighbors Bona and Kujtim were a retired married couple who had recently returned to Tirana after living in New Jersey for several years. They tried living in the States, Bona explained to me, but found that in their older age, they felt more comfortable living in Albania. Their current bank cards, still linked to their US accounts, had expired, and they needed to make a call to their American bank so that the updated cards could be sent to their new address. Bona was especially anxious about the task at hand and told me that she did not feel confident that she and Kujtim could do it alone. She had already tried to call once, and it caused such a headache that she feared trying again on her own. This is why they invited me to have a coffee. As we decided on the time and place, Kujtim said something along the lines of "You can help us because you are young, and you speak English better than we do."

We met at a nearby café later that week just before sunset. Bona retrieved the card from her wallet and handed it to me. We tried dialing the number on the back with her phone, but she quickly grew dismayed when I told her that we would have to dial the bank using an 800 number as there was no direct number with an international code for Albania. The bank only offered codes for nearby countries like Italy and Greece. But Bona's current Albanian phone provider did not allow 1-800 calls. Bona and Kujtim hung their heads low, a sigh lurching from deep within. "It is because we are not *really* in Europe," Bona said. "We are a bit behind," Kujtim added. I pulled my laptop from my bag and began to search for alternatives online, eventually finding a private number for the bank that we could call directly. Bona tried to dial it, but her phone was unable to connect. She kept hearing an operator inform her that the call could not be placed. "If we were in Europe this would not be a problem," Bona further lamented.

She was soon connected with a customer representative from the phone carrier who informed her that she likely needed to enable international dialing before making a call to the United States. This brought temporary relief. "But you will need the PIN code to change that setting," the representative said. Bona responded that she did not have a PIN, and the dejection returned once again. She ended the call with the service provider. "I have a phone!" I announced. "And I call the US often, so I know I can do that now." Lively objections ensued as Bona and Kujtim refused my offer, letting me know that I had already given much of my time and they would not let me be burdened any further. I told them that I had prepaid minutes on my phone, and while they continued to object, I started dialing.

We went back and forth, me on the phone with the bank, me conversing with Bona. English. Albanian. English. Albanian again. Bona got overwhelmed. We ultimately learned that the bank would not send the cards to their Albanian address; they could only mail them to the address on file in the United States. A relative or friend would have to go to their New Jersey apartment, retrieve the cards, and mail them to Albania. Bona and Kujtim were disappointed but somewhat resolved. "Well, we tried to do it," Bona mused. "If only we were in Europe and not in Albania."

A Wasted Coffee

I initially met Bujar in Tirana when I was invited to give a presentation about anthropology at his daughter's school. He approached me as I finished the presentation and immediately asked about my experiences in Albania thus far, whether I was enjoying the country, the typical questions I receive when I first meet people. He asked me about my impression of Albanians and then joked that though he shared a last name with a recent well-known political figure, the name was "just a coincidence" as he flashed a devilish smile. He would later tell me that he and this former prime minister were in fact distant cousins. "You are from Texas?" he excitedly asked me. "Oh, the great state of George Bush!" he proclaimed. "We *must* meet for coffee to talk more about anthropology!"

The following week I arrived at a café to meet Bujar, and since I got there before he did, I used the time to jot down some fieldnotes. When he arrived, he greeted me with an eager handshake and then quickly made himself comfortable. "I know the owner here," he said, as a man swiftly walked over to greet him. They exchanged pleasantries before Bujar returned to his seat. He ordered an espresso while I ordered a macchiato with cold milk instead of steamed. He then jumped straight to it: "Tell me about anthropology in Albania." I began with my research foci, explaining how I first got interested in Albania. He seemed to follow along at first but his faced soon showed dissatisfaction. I started talking more about race and national identity when he fervently stopped me, saying, "Yes, race, tell me more about the race research." I began to talk about racialization when he interrupted me: "No, tell me more about the types of Albanian races, you know, about the race of Albanians who are shorter and have darker features, and then about the blonde and blue-eyed race . . . What does your research say about our Illyrian heritage?" I informed him that unfortunately I did not necessarily conduct that kind of research, but I did acknowledge that understandings and beliefs about heritage were connected to my project. "But I thought you said you were an anthropologist," he interjected. "Why can you not tell me about our racial features, about how we were the first people in the Balkans?" I explained that my research pertained more to the social and political construction of race. "So you are saying that you cannot tell me about my racial background and about the strongest races of people?" "No," I slowly offered as I clicked my tongue. "So why are we even having this coffee?" he asked.

After some awkward hesitation we did continue to talk. It turned out that Bujar really enjoyed sharing his thoughts about Albania: "Albania has been persecuted; we have suffered a lot. We have been very unlucky. Not in the same way as Black people in the US, but there are some similarities. It has been so bad, I mean, over five hundred years under the Turks! We have been really unlucky. And then we went from the Turks to the communists. In literature communism sounded nice, but that is not at all what it looked like." He went on to share that Albanians had no ownership of property, no religion. "So what were we supposed to connect to, you know?" he asked me. "Now we are like lions in a cage set free. You know how a lion, if he has been in his cage forever, even when he is set free, he still walks around like he is in the cage." Similar to many of my interlocutors, Bujar used these kinds of analogies to describe Albania, like Mimoza's assertion that Albania is like a new bride with dirty clothes. Though our conversation at one point took a rather tepid turn, by the end of our coffee he was enthusiastically chatting, even encouraging me to write down more notes as he shared. Before I left, he joked one more time that I was not doing *real* anthropology and that perhaps we could chat about that research at another time.

At first read these coffees may seem mundane or disconnected from the discussion of race, but I use these two ethnographic examples to explore this anxious self-definition as Europeans. Very often race is framed in terms of the spectacular, those moments or incidents that loudly signal that someone or something is racist. Yet a study of race-making requires an attunement to these everyday conversations, processes, and rhythms, which can offer insight into how people negotiate race, and in particular the peripheral whiteness that shapes the anxiety surrounding what it means to be European. We see this angst emerge in Bona and Kujtim's failed efforts to make a phone call and obtain their bank cards, which they ultimately attribute to their European outsiderness. Similarly, Bujar wanted me to offer some kind of expertise about the race of Albanians, as a means of refuting any notions of Albania and Albanians as inferior. Relatedly, Mimoza once told me a story about an Albanian bus driver who once stopped his bus midroute and told all passengers to get off because there were not enough aboard for him to want to drive, since he would not make much money. She said that the driver only did this because of a unique Albanian mentality, one that was not reflective of being European. "Mbraptshë!" Mimoza yelled. "We're backward!" I sometimes question how much my interlocutors might overemphasize or exaggerate these sentiments with me, a foreigner and an American. But when I follow up with Mimoza and ask her why she says Albanians are backward, she responds, "We have internalized it since the Turks!" These examples demonstrate how my Albanian interlocutors see themselves as not *quite* European and white (Kalmar 2022) and instead articulate these peripheral positionalities. But such racialized understandings of marginality are not new, and as I demonstrate in the next section, they have a longer history.

Albanians as Historically Racialized Outsiders

There is not significant scholarship on the Balkans that attends to the historical racial logics that have rendered Albania outside of whiteness, but these logics have operated historically and continue to do so, whether they have been named or not. These racial logics have emanated from race theories common to Europe during the late eighteenth and nineteenth centuries, shaped by practices of both explicit and silent ordering of peoples (Wekker 2016). The Balkans are Europe's periphery, what Dušan Bjelić (2021) characterizes as Europe's "abnormals." I use the idea of peripheral whiteness to analyze how Albanians have been excluded historically and as an attempt to capture the attachments to white and European racial belonging. Whiteness is a shifting category, and the notion of European whiteness must be framed as fluid and multiplicitous rather than fixed (Boatcă 2010), yet this fluidity does not minimize the extent to which whiteness and European racial hierarchies have reshaped and continue to shape the modern world.

In her book about early twentieth-century Albania, British anthropologist and writer Edith Durham wrote: "Such backwaters of life exist in many corners of Europe—but most of all in the Near East. For folk in such lands time has almost stood still. The wanderer from the West stands awestruck amongst them, filled with vague memories of the cradle of his race, saying, 'This did I do some thousands of years ago; thus did I lie in wait for mine enemy; so thought I and so acted I in the beginning of Time'" (1909, 1). Statements like Durham's demonstrate the widely held anachronistic and Orientalist viewpoints of this period, whereby, even though the word "white" may not be used explicitly, whiteness becomes temporal, illustrating how Western Europeans have understood white Europeanness as civilization and arrival.

The boundaries of Europeanness rendered backward and uncivilized Albanians as racial outsiders, shaping cultural markers that continue to manifest in the contemporary moment in what are still framed as Europe's backwaters. These constructions of Albania were not limited to the viewpoints of those from Western Europe, as writers from Central Europe articulated similar beliefs. Travel writer Johann Georg von Hahn was an Austrian imperial-royal consul in southeastern Europe during the early to mid-nineteenth century and was regarded as one of the leading experts on Albania. Among his many writings about the nation, some of his publications included dehumanizing depictions of two so-called types of Albanian men with tails, those with goat tails and those with horse's tails (Jezernik 2004). Such ideas of animallike men are derived from eighteenth-century thinkers like Linnaeus, discussed in this book's introduction, who wrote about the so-called Satyr species of hairy, tailed men, not thought to be fully human.

Travel writings by such figures as von Hahn reinforced racist and dehumanizing perceptions that lasted well into the nineteenth and twentieth centuries. They also shaped intra-Balkan attitudes and beliefs about Albanians. An example comes from the Serbian Academy of Sciences during the late nineteenth century, in which one member characterized Albanians as "bloodthirsty, stunted, animal-like . . . modern Troglodytes who slept in trees, to which they were fastened by their tails" (quoted in Jezernik 2004). Examples like this illustrate the overlap between Western and regional racial logics that were produced by European sociopolitical structures, whereby Albanians were considered uncivilized, not fully human, and not white. Whiteness in this case once again replicates a type of temporal logic, such that those deemed backward and undeveloped are external to a refined, sophisticated, and civilized European whiteness. The timing of these mid- to late nineteenth-century observations provides insight into Albanian nation-building projects. During this period of the nineteenth century the Ottoman Empire was in decline, and other Balkan countries had either gained independence or were in the process of seeking it. As part of their nation-building efforts, Albanian leaders had to construct a singular national identity, one that was closely aligned with Europe and the West. These types of strategies illustrate a duality that animates the realm of peripheral whiteness and its complexities: Albanians at this time were striving for white European racial belonging while being situated outside of it.

Racial Belonging and Nation-Building Projects

The above examples demonstrate the ways that Albanians have occupied a subaltern position external to notions of European racial belonging. I argue that there are historical instances that illustrate how some conceptualizations of Albanian national identity were shaped by this exclusion and by desires of European white inclusivity. The study of race itself in Albania is complex, and there is little in the historical record that includes the explicit language of "white" or "whiteness." If someone would have asked an early twentieth-century person in Albania how they might describe themselves, they would have likely used words like *Shqiptar* (Albanian), *mysliman* (Muslim), *katolik* (Catholic), or *ortodoks* (Orthodox Christian). Yet I argue that racial ideologies of whiteness,[2] underpinned by notions of modernity and civility, shaped Albania's early twentieth-century nation-building projects.

Facets of this racial imaginary are especially salient when examining how Albania was constructed by those nationalist leaders who were located outside of Albania. Albania was the last country to declare independence from the

Ottoman Empire, and like other Balkan countries, its national leaders sought to obtain formal statehood recognition from the Great Powers (the United States, Great Britain, and France) in the early twentieth century. One method that Albanian leaders used to influence the Great Powers was the adoption of the Pelasgian theory within nationalist discourse. For those Albanian nationalists who resided in Western Europe and the United States in the 1910s, the theory that Albanians were direct descendants of the Pelasgians, and therefore the earliest inhabitants of the Balkan region predating Slavs and Greeks, became a means of affirming the status of Albanians as the "lawful owners of Albania" (Malcolm 2002). In many ways this was an attempt to proclaim authentic and original Europeanness, which contrasted with the uncivilized and barbaric Ottomanness they vested in their Turkish imperial rulers. Albanian writers such as Konstandin Çekrezi, who resided in the United States in the early twentieth century, wrote at length about Albanians' perpetual struggle to protect their land and identity against foreign oppressors (Malcolm 2002). I do not draw attention to this Pelasgian theory of descent to enter a debate about its legitimacy but rather to highlight how such theories were employed by nationalist leaders to fight against expansionism from nearby countries and to assert an Albanian identity that was distinct from the Ottomans, the Greeks, and the Slavs.

This Albanian identity, as shaped by the latter period of the country's Rilindja (Rebirth), illuminates facets of the early twentieth-century racial imaginary, in which both Albania and Europe were constructed against Islam. One of the best illustrations of this lies in the figure of Albania's national hero, Gjergj Kastrioti Skënderbeu, more commonly known as Skanderbeg. The story of Skanderbeg dates to the fifteenth century, when it is believed that he led a series of battles against the Ottoman Empire. Nationalist leaders, particularly those who were Orthodox and from Southern Albania, celebrated Skanderbeg as the valiant defender of Christian Europe, the hero who had vigorously fought against Muslim invasion, defending Europe from "vile Asiatic hordes" (Misha 2002). These constructions of Skanderbeg as Albania's and Europe's savior gained significant currency to appeal to the Great Powers during the nationalist period. Writers both inside and outside the country produced material trumpeting Skanderbeg's story. Political leaders further employed Skanderbeg's story to cement authority. King Zog I, for example, who led Albania in the 1920s and 1930s as prime minister, president, and eventually king, was heralded as the direct descendant of Skanderbeg. Some even referred to him as Skanderbeg's grandson and the country's savior who could defend Albania against invasions (Fishta and Schmidt-Neke 1997). As such, the story of Skanderbeg was used to position Albania as the protector and preserver of Western identity, as a mechanism for sealing Albanian national identity as anti-Ottoman and authentically European.

Early twentieth-century attempts to modernize the nation further reveal connections between Albania's nationalism and whiteness. Toward the end of the nineteenth and into the early twentieth centuries, the New England region of the United States played host to a burgeoning community of Albanian nationalists, primarily those who had relocated from Southern Albania. Groups such as the pan-Albanian organization Vatra, led by figures such as Bishop Fan Noli and Faik Konica, believed that they possessed a duty to reform the Albanian nation-state and develop a more cohesive national citizenry (Tochka 2015). The stances taken by Vatra contrasted with those of Albanian leaders in Albania and provide insight into the ways that certain Albanian migrants in the West tried to align with Western whiteness.[3]

Speaking on behalf of the national assembly in 1912, Ismail Qemali, the country's first prime minister, gave a speech about Albania's newly developed nation-state. He argued that the path toward progress was a more diverse, collective national identity that transcended religious distinctions. These statements were not eagerly received by Albanian leaders in the United States (Tochka 2015). Acting on behalf of Vatra, Faik Konica wrote a telegram urging the national assembly to take a different approach when choosing a path for Albania's future: "Vatra begs the Assembly to avoid accepting a Mohammedan Prince. Do not make the

FIGURE 10. Vatra's official seal. Public domain: https://commons.wikimedia.org/w/index.php?curid=64247776.

Albanian state like Khiva, Bokhara, Afghanistan, and Tunis. Our ideal is a European Albania like Norway, Denmark, Holland, or Belgium: therefore, we strongly advise the selection of a decent European prince from a royal house, who will bring into Albania western culture and traditions" (Federal Writers' Project 1939; see also Tochka 2015). Konica's statement depicts the ways that some Albanian leaders and thinkers desired to distance themselves from the Ottoman Empire and align Albania with understandings of Western culture and traditions, that is, elements of whiteness. Their fears of Albania becoming like Afghanistan or being led by a Muslim prince further highlight how Europeanness was configured in opposition to Muslimness.

One method used by these nationalists to further Westernize Albania was through the importation of classical music and dance as a means of transforming the souls of Albanian individuals. The Vatra band organized concerts and performances in Southern Albania, in the city of Korça, to introduce European melodies in order to civilize the Albanian population. An editorialist from a local newspaper went so far as to implore Albanians to demonstrate a closer proximity to the "civilized world," to show the world that Albania "[has] given up the Turkish airs" (Tochka 2015, 411). Vatra thus became an organization representing Albania as modern, once again reiterating the notion of whiteness as temporal. Researcher Nicholas Tochka is quick to acknowledge that there is no explicit evidence that these performances had a direct influence on the political decisions of the Great Powers, but this analysis provides examples of how Albanian nation-building projects and efforts to secure territory and autonomy may have been shaped by forms of whiteness.

While groups like Vatra were using the arts as a vehicle for introducing Western culture to Albania, Bishop Fan Noli used the realm of performing arts, specifically theater, as a means of explicitly engaging the subject of race. In 1916 Noli translated and directed Shakespeare's *Othello*, which was the first play translated into and performed in Albanian (Golemi 2020). Noli was among those Albanian nationalists who resided in the United States and was influenced by racial discourse there. It is believed that he was motivated to translate *Othello* after witnessing anti-Black racism in the US.[4] Noli believed there was a connection between the experiences of Black Americans and prejudice experienced by Albanians who had migrated to other countries, and he was prompted to translate and perform *Othello* to address racial discrimination in Albania. In Noli's version of the play, the character of Othello represents processes of othering; his alienation in Venice was intended to resemble the marginalization and discrimination experienced by the Turkish, Muslim, and Albanian other (Golemi 2020). At the same time, Marinela Golemi argues that Noli desired to confront racial discrimination in

Albania, as experienced by groups such as Roma and Egyptians. While the Albanian translation does not include explicit language naming Roma and Egyptians, Noli's configuration of blackness is one that speaks to racial, ethnic, geographical, and religious alienation and marginalization. Noli's version of *Othello* illustrates the complexities of peripheral whiteness, in that Albanians were positioned outside of European whiteness, a whiteness that was yearned for, as demonstrated by an exploration of early nation-building projects. At the same time, we can see how Albanians were locally positioned as white in contrast to those outside of white racial belonging. An examination of the country's socialist period further elucidates these paradoxes of the white periphery, as we consider how outwardly anti-colonial and anti-racist sentiments emerged alongside attempts to embed forms of European belonging within the national identity.

National Narratives and Racialization in the Socialist Period

As was discussed in chapter 1, the communist period, the Time of Enver, featured endeavors to solidify Albania's antique foundation within Europe in an effort to build a sociocultural and national coherence that had been unknown during the Ottoman and interwar periods (Blumi 1998; Galaty 2018). Similar to Albanian nationalists of the early twentieth century, Hoxha crafted a narrative in which Albanians had fought to preserve their identity for centuries, against the Ottomans, the Italians, and the Germans, evoking both anti-colonial and anti-Ottoman discourses (Nishku 2020). As a result of these occupations, there was a national obligation for Albanians to continually fight for and maintain their Albanianness under the party's guidance (Galaty 2018; Mëhilli 2017). Such narratives lasted well into the 1980s and 1990s, as illustrated by primary school textbooks that framed groups such as Ottomans and Greeks as "saboteurs of the Albanian national identity construction" (Peshkopia and Giakoumis 2021).

Hoxha initially began his tenure by rejecting the past, but he quickly realized that a particular version of history could be advantageous for party rule (Misha 2002). He emphasized Albanians' primordial presence in Europe, but, unlike the leaders of the early twentieth century, he depicted Albanians as the direct descendants of the Illyrians, an ancient Indo-European speaking group that inhabited the Balkan Peninsula around 1000 BC. This Illyrian–Albanian ethnogenesis was employed to lay claim to antiquity, as a means of asserting a belonging that framed Albanians as the original or first Europeans. The work of ethnologists during this era was used to illustrate that Albanians were a *pure* race of people, people who had fought and persisted to survive and preserve the Albanian race in the face of oppression (Hysa 2010). And, as happened in the early twentieth century, the story of Skanderbeg was used to assert Albania's role in safeguarding Europe from so-called Muslim expansion. Hoxha, like Zog I, perpetuated the idea that he was a distant descendant of Skanderbeg, the only one capable of defending Albania (Blumi 2018).

Hoxha's efforts to civilize and modernize Albanians are further demonstrated by the internal relationship between Northern and Southern Albanians. Recent years have witnessed an increase in scholarship on the historical study of eugenics and racial nationalism in southeastern Europe (Bucur 2010; Turda 2010; Turda and Weindling 2007). As it stands, the documented historical record does not illuminate a similar history in Albania, though there remains a need to interrogate the subject more fully as it pertains to Roma and Egyptian populations during the communist era. Despite Hoxha's policies, these groups have largely been considered culturally and biologically inferior to Albanians, a subject that will be further addressed in the next chapter. The historical record does, however, highlight how throughout Hoxha's reign, the party leader targeted Northern Albanians, those often referred to as Gheg, for their supposed backwardness (Blumi 1997). One of Hoxha's obstacles included rectifying how Albanians were seen, not just with the Western gaze but even by the Soviet Union, as he wanted Albanians to be seen as Europeans versus Muslims with connections to the Arab world (Mëhilli 2017). Hoxha's attempts to craft a new, more civilized identity included efforts to bring the Ghegs of the North out of what was considered "feudal isolation" through coercive labor that could sanitize Albania and develop within it a modern society; such endeavors included public ridicule of Northerners or mandating Catholic priests to clean toilets or don signs that they had "sinned against the people" (Blumi 1997). Hoxha's efforts to revolutionize Albania and extinguish religion were not limited to Catholic priests of Northern Albania, as Hoxha targeted Islamic religious leaders and called for the destruction of mosques throughout the country. But as historian Isa Blumi (1997) argues, in some ways these forms of violence perpetuated by the regime against Northern Ghegs reinforced a Tosk (Southerner) sense of power and later superiority.[5] These practices may illustrate how the hankering for modernization was bolstered by a desire for Albania to be seen as more European.

Hoxha crafted an anti-capitalist Albania, accentuating a distance from the West. In fact, for many, the emergence of the party, in the aftermath of fascist occupation, represented optimism for a liberated, anti-colonial, and anti-racist Albania. Communist leaders across Eastern Europe saw the proletariat's struggle and commitment to Marxism-Leninism as naturally anti-racist (Mark 2022). Indeed, African leaders such as Kwame Nkrumah and Haile Selassie made official visits to Albania during Hoxha's regime. At the same time, recent reporting from *Balkan Insight* has shed light on the experiences of Congolese students in cities such as Vlorë and Elbasan in the 1960s. Though the Albanian state maintained a position of anti-racism and solidarity in the global fight against imperialism, letters from officials in these cities described these students as unpleasant and undesirable. One of the Congolese students experienced such marginalization and exclusion to the extent that he began cutting himself with glass; another of the students was accused of committing immoral acts with Albanian girls and was ultimately expelled from the country (Bego 2023).

I believe there is still a need to further examine the historical record of Albania's socialist period, as there are remaining questions and gaps in the understandings of how race locally operated during this time period. Yet tracing dominant national narratives and quests to liberate the country from backwardness provides an opportunity to consider whiteness as civilizational arrival. Examining the experiences of African students further destabilizes ideas of racelessness and reveals how race and racism shaped social relations. Furthermore, despite Hoxha's articulations of anticoloniality and antiracism, and the welcoming of famous Black leaders in Albania, the treatment of Northerners and villagers, as well as African students, Roma, and Egyptians (elaborated further in the next chapter), reveal a more complex and nuanced reality involving European racial belonging and whiteness during the communist period.

Becoming White, Performing Whiteness in the Contemporary Moment

Peripheral whiteness attends to a shifting whiteness, one that captures the perplexities of racial imaginaries that have excluded and included Albanians as *really* European. Terms such as "post-Ottoman" (which in Albania's case is often read as "Muslim"), "Balkan," and "post-communist" become cultural markers that further underscore the boundaries of authentic white European belonging. Returning to Blumi's framing of Albanians' anxious self-definition as European, contemporary aspirations for European belonging are shaped by intense desires to transcend these cultural markers determined by Albania's past—to shed baggage that precludes full inclusion.

Today, the figure of Skanderbeg could be viewed as a type of talisman for European belonging. He is a fixture in everyday life, ranging from monuments and squares in his honor to his face on the country's currency. Skanderbeg's narrative is used by politicians and leaders to reinstate Albania's position in Europe, and to splinter its relationship with the "alien" Ottoman Empire and Islam (Blumi 2018).

FIGURE 11. Skanderbeg in Skanderbeg Square in Tirana. Photo by Diego Delso, http://delso.photo/.

Skanderbeg demonstrates that Albania has always been European, and, for many Albanians, European Union membership would signify a more legitimate Europeanness (Nixon 2010). There are of course significant socioeconomic and political gains that would come from membership in the EU, particularly regarding travel, common trade policies, and standardized systems of laws, but membership in the EU carries meaning beyond these material benefits. As was discussed in chapter 1, during his inaugural speech as prime minister in 1992, Sali Berisha proclaimed, "The greatest dream of every Albanian is the integration of Albania into Europe" (Kajsiu 2011). The EU itself has fortified the boundaries of European belonging along racialized and immigrant lines (Garner 2007), and I argue that Albanians have sought EU membership because it could confer that same racial inclusion. Peripheral whiteness, then, speaks to the ways that Albania is marginalized and that its status as European and racially white is made ambiguous. At the same time, this framework elucidates how this liminality is due to the shifting nature of whiteness itself. As the history of Albanian national movements illustrates, this European white racial inclusion is both conditional (Europeanness must be authenticated) and also necessitates the (re)production of an other, against which whiteness is constructed (Essed and Trienekens 2008; Frankenberg 1993).

The Albanian-Greek border has been imagined in numerous ways: as the boundary between Christian and Muslim, between socialist and not, between

Europe and *not* Europe. It is a contested geopolitical border (Green 2005; Dalakoglou 2017), and as it pertains to ethnicity and nation in Albania, Albanian-Greek relations are often immediately evoked, as shaped by these territorial disputes, questions of citizenship, and political power. I previously mentioned the 2011 Albanian national census and how multiple political groups successfully lobbied government officials to enact steep fines for respondents who answered the question of ethnicity with anything that differed from what was written on their birth certificate. Similarly, Greek minority organizations in Albania encouraged census respondents to skip questions about ethnicity because they worried that the results could potentially weaken Greek political power or territorial claims in the region (Likmeta 2011c). Similar tensions have continued to mark census counts, and as of spring 2024, officials from the country's Institute of Statistics (INSTAT) have yet to release preliminary figures, with Albanian-Greek political relations being among the reasons as to why (Sinoruka 2024).

In 2014 I developed a survey on race, nation, and belonging that was administered to college-aged students in Tirana, the majority between the ages of eighteen and twenty-five. The sample size was nearly three hundred. One question addressed the conceptualization of the word "Albanian" and asked whether the term could refer to both an individual's national identity and race. Sixty-one percent of respondents said no, that "Albanian" only indicated nationality, while the remaining 39 percent said yes, that the term could refer to both. A different question asked if Albanians and Greeks were members of the same race, which elicited a significant amount of angst nearly every time the survey was conducted.[6] Approximately 45 percent of respondents indicated that they felt Albanians and Greeks *were not* members of the same race. When juxtaposing the results of these two questions, the data reveal that almost a quarter of all survey respondents believed that the term "Albanian" could not refer to both nationality and race, that it only meant nationality, but at the same time, that Albanians and Greeks were *not* members of the same race. While this is just one data point, it illuminates more about the ways that race is imagined. There is a tendency to view the relationship between Albania and Greece as simply a political dispute, but I argue that this relationship yields insight into those processes that give race its meanings.

There remains an additional need to further probe the ways that the geopolitical border, as well as the bodies that traverse it, is racialized. To return to multiple articulations from chapter 2, many of my interlocutors exclaim, "The Greeks are racist!" I do not argue that such discursive constructions are detached from ethnicity and nation; rather, I maintain that the interconnections between ethnicity, nation, language, religion, and territorial attachment speak to the ways that race is constructed, how diasporas are read, and the ways that certain bodies are allowed to embody Europe. Particularly in the case of Albanian migrants and return migrants, how does border crossing register in their everyday lives? How do these individuals carry the border with them, and in what ways are borders inscribed on their bodies (Anzaldúa 1987; Stephen 2007)? Race is invented, but these invented ideas have material consequences.

As was discussed in chapter 1, movement outside of the republic was tightly restricted during Hoxha's regime, and ownership of private cars was outlawed. In some ways these restrictions instilled a sense of boundedness, one that was ruptured in 1991. The Albanian out-migrations of the early 1990s were at that time the largest migrations in Europe since the displacement of persons following World War II. Though Albania's post-communist migration parallels that of other countries in the Balkan region, Albania's abrupt shift from boundedness to openness and the intensity of its post-communist out-migration distinguishes it from other countries in the region (King and Mai 2008). The events of '97 and the Kosova-Serbia war in 1999 further increased out-migration. Greece has served as a primary haven for socioeconomic refugees and migrant laborers from Albania in search of economic betterment. Additionally, throughout the 1990s and early 2000s, Albanian citizens who were able to "prove" their Greek origins were given free movement across the newly opened geopolitical border in order to live and work in Greece (Bon 2008; Kapllani and Mai 2005).

In the wake of the 2008 and 2009 financial crisis across Europe, which intensified in Greece in 2010, many of the same Albanian migrants found themselves without work and in various states of socioeconomic precarity. Tirana played host to many of those migrants who chose to return to Albania, and I encountered numerous people intensely grappling with angst due to looming socioeconomic instability. Through conversations with these return migrants, I gained more insight to this precarity and uncertainty but also their sentiments about race in Greece. "We are not racist; the Greeks are racist!" It is a statement I frequently hear. These sentiments about Greece are often parallel to Albanian experiences in other countries in Europe. In their studies of Albanian migration in Italy, Russell King and Nicola Mai (2008) write at length about what they deem to be racist attitudes displayed toward Albanians. "Albanian migrants' overall experience of social inclusion and exclusion in Italy," they note, "has been continuously filtered through a thick veil of prejudice affecting all spaces and moments of social interaction" (187). And as I highlighted in this book's introduction, recent comments about Albanian migrants by members of the British Parliament have prompted widespread backlash and critique, with many considering the rhetoric in line with commonly held beliefs about Albanians across Europe.

In the next section I highlight two different ethnographic stories. The first is a shorter moment, emanating from a conversation I once had with a taxi driver in Tirana; the second draws from extended discussions in 2013 and 2014 with Albanian return migrants from Greece.

"The Greeks Are Racist"

"It is not Albanians that are racist. I will tell you who is racist: the Greeks are racist!" The Greeks are the *real* racists!" I once caught a taxi in the Pesë Maji (May 5th) neighborhood,[7] and as soon as I got inside the driver began asking me the usual questions. "What do you think about Albanians?" he asked, giving me a somewhat sly smile. I returned the smile, telling him that I really like Albania and people in Albania. "I lived in Greece for ten years," he began. "The country is beautiful, but the people are very racist," he emphatically stated. "What a shame that *they* are in Europe! Most of the people are not friendly. All the women I knew could not date or marry men who were not Greek. And the Greek men were especially racist!"

I offer this ethnographic story to introduce conversations I had with a group of Albanian return migrants in 2013 and 2014. These discussions are dynamic, emanating not from a predetermined list of questions and not shaped as a particular measurement; instead, I view this as an engagement in participatory forms of critical dialogue and listening (Craven and Davis 2013) that attunes to sentiments, sites, and stories, and that maps the traversing of boundaries and space, and the space of the in-between. This type of engagement helped me capture how my interlocutors expressed an embodiment of borders, and to articulate the deeply embedded forms of *mall* (longing) that configure how belonging is enacted (Yuval-Davis 2006). The next section uses numbers to identify the four speakers. In addition to the speakers' statements, there is also italicized dialogue that represents rhetorical questions and thoughts from our conversations.

On Returning

All four of the return migrants are close friends that have known each other for many years. "These guys are my best friends—we all have similar stories," Speaker 2 said. Like everyone else in the group, Speaker 2 was a late-twenty-something Albanian man who ventured to Greece as a young child with his family in the 1990s and spent many years there until recently returning to Albania. His family came from a small town in Southern Albania, the region that the other migrants also claimed as their *origjinë* (origin). When asked why his family first went to Greece, Speaker 2 quickly responded, "Well, we went for money." His family traveled there by night, trudging their way through mountains, mostly by foot, seeking places to hide here and there until they were able to make their way across to the other side. They eventually found refuge in a small city not far from Thessaloniki. Speaker 1, whose family also left in the early 1990s, offered a similar story. Speakers 3 and 4 left Albania a bit later, shortly after '97. All four said that financial reasons were primarily why they ended up with their families in Thessaloniki, the largest attraction for Albanian migrants in Greece.

"It was like night and day," Speaker 2 recounted. "That is what Greece was like compared to Albania." Speaker 1 added, "Seriously, it was really like night and day because over there [in Greece] there were lights. We did not have any lights in Albania." Speaker 1 stayed in Greece for almost eighteen years. Of the four, he was the youngest when his family first left Albania, around seven years old. "I did not know one word in Greek," he said. But he told us that he knew what people meant when they used the word *shiptar*,[8] describing it as a literal slap to the face, the labels of "criminal," "wrongdoer," or "perpetrator" leaving their sting. "They do not mean it in a good way when they call us *shiptar*—it is a slur." All four had to begin primary school before they fully learned Greek. "The racism began early in elementary school," Speaker 1 said. "But kids are kids," he added, somewhat hesitantly. Speaker 2 interjected, "Those that are older, around age thirty or so, they are more racist . . . I have witnessed that they just do not like Albanians." "Racism does not just refer to people of different colors," Speaker 2 continued. "Greeks and Albanians have similar traditions . . . They are more alike than, say, a Greek person and a Pakistani person but when it comes to Albanians . . ." "They are unwelcoming," Speaker 4 chimed in. "They are unwelcoming in supermarkets, in public places—they do not want us there."

I asked how they were identified as Albanian in public places. "In the beginning, it was from our outward appearance," Speaker 2 said. "We did not have as nice of clothes as Greeks when we first got there. After that they could tell by the way we spoke; even once we learned Greek, we still spoke it with a certain accent." "The Greeks are big on assimilation," Speaker 4 offered. "And they care about baptism; they want everyone to become Greek. The Bible is just as important as the passport when talking about what it means to be Greek," Speaker 1 said before all four of them laughed. Two of the migrants were baptized as children in Greece while the other two have never been baptized, though their families identified as Orthodox. All four of them, however, downplayed the role that religion currently played in their lives. Yet they all acknowledged that their family's religious identification played a role in their overall experiences in Greece, stemming from the initial motivations to go to Greece, and even shaping the communities that they were connected to in the country. Despite this shared religious identity with Greek communities, all four of them continually echoed sentiments of outsiderness and ostracization.

At some point Speaker 1 spoke up: "The media are the worst offenders! The media is racist!" His voice was animated by intensity and passion. When it comes to the news, all the bad things that happen are attributed to Albanians, even saying things like, 'A robbery has been committed, and it is very possibly that the Albanians are at fault.'"[9] Speaker 1 reiterated that in his opinion, the Greek media is very racist. "But it is not just racism but a fear of outsiders and foreigners," Speaker 4 maintained. He connected the reaction toward Albanians to a larger problem of xenophobia. "It is difficult to separate racism from other expressions because of the current [financial] crisis." More comments emerged as discussion ensued. The conversation was imbued with accusations, apprehensions, melancholy, assuredness, doubt, anger, and cynicism as they debated what constituted racism as opposed to phobias of all different groups. Speaker 3 said he certainly knew one area where he believed he experienced racism. "There are many problems dating Greek women," he began. Speaker 1 added, "Everything with you could be perfect except that you are Albanian. And their families are all racist." Widespread agreement surged about this subject. Dating struck a chord with each migrant, as they all offered stories of rejection, of what it was like when some girls learned that they were *really* Albanian, after initially thinking that they were Greek. Speaker 1 lamented a relationship that ended because the young woman's family did not want her dating an Albanian.

Speaker 4 wondered aloud if there was a difference between racism and ignorance, and whether the two could be separated. The word ignorance continued to loom over the conversation: Could it be that Greeks are just ignorant of others? That they are just not open to other cultures and to other people? Is it fear? Speakers 1 and 2 referenced the things about Albania and Albanians they have heard both quietly and loudly whispered in Greece: "But why would anyone go to Albania? To Tirana? Do they not know that Albanians are thieves? They will kill you!" "Greece is a very closed place—they do not know anything about any place other than Greece," Speaker 3 mused. Speakers 1 and 2, however, felt that the bigger social problem is that Albania is a backward country at the bottom of Europe. "Albanians," he said, "long [kanë mall] for Greece, for Greek songs, Greek celebrations, Greek customs, but the relationship is not reciprocal . . . The Greeks do not feel this way, and Albanians are not celebrated in Greece." Speaker 2 added, "The Greeks may be in Europe, but they still have the Balkan mentality, though." Balkan mentality: the definition seemed slippery and elusive, difficult to pin down in terms of what constituted Balkan mentality,[10] but without a doubt all four speakers felt that both Albanians and Greeks possessed it.

Thessaloniki, all four agreed, was not quite as "European" as Athens, as Speaker 4 put it. Many Albanians lived in Thessaloniki, which was also home to more far-right extremists, many of whom advocated for a Greece for Greeks.

"Albanians cannot get a 'Greek job,'" Speaker 3 offered. "Albanians work jobs that the Greeks do not want to work." When I asked them to elaborate on a Greek job, Speaker 2 added that Greek jobs were *good* jobs, like businessmen, salespersons, managers, attorneys, or engineers. When I asked whether the idea of a Greek job meant that there was such a thing as an Albanian job, Speaker 2 said, "Well, an Albanian job is a job that is half-done," as all four erupted with laughter. This kind of joking was common in our discussions, as the four of them rarely missed an opportunity to interject a joke. The laughter faded as we returned to our discussion about jobs. "No money, no funny," Speaker 3 said, in English. This elicited some laughter but this time lighter, more hesitant. At that time, none of the four migrants had permanent employment, and they were constantly trying to piece together whatever short-term opportunities they could find. Some were relying on family connections; others were looking for interview opportunities with new companies in Tirana. Though they all claimed to have left Greece because of the financial downturn, Speaker 2 said that he was bored and upset with Greece even before the crisis began: "My work slowed a few years ago. The women were also boring me," he joked, which once again caused all four of them to laugh. Speaker 4 agreed with Speaker 2 about becoming more disillusioned with Greece. The opportunities that his family had previously hoped for had begun to dissipate.

We shifted to talking about what it meant to return and how they understood temporality in Albania. Did they think of the return as temporary, long-term, or an idea of a continuous back-and-forth? Speaker 3 expressed that some people in Albania had mocked or teased him about not really belonging in Albania. He said he felt that he was still in between. The other respondents agreed. Speaker 2 offered, "I am Greek because I have Greek culture, but I am not *authentically* Greek." When I asked him why not authentically, he replied, "Because I have Albanian blood. I am Albanian." They started to muse more about their understanding of identity. "Communism made us backward," Speaker 4 said. "It has given us an inferiority complex that manifests between Albanians and others. It is why we have a weak national consciousness." It seemed that Speakers 1 and 2 were not so sure about this framing, noting that they believed there was an Albanian identity that they and their families expressed. "When it comes down to it," Speaker 2 began, "When we are in Greece, *njerëzit kanë mall për Shqipërinë* [People miss or long for Albania]." This longing was described as deep and tender, a fragile yet incomplete kind of yearning.

Like many others with immigration and migration stories, this longing factors into the processes of belonging, shaping social interactions and modes of being. It structures what it means to belong to one place or another, or as in the case of these four men, to be stuck in the in-between. These forms of longing are at times elusive, difficult to capture or fully grasp. There is a longing for inclusion, a longing that drives financial earning, a longing that motivates, that shapes desire and attachment—and at the same time a longing that drifts, that may never dissipate, an unpredictable longing always lingering with a potential to act but not predictable in its emergence. Throughout our conversation all four speakers shared at length about the unwelcoming nature of Greece, the racism expressed toward Albanians, and the ways that they felt Greece was never really their home. But their final words as we closed all returned toward the idea of *mall* and what it means to express a fragmented yearning, to negotiate spaces of belonging, and how to ultimately get to a place of home.

I present these migrant stories not as a means of painting a representative sample of Albanian migration experiences, nor do I necessarily frame this section as only a migration analysis. Rather, as I trace race and racialization, it is my hope that these ethnographic stories would lead to further inquiry of peripheral whiteness, particularly highlighting the notion of temporality and race, returning to the discussion of whiteness as arrival. I further hope to problematize ideas of racelessness, as these migrant experiences reveal how race is constantly negotiated, how racism is named and understood. The stories further illuminate the ways that Greece has represented arrival to Europe, the path toward European whiteness as shaped by longing. Greece served as a primary economic haven for migrants in the wake of the communist collapse as well as after '97, but it also symbolized a yearning to arrive and become European. As illustrated by the earlier story of Bona and Kujtim's phone call, as well as the stories from these migrants, peripheral whiteness speaks to the whiteness not fully configured, the ways that Albanians are relegated to the margins of whiteness and at times racialized outside of it.

Peripheral whiteness speaks to the socioeconomic disparities across Europe, the ways that Albania itself is configured outside of Europe—how, for example, Albania has been imagined as akin to Africa. About Albania in the early 1990s, Robert Elsie once wrote, "When the Albanian communist system finally imploded and multi-party democracy was introduced in 1990–1 . . . it left behind a land with a sub-Saharan economy, a country where extreme poverty was the norm" (Fevziu 2016, xi). Albania continues to be similarly imagined as "Europe's last true wilderness . . . the back-of-the-wardrobe secret land that had somehow evaded the attention of the outside world" (Elia 2023). And as highlighted in this book's introduction, Albanians are imagined and socially constructed as criminals, gangsters, traffickers, and invaders—as perpetual foreigners, migrants, or Muslims. To return to Cedric Robinson (2000) and racial capitalism's genesis *within* Europe, those othered as Eastern/Balkan/Albania/Roma were the first to be racialized outside of whiteness, shaping hierarchical groups thought to be natural. Albanians, as a result, occupy a space of externality: external to Europe

(Goldberg 2006) and external to Slavs, at times *in* Europe and at times not, but rarely considered *of* Europe. As I will show in the final section about whiteness, Albania's position within the framework of global racial capitalism must be nuanced, as Albanians do occupy spaces of whiteness in relation to Roma and Egyptians, and at the same time, there are global racial logics that situate Albanians outside of European whiteness, illustrating those forms of dehumanization produced by the geographies of racial capitalism that configure variegated forms of inequality and exclusion (Bhattacharyya 2018; Gilmore 2020).

My conceptualization of peripheral whiteness speaks to paradoxes of whiteness, whereby Albanians are at times racialized outside of whiteness yet *locally* occupy a space of whiteness. Whereas much of this chapter has historicized and contextualized whiteness, in this final section I now turn our attention to the ways that Albanians in Tirana locally perform and assert whiteness. In doing so I also set the stage for analyzing the subject of blackness, which is the focus of chapter 4.

Dorë e Bardhë

As this chapter has shown, and as later chapters will further reveal, it is important to trace the history of whiteness in particular contexts. I argue that the racial logics of the communist afterlife have shaped these forms of whiteness and the ways that Albanians take part in the fantasies of whiteness (Mbembe 2017; Rexhepi 2023). The notion of being European is not just an allurement; the very process of becoming European mandates the embodiment of white fantasy. Albanians have supported these European visions as a means of securing formal recognition of their country and their own survival, performing whiteness because, as Piro Rexhepi argues, "Albanian existence hangs on the thread of Western support" (2023, 91). Albanian adulation for Western Europe, and the West broadly, reflects the ways that Albanians experience forms of structural violence in the Balkans, as is the case with Serbia and Kosova (Rexhepi 2023). At the same time, Albanians maintain and occupy whiteness in the ways that they affirm what it means to be white, to be *bardhë*. *Dorë e bardhë* can be translated as "white hand" or "white side," and in Tirana is used to refer to Albanians, who are racialized as white, in opposition to "black" (*dorë e zezë*) Roma and Egyptians. Whiteness gets defined by blackness.

The European Values Study (EVS) is a large, multi-country research survey administered in most countries in Europe. The project began in the 1980s at a small scale, with surveys conducted in only ten countries at the inception, and later spawned the global World Values Survey. One of the primary goals of the survey is to measure attitudes, opinions, and values, particularly how they change over time. Topics include family, work, politics, religion, and the environment. Between 2008 and 2011, during the EVS's fourth wave, data were collected from forty-seven European countries (including the Russian Federation and Turkey), including 1,534 participants in Albania. The survey included the following question: "On this list are various groups of people. Could you please mention any that you would not like to have as neighbors?" [*Në listen e mëposhtme paraqiten grupe te ndryshme njerëzish. A mund të zgjidhni se cilët prej tyre nuk do t'ju pëlqente të kishit si fqinjë?*]. Respondents were instructed to select any that may apply from the following choices:

People with a criminal record
People of a different race [*Persona të një race të ndryshme*]
Left-wing extremists
Heavy drinkers
Right-wing extremists
People with large families
Emotionally unstable people
Muslims
Immigrants/foreign workers
People who have AIDS
Drug addicts
Homosexuals
Jews
G-----s [*Evgjitë/Romë*]
Christians

Of the 1,534 survey respondents in Albania, 514 (roughly 33 percent or one-third) responded that they would not like to have people of another race as their neighbors. An even higher number of respondents, nearly 38 percent, indicated that they would not want to have Roma or Egyptians as neighbors. This is compared to 28 percent who also listed that they would not want foreign immigrants as neighbors, and 53 percent of respondents who said that they would not want LGTBQ people as neighbors.

In 2013 the *Washington Post* ran a story with a featured infographic titled "A Fascinating Map of the World's Most and Least Racially Tolerant Countries" (Fisher 2013). The story's author wrote that the idea for the map emerged from a Swedish study that used data from both the European Values and World Values surveys to gauge levels of racial tolerance. That study and the map in this *Washington Post* story were both based solely on the answer to this question about neighbors, a question that appears on both surveys. The *Washington Post* news story included an infographic with a color-coding system whereby the most racially tolerant countries were shaded with blue hues and the least racially tolerant with red hues. Albania was the darkest red country in Europe and presumed therefore to be the least racially tolerant.

It is important to remember that these data reflect opinions and attitudes between 2008 and 2011, and data from the most recent EVS are forthcoming but at the time of writing had not yet been released. I have presented talks about these findings and this map before, often joking as to whether Albanians in fact might be more honest than respondents in other countries, as this map includes the United States among the most racially tolerant countries, where neighborhood and school racial segregation remain deeply entrenched in US everyday society (Frey 2020; Massey 2020; Trounstine 2018), amid ongoing police state violence, health disparities, and poverty that disproportionately impact Black Americans. The average white American, for example, is more likely to reside in a majority-white neighborhood, where the neighborhood population is 75 percent white or higher (Frey 2020). As such, I have often wondered whether respondents in the United States and Western European countries are more aware of the social implications of officially recording racist sentiments on a survey. Moreover, as some such as Stephen Saideman (2013) have highlighted, to assess a country's level of racial tolerance based on responses to one survey question provides a superficial understanding of race and racism and further ignores the complexity of the subject through an assumption about the findings of a single measure.

Still, the responses to this question are illuminating. The question does not ask respondents to list the race(s) of their neighbors but rather asks people to select those to whom they would not want to be in close proximity. As I have already underscored throughout the book, the word "race" itself is a multifaceted word, comprising multiple understandings and meanings. We must then question *who* is envisioned as belonging to a different race, as for some Albanian respondents this could be someone who is Serbian, Greek, a person of Black African descent, or a person of another *fis* (family clan). The percentage of those respondents who indicated that they would not want to have Roma and Egyptians as neighbors, however, is even higher. Most Albanians, and in Tirana in particular, do not have neighbors who are Egyptian or Romani, as many of them are in segregated neighborhoods (like Kinostudio) or relegated to the margins of the city, those spaces marked undesirable. Still, the survey responses illuminate the desires for and attachment to whiteness through the ways that respondents are asked to even imagine those they would not want to live nearby.

Underscoring articulations of racelessness is a persistent belief that race is a problem of elsewhere. Returning to my conversation with the taxi driver in the 5 Maji neighborhood, after he finished his denouncement of Greek racism, he followed by saying, "But in Tirana there are no problems with race . . . Everyone gets along in Tirana. Life is beautiful here." The taxi driver believed that Albanians occupied a perpetual outsider status and were the *true* victims of racism as a result. And like other Albanian interlocutors, he framed racism as hate or personal animus that someone held in their heart, and as ugly (as opposed to beautiful), the opposite of what he considered a hospitable and welcome space of Tirana. The refusal to recognize and reckon with racial exclusion of Roma and Egyptians is shaped by the deeply held longing to be included in white Europe, a whiteness that requires the denial of racism.

Roma and Egyptians are imagined outside of whiteness, but such constructions are often unacknowledged. Consider the following statements that Albanians have shared with me during fieldwork:

> There was a time once when I was a younger girl. I used to live in a neighborhood in Tirana where many of them stay, you know, the Jevgjit. One day while walking home I passed some of my neighbors who were seated outside. One person said, "Je bërë si jevg" [you have become like the jevgjit] regarding my tanned skin from being outside. You know, I went home and I cried and cried until my grandmother came into my room and said, "Do not cry, you are not dark, you are beautiful."

> You spend time with them [speaking about Roma]? Inside their homes? Oh please, O Zot [o God], be careful with them.

> Do not walk close to the house where those jevgjit live. You will not be able to breathe. You can smell them from a hundred meters away.

The next two chapters will provide a more-in depth analysis of racialization and categorization as it pertains to Roma and Egyptians, but here I want to draw attention to how the racialization of Roma and Egyptians cements whiteness for Albanians. It is not uncommon to receive cautions about Roma and Egyptians: warnings about sun exposure, about proximity in terms of physical space, about safety shaped by the fear of the other. Space in Tirana is racialized, in terms of both neighborhoods and the sites of begging and collecting. Such spatialization is reflected in the ESV survey responses as well as the sentiments of not going over *there* or *with them*. The above statements also elucidate how phenotypic markers, along with class inequality, the practice of waste collection, and a type of olfactory racism (Kettler 2020) racialize Roma, Egyptian, and "black" bodies unlike more normative white ones.

The socioracial categories of "white" and "black" are not used in formal or official governmental discourse, and as I have illustrated, common means of naming difference often include nation, language, religion, and ethnicity. At the same time, whiteness and blackness do index race in Albania, particularly in the everyday contexts of Tirana. The discursive practices of *dorë e bardhë* and *dorë e zezë* highlight how race operates, and not simply as a means of phenotypic differentiation but as a way of marking social difference, including along the lines of cultural practices, the boundaries of marriage, and the racialization of space and housing. The Albanian terms *zezë* and *bardhë* directly translate as "black" and "white," respectively, but it would be too simplistic to assume that they carry the same meaning of whiteness and blackness in a transatlantic context. Like many other lexicons, these terms are contrastingly used to denote morality, luck, and superstition, with white being associated with goodness and purity, and black meaning accursed or stigmatized. And like other languages, blackness, in the Albanian language, often carries with it notions of misfortune or disgrace (Golemi 2020). To recall Stuart Hall (2002), because race is a floating signifier, the discursive practices and differentiations of whiteness and blackness do not tell us everything we need to know about race, but they do illuminate contours of local racial imaginaries. The formations of *dorë e bardhë* and *dorë e zezë* draw attention to phenotype and appearance, and further, what it means to become white or black, what it means to be Albanian, to be included or excluded, and to be rendered as the nonbelonging outsider, or in the case of the often-used term I discuss in the next chapter, the *gabel* (stranger).

Albanians are imagined as external to European whiteness, and many use the language of blackness to speak to this racialized peripheral whiteness, especially shaped by transnational experiences. At the same time, those racialized as *dorë e bardhë* use the language of *dorë e zezë* to denote the actions of those who are othered and marginalized along residential, socioeconomic, linguistic, and hygienic lines, ultimately those that do not demonstrate the cultural markers of whiteness. In some ways, the constructions of whiteness and blackness become a way to make Albanians white, in a way that ethnicity cannot do. These local formations cement socioracial superiority with European belonging, reiterating the ways that historical and contemporary borders of whiteness define Europe.

Roma and Egyptians in Tirana often employ the language and position of blackness to distinguish themselves from white Albanians, and to draw attention to the everyday racism experienced by racially marginalized groups (West Ohueri 2021). These examples include the ways that blackness is articulated during collective protests or on social media. At times blackness is employed as resistance, as Roma and Egyptians combat forms of racial injustice, such as was the case when Roma communities responded to an incident of police brutality in the Yzberisht neighborhood in Tirana in the spring of 2020 (Erebara 2020). My ethnographic research has found that the language of blackness is most salient when interlocutors discuss what it means to be *feel* black, and what it *feels* like to be made other by the antiblackness and anti-Romani racism that shape the social landscape in particular and localized ways. I examine these social relations in the context of whiteness, not as a means of equating the experiences of Roma and Egyptians with Black Americans but rather to offer insight into local manifestations of broader racial arrangements of Europe, and how the Balkan region, despite claims of racelessness, is shaped by global racial structures. This thus offers an opening for scholars to analyze race, whiteness, and social differentiation from a relational rather than comparative perspective (Vargas 2018).

I once had a conversation with an Albanian interlocutor from Tirana who felt that Albanians are not necessarily white because they do not regularly refer to themselves as white people. She said that she herself rarely used the language of *e bardhë* to describe herself, unlike the ways she thought of race in places like the United States. When I asked her about the ways that Roma and Egyptians are named as "black" or racialized outside of a national Albanian identity, she acknowledged that they were associated with blackness, but this was not necessarily about race. In many ways her thoughts reflect the ways that race operates in broader contexts, in places like the US where white people distance themselves from race or might call themselves colorblind, or places like France where officially there are no races but rather a hegemonic denial of race (Fleming 2017). Whiteness in many ways still functions as the unmarked and unnamed, producing asymmetric racialization, whereby whiteness is invisible to those who are white but unequally recognizes other racialized groups (Mills 1997; Fleming 2017). In the case of Albania, whiteness can be rejected, avoided, or seemingly made to be irrelevant and nonexistent but then at times explicitly named and desired, embraced, and performed. These are the facets of peripheral whiteness.

What it means to be white has not necessarily always meant the same thing, and further, what it means to be white in one place might mean something very different in another. Yet the superior hierarchical racialization of whiteness and blackness as its counterpoint has been shaped by global forms of white supremacy and antiblackness. Through the articulations of "the n*ggers of Europe," we can witness the utterances and expressions of feeling or not feeling white, and the desires for whiteness and white belonging. In the case of Albania, we can trace how these forms of whiteness work to exclude Albanians, but then also chart the ways that Albanians assert and perform whiteness as a means of claiming Europeanness through racializing Roma and Egyptians as "black." In the next chapter I turn our attention to the constructions of blackness through six key terms and their usages over time.

4

ON BLACKNESS
A Story in Six Names

Race is an idea, an idea of people, of peopling, about the racialization of peoples. Race is about lineage, history, nation, and language. It is about understandings of who and from where and when. Race is not just skin color, and skin color alone does not illustrate race. Race is ascription. It is assignment. Race is categorical, but categories change, mutate, and fluctuate. The idea of race is about bodies: the size and shape of skulls, the type of bones, the length of arms and legs, the size of lips and the width of hips. Big lips, wide noses, big hair, coarse hair, nappy hair. Straight hair, white skin, right skin. Skin like ash, like the pitch-black night. Race is about bodies that are proper, foreign, unclean, and ugly. Groups of bodies, types of bodies, belonging bodies, bodies that don't belong. Race is about borders, barriers, and limits. The boundaries of whiteness shift: they are guarded and patrolled, but race is not bound nor restricted by borders. Race travels.

Words. Words are units and compositions. Words are created and developed. Words are agentive. They function, they signify, they morph. They coalesce. They travel. Words are soft and heavy. Sometimes loud, at times imperceptible. Words illuminate. Words silence. Words name. Words may be used to erase, but they retain their latency, buried but not bereft. Words move. Words linger. Words travel.

What are some of the ways that race travels and shapes social worlds? One way is through names and words. In this chapter I explore this aspect of racialization through an examination of blackness in six key names. The previous chapter examined whiteness and concluded with a discussion about the ways that Albanians are locally racialized as white in relationship to Roma and Balkan Egyptians, who are racialized as black. This chapter continues that conversation about blackness, about Roma and Egyptians who are racialized as *dorë e zezë* ("black hands" or "black side") in Tirana. I use ethnographic data as well as historical and theoretical analyses to interrogate how the collective categorizations (Trubeta 2003) of Romaniness, Egyptianness, and ultimately blackness are shaped by distinct racial logics. In this book I have asked you, the reader, to at times suspend preconceptions of whiteness and blackness as shaped by Western racial frameworks. At the same time, I have argued that though whiteness and blackness emerge differently in local contexts, racialization is shaped by global social processes and structures that hierarchize notions of humanity, civility, belonging, and worth. It is my hope that this chapter's focus on blackness and otherness will do two things: The first is to use an analysis of names to demonstrate how locally racialized social landscapes in Albania are connected to global racialization processes. Second, I call attention to the ways that Roma and Egyptians understand, articulate, embrace, and reject blackness, as a means of illustrating that racial logics actively animate the Albanian social landscape, but these logics are complex and need to be locally and historically contextualized.

For this book I considered writing two different chapters to discuss blackness, one about Romani populations and the other about Balkan Egyptians; when I have tried to write separate chapters, however, or even when I have given talks about each socioracial group, audiences and readers have often experienced more confusion than clarity. Part of this is due to the limited history of Romani and Egyptian populations in Albania in particular, but it also reflects the difficulty in creating neat and well-defined, delineated groups. This is not a chapter that examines the history or culture of Roma or Balkan Egyptians in Albania, as this is not within the scope of this book. As an ethnographic study of race-making, this chapter traces racialization processes through an exploration of names, how they emerge, and what those names do.

When we consider racialization and how people are named, we must think about the "continual impositions of old and new racial meanings" (Briggs 2005). There is a multiplicity of racial meanings and racial discourses that organize social relationships in Tirana, and one of the ways to explore them is through names and language. As such, I invite you on an inquiry into some of the naming practices and semantics that signify blackness and produce racialized otherness and marginality in Albania. Words play a significant role in the context of racialization. Words are not just produced by racial logics; they themselves are active—they shape social worlds as they name, signify, circulate, construct, and reiterate. These historical and ongoing six names explored here have marked Roma and Egyptians in particular ways—I ask, what can they tell us about race-making in

Albania? And what they may illustrate about the ways that blackness travels, how it is imagined, and how it animates social relations?

H. Samy Alim's extensive work on race and language (Alim 2009; Alim, Rickford, and Ball 2016; Alim, Kroskrity, and Reyes 2020) has demonstrated how race and language are not separate entities but in fact are co-constitutive processes. The racialized ways of seeing or categorizing reveal how global notions of whiteness and blackness, for example, mark everyday livelihoods. Racial logics shape how we speak, how we name, and how we articulate categories of social hierarchies; communicative practices and discursive naming play a critical role in how racial imaginaries take shape. Ethnography can reveal how race and language both become naturalized as certain linguistic signs over time correspond to racial categories (Alim, Kroskrity, and Reyes 2020; Rosa and Flores 2020). Tracing these selected terms enables us to interrogate how these names become meaningful and solidify social distinctions; tracing the names becomes a way to trace racialization itself (Alim, Kroskrity, and Reyes 2020). As Alaina Lemon (2002) has noted, when studying race in regions often thought to be raceless, naming practices, that is, "discursive practices of recognition and misrecognition" can illuminate how racialization and/or nationalizing occur (55). Further, to analyze race and language requires us to resist a singular focus on individuals and discourse at the individual level; such analyses must be properly contextualized by broader social and historical structures that organize livelihoods in multiple ways (Rosa and Nelson 2020).

A key aspect of this chapter underscores how Roma and Balkan Egyptians are at times considered distinct groups but are also collectively racialized as "black." These racial formations and claims to and articulations of blackness, however, can vary. As such, logics of blackness, and further, antiblackness, do in fact shape race-making in Albania, but the formations of blackness emerge differently for these two social groups. I follow historical and contemporary accounts, including archival material, theoretical analyses, and ethnographic data, to highlight how these socioracial identities have been produced and reproduced over time. Following Kóczé et al. (2018), I acknowledge that Roma and Balkan Egyptians in the Balkan region have varying life experiences and different identities. While I acknowledge these differing identities and affinities, I do highlight formations, groupings, localities, and collectivities that are shaped by shared and parallel experiences of racism and marginalization (Kóczé et al. 2018). In doing so I also share moments where Roma and Egyptians in Tirana have expressed a shared relationship with me, highlighting how both Roma and Egyptians have expressed that "*We* are all 'black' folk." When I engage in this type of analysis, I am not arguing for a monolithic, homogenous, or superficial understanding of blackness; rather, I am interested in the ways that blackness itself is configured, utilized, embraced, rejected, fashioned, and refashioned. While I aim to show how the language of blackness is meaningful for both Roma and Egyptians, I also use ethnography to elucidate how blackness is not necessarily articulated in the same ways for both groups. My use of the term "black" illustrates the language that is used by Roma and Egyptians, but by employing this term I am not arguing that Roma and Egyptians share the same racialized identity, history, or life experience as African-descended populations in the Americas or Western Europe. I am interested in the processes that determine who is or becomes Roma, Egyptian, black, or white. I ask what certain bodies index about race in Tirana, and what this reveals about the ways that both blackness and whiteness are imagined. I draw attention to local manifestations that I believe yield insight into categorizations and understandings of blackness, black people, blackened people, and ultimately the ways that antiblackness and anti-Roma racism shape everyday life.

A few notes about this chapter: Like previous chapters, you will find ethnographic material of varying lengths woven throughout each section, which helps introduce topics, frame broader inquiries, and illustrate key points. Ethnographic research often involves a great deal of sitting and listening. Sometimes that means carrying out short or long conversations with different people; other times it means listening to sounds, to sentiments, to the road, to pauses and gaps. The research can also involve a great deal of waiting. In this way, it is important to trace race through a multifaceted lens, for example, when someone may refer to themselves as "black" but may change their articulations at another point in time. It is also just as important to document moments of confusion, of refusal, of disengagement, of silence in response to a question—to ethnographically map those parts of everyday life that shape its rhythms and cadences. This chapter does not revolve around the lives of just one or two main figures as much as central and key terms and questions. You will notice that perhaps more than prior chapters, this chapter refers to several different people. There are those such as Shpresa who have appeared at earlier points in the book, but there are many others, nearly all Romani and Balkan Egyptian, whose lives I have followed and with whom I have had relationships for over a decade. There have been times when I have sat with families in the streets for hours with interlocutors, and there are neighborhoods, like that of Kreshtë, which I have visited routinely and where I have built relationships over time.[1] I try to provide context for the people I introduce, but I do not expect readers to keep track of each person. These are all real people, and telling the stories of real people provides us with insight and knowledge about subjects like racialization. But more than an exercise of recalling people, I want you, the reader, to grapple with these stories and what they reveal about the ways race operates.

In the same way that Enon, the TV host of *Wake Up Tirana*, cautioned me not to view Albania through an American racial lens, I am attuned to the moments when Roma and Egyptians have rejected blackness and at times have rejected my inquiries. It is my hope that this chapter illuminates articulations, claims, and understandings of blackness but also the ways that blackness is contested, negated, and at times in question. By ethnographically tracing race, and in particular blackness, I hope to illustrate the ways that formations of blackness are globally shaped but emerge locally in particular and distinct ways. In this way the chapter extends the conversation beyond race as feeling to demonstrate how multiple aspects of social life in Tirana are organized and shaped by racialized processes even when the word "race" itself is not utilized.

Finally, this chapter is not a history of the Roma people, nor is it even a concise history of Roma people in Albania. Noted scholar and community leader Marcel Courthiade (also spelled Kurtiade [1995]) has made significant contributions to the study of Roma communities in Albania, and groups like the European Roma Rights Commission have sponsored numerous reports on Roma and Egyptian groups, some of which are cited in this chapter. Despite these publications, as scholars like Ervin Kaçiu (2022) have recently pointed out, the history of Roma in Albania remains largely underexplored. I do explore history as a way of tracing language and race, but there remains a need to further study the history of Roma and Balkan Egyptians in Albania. This chapter is also not a close analysis of Romani cultural practices, though there are numerous sources that engage such topics (Crowe 2007; Marushiakova and Popov 2013; Qirici 2004; Hancock 2002; Silverman 2012).

Cultural analyses alone can sometimes be used to obscure discussions of race and racism, particularly those by Western and non-Romani scholars without a critical lens. Further, there is a long-standing practice of Western scholars and writers producing texts that exoticize and fetishize Roma populations. Taking the lead from critical analyses of race and Romani subjectivities, particularly from scholars who engage with critical Romani studies (Chang and Rucker-Chang 2020; Costache 2018; Hancock 2010; Kóczé 2018; Matache 2017; Sula-Raxhimi 2021; Vrăbiescu 2014), I interrogate how processes of racialization shape belonging, access to resources, configurations of space, and ultimately understandings of how people are denied full humanity. At the same time, I am aware that analyses of racial inequality can at times reiterate stereotypes about Roma and further contribute to ideas of Roma as only oppressed subjects. The following pages do speak to racialization in an effort to highlight how racial logics and racist practices are present in the often-presumed raceless region; yet, recalling Ioanida Costache (2018), I want to emphasize that Romani identities and subjectivities are plural and multiple. They speak to diverse histories and experiences that do call attention to oppression and violence but also resistance, reclamation, cultural vitality, and survival. Research about racialization is necessary to critically examine the continued production of social inequality, exclusion, and nonbelonging. To discuss structural marginalization and injustice, however, is not an erasure of agency, and Roma groups in Albania have a deep history of organizing and activism, particularly in Central Albania. As Costache (2018) reminds us, in scholarship about race and racism, there is a need to also draw attention to that agency and the ways that anti-racist mobilization can shape reclamation efforts and social justice. Later sections of this chapter will draw attention to some of this type of work as it takes place in Tirana.

I now turn to the next sections, which are organized by six key words that guide the remaining parts of the chapter. I begin with the term *arixhi*, followed by *gabel*, *Romë*, *jevg*, *Egjiptian*, and finally *dorë e zezë*.

Arixhi

Anti-Romani racism is not a recent manifestation but rather a continuation of oppression of Romani groups for more than six centuries (Hancock 2010; Trehan and Kóczé 2009). In the social landscape of Central and Eastern Europe, this long-lasting, racialized social exclusion, can be seen as naturalized and unquestioned. Few people are aware of the history of racialized enslavement of Romani people in southeastern Europe, and literature in this field is still emerging. As Parvulescu and Boatcă so aptly note, "Being written out of history has been the lot of subaltern, colonized, and enslaved populations" (2020, 1). Roma have endured centuries-long othering as foreign outsiders, being dehumanized and denied the possibility of full humanity. And it is these imbricated and deeply embedded racial logics, like those racial logics that underpinned the transatlantic slave trade, that justified enslavement of Roma groups in Europe.

Beginning in the fifteenth century, Roma were enslaved across Eastern Europe, with the majority enslaved in the Wallachia and Moldovan Empires, in what is present-day Romania. Slavery and servitude took many forms across Romania and the Balkan region, with Roma serving as gold washers, bear trainers, wood carvers, or fiddlers (Hancock 1987). Though occupations varied throughout the region, the cruelty and violence that Roma experienced followed similar patterns. Most Roma were not property of individual owners but were considered property of the state or monasteries. In this way, Romani livelihoods became synonymous with enslavement and property. Similar to slavery in the United States, the children of enslaved Roma were also enslaved from birth (Hancock 1987), drawing attention to the ways that Roma children inherited their slave subject positions from their mothers. Consider the following decree from the code of Wallachia at the beginning of the nineteenth century: "G-----s shall be born only slaves; anyone born of a slave mother shall also become a slave" (Petcut n.d.). Moreover, the Crown issued decrees whereby any non-Roma person who got a Roma woman pregnant, and subsequently married that woman, also became a slave (Crowe 2007).

Roma women experienced sexual violence by their enslavers, while Roma men were widely considered a threat to Romanian women (Hancock 1987). While there remains some ambiguity about who was considered white in the Balkans during this time, nineteenth-century anti-miscegenation laws, such as those in Moldova and Romania, forbade marriages between Roma and those with fair skin and blonde hair or those who were considered proper Christians (Hancock 1987). Later decrees outlawed marriage between free persons and slave persons altogether (Crowe 2007). It is difficult to homogeneously group Roma populations across the Ottoman Empire as the empire was vast and diverse, but research has shown that Ottoman-imposed rulers in places such as Moldova also codified laws that enslaved Roma (Parvulescu and Boatcă 2020). Further, archival documents from as early as the fifteenth and sixteenth centuries reveal that at many times, Roma were referred to as "slave" through Slavic and Romanian terms such as *sclavi* and *robie*, respectively (Hancock 1987). Though these two examples do not necessarily indicate that Roma were consistently named "slave" across the Balkan region, they do illustrate how Roma were socially categorized across multiple spaces of Central and Eastern Europe broadly.

The enslavement of Romani people across the region ended in the mid- to late nineteenth century. There are additional texts that provide a more comprehensive history of Romani enslavement (Crowe 2007; Mudure 2003; Hancock 1987; Parvulescu and Boatcă 2020), but the overview that I have shared here is important for understanding historical and contemporary naming practices in Albania. It is believed that Roma have lived in and around Albania since at least the seventeenth century, with many arriving around the early to mid-eighteenth century (Vukanovic 1959). At that time, many of those Roma who settled in the area performed labor with animals, particularly bears, which is translated as *ari/arushe* in Albanian. While there is not, as of this moment, any historical documentation of enslavement of Roma populations in Albania, this section's term, *arixhi*, reflects the ways that this racialized term has traveled across space and time.[2] Translated as "bear tamer," "bear man," or "g----," *arixhi* is a remnant of the labor performed by Roma, as animal keepers or bear tamers. The term is also a marker that signifies proximity to the realms of barbarism and animalism. Such meanings are crafted and cemented over time, shaping understandings of who people think Roma are. Documentation from the Balkans reveals that Roma have been described as uncivilized and unfit, or as g-----s, savages with "primitive needs" (Trubeta 2003) who feed off cats and dogs (Ozanne 1878).

As numbers increased across Europe throughout the nineteenth century, many European countries became distrustful of Roma, and while slavery had been abolished, Roma were subject to flaggings, whippings, expulsion, and harsh prison sentences (Silverman 2012). But in the nineteenth-century Balkans under Ottoman rule, policies toward the Roma were viewed as more lenient (Marushiakova and Popov 2001a), and Roma converted to Islam in large numbers. Most Albanians also converted to Islam during the Ottoman period, and some scholars have suggested that due to this shared religious identity, Albanian provinces of the Ottoman Empire provided some refuge for Roma fleeing persecution from elsewhere across Europe (Kolsti 1991). These movement and migratory patterns perhaps illustrate the development of other Albanian terms that were used for Roma during this time include *kurbat* ("bohemian" or "traveler") as well as *magjyp/maxhup* (thought to derive from the word "Egypt"). There are long-held beliefs in Albania that nomadic lifestyles are innate to the Roma spirit (Qirici 2004).

It is the term *arixhi* that is later cemented as the official designation and delineation of Roma. One thing that has marked Roma and g---- identities over time is that they have often been named not as they imagine themselves but rather as they are imagined by others whom they live alongside (Marushiakova and Popov 2013). *Arixhi* is one such example of this racial imagination, one shaped by various social and historical processes of enslavement, labor, and segregation. After the fall of the Ottoman Empire, with the creation of the Albanian nation-state and emergent forms of nationalism, those imagined as g----/*arixhi*/*magjyp*/*kurbat* were also increasingly imagined as foreign, as outcasts, as strangers who do not belong.

Gabel

An official government document from the then-Italian protectorate of Albania during World War II stated in 1943: "A large number of thieves, especially the *Arrixhi*, have gathered here in the capital city. In addition to this negative trait [of thievery], this category of people, who are known to have bad health hygiene [and] cause the spread of epidemics, are thus therefore a threat to public health" (Mbretnija Shqiptare Ministria e Brendëshme 1943a). You may remember from the book's introduction and first chapter that Albania has been occupied by multiple entities, including the Italians, whom Hoxha framed as colonial occupiers. While the Italian occupation is not a focus of this chapter, it is important to contextualize the quotation, which was shaped by a fascist government intent on creating a modern and Italian Albania. Removing Roma people was one aspect of this modernization, and in fact it was not a new practice as the same agenda existed during the reign of King Zog in the 1920s (Kaçiu 2022).[3] This official notification illustrates the government's sentiments about *arixhi*, a specific social grouping of thieving people with poor hygiene—a group considered a threat to Albanian society on multiple levels. In the notification the office mandated that this group of people should not be allowed to stay in Tirana and that all of the *arixhi* thought to have come to Albania from other places needed to return to those countries. For those who had to stay in Albania, the government recommended that they get housing—but in the outskirts, away from Tirana, as these people gave the country a bad image (Mbretnija Shqiptare Ministria e Brendëshme 1943b).

Roma have lived in Albania for more than four centuries but in many ways remain fixed as bohemian nomads (see also Qirici 2004; Sula-Raxhimi 2021). Much of the labor during the period of Romani enslavement required movement from one place to the next, and even in those provinces where Roma were not enslaved, many took up trades such as music, blacksmithing and metalworking, and basket weaving, which required seasonal travel (Silverman 2012). This, coupled with the large numbers of Roma who fled slavery and those who have migrated because of ostracization and marginalization, has meant that many dominant populations view Roma as naturally itinerant. While there are some Roma groups who prefer a more nomadic lifestyle, a significant number of Roma in Albania have been sedentary for multiple generations. Yet Roma have been and still are considered the wanderers, the outsiders, the *gabel* (stranger). In 1947, an arm of Hoxha's somewhat new regime, the Branch for the Extinction of Crime, released a decree to create a commission that would solve the problems for the nomad *arixhi* who gave the country a bad reputation (Republika Popullore e Shqipërisë 1947). Such decrees would continue under the regime into the 1970s and 1980s (Republika Popullore Socialiste e Shqipërisë 1979). The historical decrees illuminate the ways that deeply embedded racial logics have shaped Roma and Egyptian livelihoods across time as pariahs in someone else's land (Hancock 1987).

Several of my Albanian interlocutors have pointed to history, particularly that of World War II and the years of the communist regime, as evidence that Albania, unlike other countries in the region, has welcomed Roma and Egyptians. As it pertains to the Porajmos (Devouring), the Romani Holocaust, Roma populations in Albania did not experience the same fate as did those in nearby countries. Yugoslavia, for example, was occupied by the Axis powers during the war, and Roma groups there were subject to widespread systemic persecution and imprisonment (Reinhartz 1999). In other parts of Eastern Europe, more than half a million Roma perished in labor and concentration camps alongside Jewish persons. The historical record does not demonstrate that such atrocities occurred in Albania, and as mentioned in chapter 2, at the end of the war, Albania was the only country in Europe to have a higher Jewish population than before the war started (Luku 2019). Even though there was no widespread extermination of Roma in Albania, there has been a stability of exclusion over time, the persistence of Roma as stranger and outsider.

Much of this exclusion stems from the construction of Roma as an itinerant and unstable people marked by an unhygienic and deviant culture. As Chang and Rucker-Chang note, when it comes to racial formation and the Roma, "The difference of Roma is marked in part by a color line, but equally importantly by their cultural traits and purported proclivities—chiefly nomadism and associated qualities such as vagrancy and idleness, all of which supposedly distinguish Roma from majority populations" (2020, 25). This association also mischaracterizes movement patterns as a negative, natural aspect of a Romani way of life, rather than through a lens that considers the ways that Roma and Egyptians have escaped various forms of oppression and persecution, have faced displacement and forced eviction, and have not been genuinely integrated into majority populations.

One of the biggest benefits of communist regimes was that Roma were given employment opportunities and, due to compulsory laws, were integrated into school systems in ways they had not previously experienced (Chang and Rucker-Chang 2020). Many of my Romani interlocutors remember the communist period fondly, not only because of educational and job opportunities but also because of some policy decisions made by Hoxha. "Rroftë partia, rroftë Enveri, se Mehmeti desh na therri," my interlocutor Toni once told me. (Long live the party, long live Enver, because Mehmet wanted to slaughter us.) Toni explained that he learned this saying from his ancestors, an expression that highlights the ways that in the 1960s, Prime Minister Mehmet Shehu wanted to ban Roma from entering major Albanian cities, but Hoxha ultimately rejected the proposal (see also Courthiade 1995). Some have speculated that Hoxha displayed some possible feelings of conviviality toward Roma people in his personal writings (Courthiade 1995), and it has been argued that Hoxha once said that the experiences of the Roma were the result of persecution over time (Crowe 2007).

For most of the twentieth century in Albania, Roma were not classified as nationality minorities, unlike other groups such as Greeks and Montenegrins. Instead, they were labeled a distinct group, the Arixhi/Arxhijt, a separated population outside of the majority but not necessarily an officially recognized social group. At least at the surface level, Hoxha's regime worked to suppress ethnic and racial categorizations and affinities. Roma were often considered idle; even when working, the work was not always considered work (Parvelescu and Boatcă 2020), and the communists emphasized the need to put people to work. During Hoxha's regime there were numerous proposals to study ways to solve the so-called problem of the Roma, including what was believed to be their natural disposition toward criminality (including the kidnapping of children), their unsuitable housing, and their hygiene. Many Albanians today cite Hoxha's housing policies as evidence that Roma have not experienced discrimination since the regime developed programs that they felt prioritized Roma groups. The communists did make attempts to ensure housing for all people living in Albania, including Roma and Egyptians, but this housing was often substandard and kept Roma and Egyptians isolated from other neighborhoods (Sula-Raxhimi 2021). Memos documenting the party's efforts to "stabilize" Roma populations included language about "correcting" their natural tendencies to be thieves, counterfeit storytellers, and beggars (Republika e Popullore Socialiste e Shqipërisë 1981).

Hoxha's regime outwardly rejected race and ethnicity as a means of social organization, and while it was illegal to discriminate against someone because they were Romani or Egyptian, in many ways racial logics continued to shape hierarchies. There were no Romani or Egyptian officials in Hoxha's regime at any point, and Roma and Egyptians often faced barriers when they tried to attend school beyond eighth grade (Woodcock 2016). While Romani was the first language for a significant number of the Roma population, formal instruction only occurred in Albanian. Rarely did marriages occur between Roma or Egyptians and the majority population. Romani and Egyptian interlocutors have shared with me the ways their families were marginalized, often living in secluded areas and subject to discrimination at school and work. Some of my interlocutors like Sami, an Egyptian man who worked in a factory in the late 1970s and early 1980s, told me that he would often hear slurs at work. Afërdita, a Roma woman who grew up near Elbasan, shared that though she attended school until the eighth grade and was employed at a factory soon after, she similarly experienced name-calling and everyone referred to her as *gabele*. Many Roma were formally employed, but oftentimes these jobs involved trash and waste management. As shown in figure 12, an image from the 1970s, people in communist Albania found themselves on the same road but not necessarily on the same path, with the marginalization of Roma and Egyptians remaining commonplace.

To return to race and the continual imposition of old and new meanings (Briggs 2005), Roma have been and continue to be imagined as *gabelë*: as strangers, vagrant, thieving, troublemakers, unclean, unworthy, uneducated, unemployable, criminal, sickly, a threat, not fully human. Many Roma in Albania today feel that their livelihoods are akin to the experiences of other racially minoritized

FIGURE 12. A Roma woman cleans the street as Albanians walk under banners that proclaim "Long Live Enver" and "Long live unbroken unity between the Party and the People." Credit: Wikimedia Commons/Robert Schediwy.

groups, like Black Americans. "In Albania, Roma are called *gabel*ë, which is to say, 'n*gga.'" This is how my friend O puts it as he shares with me his feelings about this word. O is a Romani community organizer and activist, and he has expressed that he feels that in Albania, animals are treated better than Roma. I have heard this comparison often, whether it is Albanians referring to Roma as pests or Roma who frequently voice sentiments of dehumanization. On my walks home in my 2014 fieldwork season I used to frequently encounter a young Roma person, Rigers, who begged outside of a market and was the target of frequent mocking and teasing. I remember one particular day when the bullying became physically violent as Albanian teenagers hurled rocks, kicks, and slurs alongside ridicule. An older gentleman from the street intervened to make the offending teenagers scatter, but not before Rigers began to bawl, the words seemingly suspended in the air: "Jam kafshë! Jam kafshë, këtu! Jam kafshë në Shqiperi!" (I am an animal! I am an animal here! I am an animal in Albania!).

Naming practices have cemented Roma in particular ways over time (Parvulescu and Boatsă 2020), including the use of *arixhi* and *gabel*. *Arixhi* is rarely used in contemporary context and many Roma consider it to be a slur, with very few using the term to refer to themselves (Cela 2021). *Gabel* is not a term that has been used as frequently in official government discourse, and most of my Romani interlocutors refer to it as a slur, but unlike *arixhi*, many of my Romani interlocutors do use *gabel* at times to refer to themselves. In this way they claim a type of agency over the term. But more than an analysis of endonyms and exonyms, what the research into these names reveals is that there is very little consistency of names used to refer to Roma broadly, which draws attention to how the state has collectively ostracized and othered Roma, holding contempt for Roma and Egyptians broadly (Kaçiu 2022). In Tirana, for example, it is not uncommon to hear *gabel* or even terms like *gabel muti* (*mut* is the Albanian word for "shit").

Roma, unlike Albanians, have not always been considered a singular racialized or ethnicized group with the same language and shared homeland; instead, they have often been characterized as a social or cultural group, which further bolsters ideas of supposed racelessness: how can there be race without races? Yet the constructions of *arixhi* and *gabel* demonstrate how racial logics shape collective categorization (Trubeta 2003), as naming practices order and reorder social meanings and configurations (Neuburger 2004). The names *arixhi* and *gabel* carry meaning beyond categorization and terming; they illustrate racialization and race-making processes. And these racial formations are shaped by the ongoing imagination of Roma as wild and uncivilized g-----s, as spreaders of epidemics, as the othered and outcast that are not of *here* but of *elsewhere*.

Rom/Romë/Roma

"Do iki jashtë shtetit! Do iki jashtë shtetit!" Xheladin Taço laughed as he retold me this story. The year was 1994, and he was preparing to travel to Hungary, a trip that marked his first time leaving Albania. "Do iki jashtë shtetit," his family exclaimed as he got ready to depart, especially his then younger daughter, who he said was the most excited. "He is leaving the country! Daddy is leaving the country!" Like most Albanians at that time, Taço had never left Albania, and for his first trip out of the country he was headed to Budapest with a colleague and friend, Marcel Courthiade. The two were the leaders of one of Albania's first Roma-focused and -led civil society organizations, Rromani Baxt, and for the first time, Taço had the opportunity to form relationships with other Roma organizations across Europe.

A Roma man from Tirana's Kinostudio neighborhood, Taço had long served Albania's Roma community while his friend, scholar and community leader Marcel Courthiade, had dedicated his intellectual pursuits to the study of the Romani language and Romani history. Officially opening its doors in 1993, Rromani Baxt was their first formalized endeavor in Albania. The word *baxt* in the Romani language means "fortune" or "luck," and while the moniker proclaims good fortune for Roma, it is also a demand for change. During an interview Xheladin told me that the group's initial efforts were aimed at cultural awareness and emphasizing dignity for Roma communities in Albania. With the end of the regime and the advent of democracy, Taço and other Roma leaders saw an opportunity to address human rights and promote campaigns that would change how majority societies viewed Roma. He told me that the trip to Budapest was very significant for their organization. Because of Hoxha's isolationist policies, few Roma had any relationships with Roma groups outside of Albania. Some Roma in Tirana were not even aware of other diasporic Roma groups across Europe (Fonseca 1995). While people like Taço were cognizant about issues (poverty, joblessness, housing) faced by almost everyone in Albania after 1991, he was also mindful of the ways that Roma were more acutely impacted. The trip to Hungary illuminated how the categorical understanding of Roma was transnational, even with limited movement across borders. "After that trip," he told me, "I had an intense motivation and desire to work harder for and with Roma youth in Albania."

The name *Rom/Romë/Roma* is translated as "man" or "person" in the Romani language. Words like "g----," tzigane, *arixhi*, and *gabel* have long been pejorative markers, racist misnomers used to render people untouchable, non-European, and nonhuman, but *Rom/Roma/Rroma* is how Roma have named themselves. In Albania it is a spoken act of recognition and reclamation that was previously denied. Whereas Roma were not officially recognized as a national minority for most of the twentieth century, this changed following the fall of the regime. In the 1990s Roma were officially deemed a linguistic minority, and later in 2011 they were formally included in the Albanian census for the first time as an ethnic group. Prior to this Roma were only sometimes vaguely counted as "others" (Koinova 2000). Groups like Rromani Baxt worked to preserve Romani culture and heritage and to change perceptions of Roma. Taço says that many Albanians perceived Roma as strangers, swindlers, and thieves, even before the fall of the regime, and such images were only more entrenched following '97. Though one of the most well-known pyramid firms, Sude/Sudja, was actually led by an Egyptian woman, many Albanians believed she was Roma, and the firm often marketed Romaniness, read as magic and supernatural gypsiness, to increase the money of those who invested (Musaraj 2021). The resulting severe economic downturn and loss further sealed negative ideas about Roma: in some ways Roma were blamed for the schemes, and in other ways the result of the schemes' implosion served as confirmation of Albanian beliefs about Roma as fraudulent and inept. Sude became representative of a type, as proof of the stereotype.

The air swelled with hopeful anticipation at the dawn of democracy's arrival. My Romani interlocutors have described feelings of excitement and hope from that time, particularly about human rights and promoting cultural awareness after the repressive regime's fall. But many have since discovered a large gap between professed human rights and everyday racism. The Rromani Baxt organization began with cultural heritage and quickly mobilized into a force of social activism and organizing. The 1990s witnessed many Roma without housing, without jobs, and lacking access to education. A significant number of Roma families in Tirana lost their homes and belongings in the Ponzi schemes, whereas many others were forced from their homes by Albanian families who wanted to reclaim land and housing that they said were stolen by Hoxha's regime. The celebrated factories of the communist era slowly transformed from celebrated sites of work to dilapidated locations of respite, as Roma families sought refuge in abandoned buildings and barracks. The 1990s turned into the 2000s, and many Roma children were not in school and lacked consistent access to food, clean water, clothing, and indoor plumbing. Groups like Rromani Baxt increasingly advocated on behalf of these matters. "Capitalism is wild," Xheladin told me. He acknowledged that there were many issues with Hoxha's regime but also said that in terms of housing, jobs, and schools, there seemed to be more predictability. "When politicians today reprimand Roma parents and say they need to send their kids to school—how are kids supposed to go to school if they do not get to eat?"[4]

Such social issues became the primary focus of entities like Rromani Baxt and its later sister organization, Rromano Kham (meaning "Roma sun"), led by Xheladin's daughter. These organizations work to address discrimination, housing crises, and unemployment, and they play a vital role for Roma communities who are inadequately served by local or national government. These two organizations have sponsored projects to try to get school instruction in the Romani language, a hard-fought effort that is still not widespread in Albania. Taço says that he has additionally led efforts to try to change the national perception of Roma in Albania, at times serving in an ambassadorial role with governmental leaders. As an advocate he is not afraid to criticize or correct. And his daughter was once dubbed "Albania's next Obama" by Tirana's local media. Some days she leads political efforts and rallies with other civil society organizations. On other days she comforts mothers who have lost babies and children in the informal settlements. She tries to find bread or beans when there is no food; she works to stop illegal evictions and provide shelter for people forcibly displaced. She leads protests and makes demands of organizations like Amnesty International to intervene in local affairs.

One of the ways that we can trace processes of racialization in Tirana is through practices and patterns of segregation that often render Roma outside of spaces of belonging (West Ohueri 2021). A significant number of Roma families in Tirana reside in the Kinostudio neighborhood, named for the first Albanian film studio built in the early 1950s. The Roma neighborhood was largely constructed during this same time, as many families were located and relocated here by Hoxha's regime, just beyond the city's main trash heap. Xheladin Taço's family's home was in this neighborhood. For those Roma that do not reside in this area, however, most live in various segregated areas, either smaller settlements located in alleyways and behind buildings, along the riverbank, or in larger, informal camps on the outskirts of the city. Many of these encampments are made up of the families who lost their homes in '97, while others have migrated to Tirana from other parts of the country in search of the work and housing they could not obtain in more rural regions. Because of the informal nature of these settlements, Roma (and also Egyptians) in Albania are easily evicted (West Ohueri 2021; see also Picker 2017 and Vincze 2014). In recent years the Tirana municipality has demolished many of these Roma settlements in the name of development and a greener future. I discuss this, and the resulting displacement of Romani and Egyptian families, in chapter 5, but I highlight it now as a means of illustrating how these racialized practices of segregation and abandonment shape the everyday life of Roma in Tirana.

When I conducted fieldwork with Romani and Egyptian families in 2013 and 2014, most of my interlocutors resided in informal settlements, like Kreshtë, located in Tirana's outskirts behind an abandoned communist-era factory. I normally traveled to Kreshtë via bus, but one day I took a cab with an Albanian driver. When he asked why I was going to that area, I began to explain my research when he interjected, "Nuk rrijnë dot në pallate! Duan të marrin gomerë brënda!" (They do not live properly in apartments! They will bring their donkeys inside!). I have heard this expression more than once during fieldwork from those who have felt that typical housing in Tirana is not well suited to house Roma because they do not know how to live in apartment buildings and would want to bring their donkeys or other animals inside. While some of my Albanian interlocutors might argue that they have articulated these sentiments in jest, these beliefs nevertheless reiterate commonly held views of Roma as uncivilized, itinerant, and more suited to live in rural areas with animals. In the case of the settlement I was visiting, Roma (and some Egyptian) families lived amid squalor: trash and excrement lined the grounds, and housing units were barely held together by metal scraps, pieces of wood, and tattered cloth. At the time of my research at least three babies had died during the winter months at this settlement. Yet the camp was surrounded by large and spacious apartment buildings, six of them, all empty. The buildings remained empty for nearly six years before occupants were able to dwell there, yet even once the units became available, none of the Romani and Egyptian families from Kreshtë were given the opportunity to occupy them.

Along with Shpresa, Gresa was one of my interlocutors from Kreshtë, and we regularly had long conversations about life in Tirana. One of those conversations included her husband Flori, who normally spent his days collecting scraps around Tirana, but on one particular day he arrived home early and decided to join us for coffee. "White people [*dorë e bardhë*] speak badly about Roma," Gresa began. "If we go look for cans or collect scraps, they say bad things about us. They think they are superior to us, in their houses and apartments, while we are stuck living under umbrellas and tents . . . For me, there is absolutely racial division and discrimination in Albania, especially Tirana. It has existed in Albania before and now."

We continued talking, my Turkish coffee long gone, Flori somehow still sipping his. As we began to wrap up, I decided to ask Flori what he thought could make life in the neighborhood better or what could be done to address inequality in Albania. I had to remind him that I was asking for his perspective or point of view, as sometimes people would assume that I was looking for an expert answer or official policy solution. Flori crumpled his face but did not answer audibly, remaining silent. We had spent the better part of an hour discussing experiences in the settlement, so I thought this question aligned with our conversation. I anxiously looked to Shpresa, wondering if I had spoken incorrectly or concerned that perhaps my line of questioning had struck a nerve of discomfort. After one or two minutes, Shpresa responded but slightly rephrased my question. "Oh, Flori, in the event that it could somehow be possible, how could things be better here for our community?" This revised question seemed to offer greater clarity for Flori as he replied, "As the days go on, things are only going to get worse. No one ever asks about us; no one cares. It is racial discrimination. Now if we were white [*dorë e bardhë*], then maybe that would make a change. Maybe then they would ask about us."

These ethnographic examples are not necessarily representative of all Roma in Tirana or Albania, and not all Roma in Tirana live in the same conditions as my interlocutors in the barracks of Kreshtë. These examples do illustrate, however, that despite persistent denials of race in Albania, Roma do articulate and emphasize their racialized positionalities in relationship to Albanians. These ethnographic stories, as well as those captured later in the chapter, reveal how racialized language is used in Tirana, as well as the ways that race shapes access to resources, home ownership, and capital, and collective racialization of Roma as black, as counter to white. For Flori, he could not even answer my question about what could make life better for those who lived in the Kreshtë encampment because for him, his daily life in Albania is intimately shaped by a color line, one that may not always be named but continues to delineate racial belonging. Flori believed that his life in Kreshtë could only be better if he were white—only then would people care about Roma.

In the fall of 2017 the Albanian Parliament passed law no. 96/2017, which officially recognized Roma as a national minority, a fiat that stemmed from numerous efforts led by activist and advocacy organizations. This legislative recognition, distinct from that of a linguistic minority, was also the first to formally recognize Roma with the name *Roma*. As a result of this legal change, Roma would be entitled to guaranteed rights to education, greater cultural protection, and increased participation in public and socioeconomic life in Albania (Council of Europe 2017). Finally, the legislation was supposed to ensure that Roma are represented by the Committee for National Minorities, which in theory regularly reports to the prime minister on policy matters regarding minoritized populations. Additionally, a new television program, *Bashkëjetesë dhe Integrim* (Coexistence and integration) was developed by a local television station, RTSH, which featured episodes about Romani life and culture. Yet, despite these shifts, as well as Albania's participation in the Decade of Roma Inclusion, Roma in many ways remain ostracized as outside others.[5] The word *Roma* is a means of claiming an identity previously denied, but for many Roma in Tirana, name recognition is not racial reckoning, nor does the formal designation preclude continued use of misnomers and slurs. Official designations do not eliminate everyday racism. As scholar Ioanida Costache (2023) has noted, *Roma* has become a negative referent for European whiteness, a term akin to savage. Segregation remains entrenched. Forced evictions and displacements continue. High rates of unemployment and hunger persist. Equal access to education is elusive.

In Albania, "racism is not seen but it acts," wrote the leaders of Rromani Baxt once in a letter to various European Union embassies in Tirana.[6] The fall of the communist regime brought a sense of hope to Roma as many looked forward to a new era of human rights and, like Albanians, the ability to participate in democratic processes. Many of my interlocutors feel they are still waiting. Some Albanian interlocutors have expressed to me that Roma in Albania very rarely experience public extremist violence from skinheads or neo-Nazis, like they do in places such as Czechia or Hungary. As a result, these interlocutors have argued that Roma are not racialized and do not experience racism. But Roma in Albania are subject to seemingly mundane, ordinary violence, which also includes police and state violence (Taylor 2020), medical violence, sexual violence, verbal and physical assault toward those who beg in the street, and as chapter 5 will demonstrate, forced displacement and raids on settlements. The racial logics of disposability and degradation shape an everyday rhythm, one in which Roma are criminalized, surveilled, and dehumanized. For numerous Roma this tempo involves familiar patterns of precarity, questioning whether they might sell an adequate number of secondhand materials, whether they will collect enough money or wash enough windows, whether there will be an encounter with the police or state, whether a family will be displaced from their home or watch their neighborhood be demolished. Marginalization and ostracization are made ordinary, becoming forms of exclusion that do not necessarily involve regularly occurring public acts of violence but forms that cement nonbelonging as natural, continually legitimized through racial imaginations that render Roma subhuman, outside of Albanianness—outside of whiteness.

Jevg/Jevgjit

"You're black like us," Arben said to me as he touched my forearm then touched his cheeks. "But your hair, how did you get your hair like that?" I laughed and explained that my hair is kind of like braids, and that in English, the word we use is "locs." I told them that over time, with twisting, palm rolling, and gel, my hair strands began to stay in place and were thus locked together. But to explain this in Albanian I had to say hair "gel," which is written as *xhel*. In Albanian *xh* makes a sound akin to the *j* sound in English, but also the Albanian letter *gj* makes a similar sound, like a hard *g*. For a nonnative Albanian speaker like me, the difference can be very slight, and I unfortunately do not always enunciate the distinction well. As such, rather than saying that my hair had *xhel* in it, Arben and his siblings heard me say I used *gjellë* in my hair, which is the word for an entrée or main dish at a meal. They were of course very perplexed. "What do you mean you have *gjellë* in your hair?" they asked in astonishment. "Why would *anyone* do that?" Eventually I was able to correct my mistake, but from that first moment on, whenever they would see me approaching in the road, Arben or his cousin would yell, "Look, here comes Chelsi with *gjellë* in her hair!"

In addition to begging for coins, Arben and his younger cousins would wash windows at traffic stops along the main boulevard in Tirana. Arben, who was roughly eleven or twelve years old, wore the same drooping sweatpants almost every day, his white T-shirt hanging ever slightly from his shoulder. He usually wore oversized slippers, known as *shapka*, that are typically worn inside of homes. Arben told me that he wore his *shapka* outdoors because they were his only pair of shoes. On many days I sat with his mom during her breaks from begging along the boulevard. We would pass the time watching the road, the kids moving up and down, sauntering along the Lana (River Road). "How much do you all get from washing windows?" I asked her during one of our first conversations. "Whatever *lekë* [money] or slur they give us," she replied. Most of the family members lived in Kombinat, an area of town located in southwestern Tirana, named for the infamous yet now defunct Kombinat textile factory, which was largely financed by the Soviets during Hoxha's time. It was the first factory to be built in Albania from the ground up. Writing about Kombinat, Elidor Mëhilli (2017) described it as "a battle against long-standing backwardness, delivering precious Soviet machines where previously there had only been mud and misery. . . . It was a factory for making workers" (98–100). "We live just past Kombinat," Flora, Arben's aunt, said, "and we take the bus here to the center every day. There is nothing out there where we are. It is just all *kot* [useless]." Perhaps for Flora, not even the mud and misery remained.

The first time I met Arben's younger cousin, Fatmir, he stood next to me in the road and extended his hand and said, "Më jep njëqind lekë" (Give me 100 lekë).[7] A waiter was standing outside, having just kicked Fatmir out of a café because he was begging for money. "Mistrec!" (Troublemaker!), the waiter yelled. I looked down into Fatmir's large brown eyes as he asked me for money a second time. "Please," he then said to me, in English. I smiled. "Where did you learn how to say 'please'?" I retorted, in Albanian. He returned the smile. "I learned it from a friend." I looked down and realized that he was not wearing shoes but instead thick socks that were several sizes too big. An oversized pink and yellow hoodie barely clung to his small frame. I asked him his age, and he told me he was twelve. I furrowed my brow and told him he looked small for twelve. "Okay, okay," he said. "I am ten." I later learned from his sister that he was eight. I asked him if he attended school, and he told me he did not. I asked what he did during the day, and he said he mostly walked the Blloku streets.[8]

Fatmir eventually became somewhat of a friend. It seemed that everyone around Blloku knew him. He helped me to create a map of sites in Blloku and Tajvani where his family members might beg or wash cars, which in turn helped me understand how everyone was related. At night Fatmir would weave in and out of nightclubs and cafés as he made his rounds. He and his sisters usually arrived in the evenings when the area was busier, which would increase their chances of getting more money. Sometimes they came with their older sister-in-law who begged with her young child on a strip of cardboard, the child's face always covered with a scarf. At other times they were accompanied by their mother, who had a heart condition and often fell asleep on the sidewalk, hands cupped and outstretched as she slumped against the gates of what used to be Hoxha's villa. "So is your family Roma?" I asked Fatmir. He scrunched his small face and clicked his tongue, resenting my inquiry. "No, I am not *gabel*. We do not speak that *gabezqe*." The word *gabezqe* is a derogatory term for the Romani language, deriving from the word *gabel*. He and his siblings spoke Albanian. "*We* do not dig in the trash like *them*—we beg for money," he explained. "We are *jevg*." During one of my few conversations with Fatmir's mother, I asked about her family background. "My father was black, real black, I mean darker than you," she said to me as she gave a small chuckle. "Do you consider yourself Roma?" I asked her. She clicked her tongue and wagged her finger just as Fatmir had done. "No! We are *jevg*. We beg because we lost our house and our money, and we cannot get jobs in Tirana. But we are not like the *others*—we are not Roma."

Jevg is a shortened form of *jevgjit/evgjit*, a word thought to derive from the Albanian word for Egypt, *Egjipt/Egjipti*. Like other names in this chapter, this one carries multiple meanings, many of which are tied to racialized phenotypes. An example comes from the Albanian novel *Jevgu i bardhë* (The white *jevg*), which tells the story of an Albanian orphan of war who was raised with a dark-skinned *jevg* family. After the war the child was placed in a home for children, but he was unhappy there and eventually fled to rejoin the *jevg* family. Well-known Albanian translator Pavli Qesku (2004) translates *evgjit* as a "dark-skinned person" and *jevg* as "darkie." My conversations with Albanian friends have illuminated the myriad ways that people delineate the meanings of *jevg*.

An example stems from a dental visit I once took with Mira in Tirana. While checking out after the appointment, I realized that I did not have as much cash as I thought I did in my wallet. I told the dental assistant I would go to the ATM and quickly get money to pay for the visit, but Mira insisted that we just combine what cash we had then pay together. We took all the bills and coins out of our purses and ultimately had just enough to cover the fees. As we were leaving, Mira laughed and said, "Jemi bërë si jevgj" (We have become like the *jevgs*), as she and the dentist both snickered. I asked Mira what she meant by this, and she said, "You know, we are like them now because they always spend all of their money at one time." On a different occasion I had coffee with my friend Agim, a local historian in Tirana. I asked him about the meaning of *jevg*, and he explained that it referred to someone who quickly spends all of their money: "[they] cannot save and do not know how to plan for a future." Agim felt the name *jevg* was not racist but said that uttering the term was not necessarily appropriate either. Another friend, Endrit, once told me that when he grew up in Tirana in the 1980s and 1990s, the term *jevg* was not derogatory but rather was equivalent to "handyman": "Every neighborhood had someone who was *jevg* who could fix things or would have scrap material. They also collected items that other neighbors had discarded." Besa once described *jevg* to mean someone who resells clothes; sometimes they might have really nice used clothes, but in Tirana people may whisper that they bought clothes from a *jevg*. At a wedding once Besa also told me that people who are *jevg* are the best musicians.

One thing that has become apparent is the way that Albanians will use the same descriptions and attributes for those they call *gabel* and those who are called *jevg*. A person who is *jevg* might be the wedding musician, the clothes seller, the scrap collector, the spendthrift, the dark-skinned person. Roma can also be described the same way. At times I have encountered Albanians who say that those who are Roma and *jevg* are the same people, that they are all *jevg*, *gabel*, or g----. Yet Roma in Albania, and those who are called *jevg*, see themselves as distinct groups. And while Albanians may at times see the two as the same, as I have illustrated in previous research (West Ohueri 2021), it is commonly understood in contemporary Tirana that there are two different groups who get grouped under a broad banner of dark-skinned, g----like others.

There is little historical documentation about the first uses of the term *jevg*. I visited the Albanian national archives in late 2013 and early 2014 on a quest to learn more. Prior to my visit I told a local historian that I wanted to find out more information about those who are called *jevg*, and she replied, "Oh you will not find anything about them in there." I made numerous visits to the archives, combing through files, viewing microfilms from as early as 1920. Eventually I came across a letter to the prime minister from 1930 from residents of the Kulla e Hirit (Tower of Grace) neighborhood in Korçë, in Southern Albania. I offer an excerpt below:

> Të nënshkurarit e pleqësisë... Kemi nderin në emër të popullsisë së kësaj lagjeje t'ju parashtrojmë lutjen e mëposhtme: Me gjithëse elementi, jevg, që përfaqësojmë, si nënshtetas Shqiptarë të bindur në urdhrat e Lart Madhërisë, Mbretit tonë të dashur, dhe ligjeve në veprim, jemi duke i dhënë shtetit gjithë taksat qeveritare, jemi duke marrë pjesë aktivisht në çdo lëvizje, si në votimin për anëtarët e Dhomës Legjislative, anëtarëve të Bashkisë dhe të Dhomës së Ekonomisë kombëtare, dhe jemi duke shërbyer si ushtarë dhe paraushtarakë, dhe me një fjalë si ushtarë të bindur të Lart Madhërisë jemi gati të sakrifikojmë dhe jetën tonë për Mbret, Komb dhe Atdhe, dhe kështu si të tillë përbëjmë një pjesë të popullsisë Shqiptare, por mjerisht deri më sot popullsia jonë nuk është përfillur për asgjë, nuk kemi parë e dëgjuar që ndonjë nga popullsia e kësaj lagjeje, edhe pse të zotë të detyrës, të kenë marrë pjesë si nëpunës të shtetit apo të përfillen duke u marrë me një shërbim të pajtueshëm me zotësinë e tyre. Kjo natyrisht na dëshpëron pa masë, mbasi me këtë vjen një mospërfillje e këtij elementi i cili është përbuzur në një klasë më të ulët. (Hazili and Myftar 1930)

(The undersigned elders... have the honor in the name of the population of this neighborhood to pose in front of you the following inquiry: Even though we represent the *jevg*, as Albanian citizens, obedient of the orders of His Majesty, our beloved King, of laws in power, we pay all taxes to the government, we are active at any movement, as in voting for the House of Lords, voting for the members of House of Laws, members of the Municipality and the Chamber of National Economy, we are enrolled as military and paramilitary, in a word as obedient soldiers of His Majesty we are ready to sacrifice our lives for the King, Nation and Country, and as such we are part of the Albanian population, but unfortunately still today our population is not taken into consideration at all; we have not heard of or witnessed anyone from this neighborhood, even those capable for the job, being hired as a State official or being considered to hold a duty at the level of their capabilities. This, of course, disappoints us immensely, because through this comes the neglect of this element [that is, being *jevg*], which is despised as a lower class.)[9]

Tracing this term illuminates *jevg* as a type of collective grouping; we can see how *jevg* has been understood as distinct from Albanian, designating not just socioeconomic status or marginalization but also socioracial and national identity. Earlier records from the 1920s detail the role that those considered *jevg* played in public executions, whereby they were tasked with carrying out the final killing acts. These actions were taken because of Albania's laws and codes regarding murders and blood feuds. It has been theorized that those broadly considered *jevg* would carry out the killings because they were not rendered as fully human or were a lower human class and therefore incapable of being involved in any revenge blood feuds in the same way as Albanians (Lame 2005).

While those who are *jevg* and Roma are considered dark-skinned others, relegated to the lower rungs of societal hierarchies, my *jevg* interlocutors claim an alternate subjectivity than Roma. This type of dualism is not new. Multiple authors have written accounts that reference two types of Roma groups in Albania. Very frequently one group is described as g-----s or Roma, while the other is described as *jevg*. Often the differentiation speaks to class, perceived assimilation, and cultural and moral practices deemed more respectable by societal standards. Writing about a similar distinction of Roma groups in Russia, Alaina Lemon has observed what she refers to as the clash between "cultured and wild g-----s" (Lemon 2000, 61). Writer Isabel Fonseca, who spent considerable time with Roma families in Tirana, wrote about a tribe that considered themselves distinct from Roma: "There was another group in Albania which was worse off, namely the *jevgs*—a small dark people, often to be seen begging in Tirana's squares" (1995, 22). Fonseca later refers to *jevgs* as a "miserable group" who begged in the center of town. Stuart Mann, a British scholar and travel writer, chronicled this type of distinction between Roma and *jevgs* in the early twentieth century. His writings from Central and Southern Albania speak to conjecture, but they also capture the ways in which Albanians differentiated between two groups (note that Mann uses the term "Arli," an older word that some Albanians use in place of *jevg* or *Egyptian*):

> The Albanians made a sharp distinction between the Arli and the Roms. The Roms are called by the Albanians "Kurbat," "Cërgëtar,"

> ("tent-dwellers"), and most commonly of all Arixhi. But they call the Arli "Jevt," "Magjyp," and (in South Albania) "Biçes." The Jevgs call the Roms "Tsikan." They [the Jevgs] are a dark, reddish-skinned people, living in humble settlements in various parts of Albania. They stoutly deny any connexion with the Roms, and to call them "Tsikan" is the worst possible insult. Their traditions seem to point to an African origin. . . . One theory (I forget whose) is that the Jevgs are descendants of Egyptian slaves who escaped from Greece and fled to Albania. They are clean, honest, and hard-working and fairly intelligent. . . . The menfolk are rather lazy, but practice smithery. The women work in houses as servants, or take in washing. . . . The women, especially, are very shy and avoid all contact with "Europeans" and even Albanians. They are despised by the latter, but feel themselves (justly) to be above the Roms. (Mann 1933, 2–3)

Writing during a similar time period, a fellow British writer denoted that there were two g---- groups in Albania: "These Cigans, as they are called, being no longer nomads, have lost their language, though they still tell the tradition that their forebears came over the sea from the direction of the sun (meaning Egypt)" (Kolsti 1991, 53).

Returning to my conversations with Fatmir and his mother, both expressed disdain at the thought of being referred to as Roma. Though they begged in the streets and lacked money for food and water, and though they felt ostracized in institutions like schools, they wanted to ensure that I was aware that they were not Roma. They did not speak Romani, and their family often squatted in older apartment dwellings and sometimes in informal settlements along the riverbank. Fatmiri further emphasized that he did not dig in trash like Roma in Tirana. His uncle and other family members were known in the area as people who could fix things, as collectors, which recalls Mann's writings as well as the comments from my friend Endrit. Moreover, Fatmir and his family rejected the idea that they were descendants of people from India, claiming instead that their origin was in Egypt. This too is referenced in Mann's writings whereby he denotes the belief that *jevgs* are from Egypt, and he goes as far as to write that some of the *jevg* women that he met were "the living image of queen Nefertiti" (1933, 3).

One morning in 2013 I took my usual route from my apartment toward the market when I stopped by a store I frequently passed. The store was run by two brothers who sold various clothing items, some new, some gently used. A dress caught my eye that day, and while I waited for one of the men to retrieve it, I began to talk to the other. Both men had always been cordial with me on my daily walks, greeting me on the street—but we had never exchanged more than two or three words. On this day they asked more questions about why I was in Albania, about my research, and eventually I asked if they were Roma. Both men had dark brown skin, and both were practicing Muslims, which I had learned during the observance of Ramadan. One of the brothers responded to me: "No, we are not Roma. Actually, we are *mullatë*." "Mullatë?" I asked, surprised to hear this word, an Albanian translation of "mulatto." "Do you mean that you have an Albanian parent and one who is not?" I asked. "If you are not Roma, are you all *jevg*?" Their friendly demeanors quickly soured as they frowned. "No, we are Egyptian. And we are Muslim. But do not call us *jevg*! That term is used for those who are in the streets, who do not have education. They are a low class of people. We are Egyptians."

Egjiptian

One of the first times that I heard the term *Egjiptian* (Egyptian) was actually from Fatmir's mother. Most of our chats were usually short as she rarely had much energy for in-depth conversation, but on the few days that she did, she spoke animatedly about her family. On more than one occasion she would amusingly touch my hair and tell me, "My father was darker than you and had hair just like yours." "Oh really?" I asked, very intrigued. "Was your father also *jevg*?" I once asked her. "Yes," she said, her facial expression an affirmative one. "He was Egyptian." Fatmir also used the term "Egyptian" from time to time but more frequently described himself as *jevg*. As was highlighted in the exchange with the two brothers in the store near my apartment, they identified as Egyptian but adamantly rejected the name *jevg* and were greatly offended at my use of it.

For many unfamiliar with Balkan Egyptians, the mentioning of the name "Egyptian" evokes an Egyptian national or someone with Egyptian citizenship in the contemporary nation-state of Egypt. As I discussed in this book's introduction, Egyptians are often included under the broad umbrella category of "Roma" or "Romani," particularly when grouped by entities like the European Union. But as my ethnographic research illustrates, Balkan Egyptians do not consider themselves to be Roma. They do not speak Romani, and unlike Roma, they do not trace their heritage to India but rather through Egypt. Balkan Egyptians largely reside in Albania, Kosova, and North Macedonia, and in 2017 the Albanian government formally recognized Egyptians as a distinct national minority. Egyptians in Kosova are also recognized by that country's constitution. Many scholars have theorized that the term "Egyptian" first emerged in the 1980s in the former Yugoslavia and Albania,[10] with its use becoming more widespread in the 1990s. In June 1992 a formal Egyptian association was founded in Korça, in Southern

Albania, which was followed by regional organizations such as the Students' Egyptian Association in Albania, later united under a Cultural Association of the Egyptians in Albania called Nefreta, after the ancient Egyptian queen Nefertiti. Though some scholars (see Duijzings 2000; Trubeta 2003) have traced the first uses of "Egyptian" to the late communist period of the former Yugoslavia, in many ways my research reveals that in contemporary Albania, "Egyptian" has emerged as a newer, more sophisticated, and socially accepted moniker for those racialized as *jevg*, those who have long claimed a distinct identity from Roma.

One of the more complicated aspects of the term "Egyptian" emanates from its relationship to the word "g----," and as such, the contemporary use of the term might better be classified as a refashioned or newly aligned discursive practice. Multiple scholars, including Ian Hancock (2002, 2010) and Elena Marushiakova and Veselin Popov (2013) have written about "g----" as an exonym, a misnomer, whereby Europeans in the fifteenth century wrongly believed Roma to be from Egypt. Sevasti Trubeta (2005) has similarly highlighted early Ottoman documents that included discussion of groups named "Çingene" or "Kipti" that scholars now tend to link with Egypt, as the term "Kipti" refers to Coptic ancient Egypt. Despite significant research that has traced Romani origins to India (Matras 2004; Hancock 2002, 2010), the misnomer of "g----" continues to circulate and get reproduced. In their work on Roma communities across Eastern Europe, Elena Marushiakova and Veselin Popov (2001b) argue that Egyptians should be recognized as they self-identify *but* assert that they are a branch of the Romani community. In one of their ethnographic and historical studies of Roma groups they wrote: "G-----s form a specific intergroup ethnic community which has no parallel among other European nations. The broader g---- community is divided into a widespread archipelago of separate groupings, split in various ways into metagroups, groups and subgroups, each with their own ethnic and cultural features. Sometimes these groupings are even opposed to each other and their problems are frequently completely different in nature and therefore cannot be generalized." (33)

For Marushiakova and Popov, "g----" is a broad and complex category that encompasses both Roma and Egyptians. The emergence of "Egyptian," they maintain, follows other models of ethnic mimicry in the Balkans whereby there exists an unwillingness among certain g---- groups to declare their own identity and instead acquire a more preferred identity. In their research they have linked Balkan Egyptians with such groups as the Agupti from Bulgaria, who also claim a separate Egypt-descended identity apart from Roma. By linking these groups, Marushiakova and Popov attempt to show that the emergence of Balkan Egyptians mirrors larger separatist movements of Romani groups who no longer want to identify as Roma/Romani.

Egyptian scholar and activist Rubin Zemon is one of the leading voices for the movement for increased recognition of Egyptians in the Balkans. He believes that to understand the Balkan Egyptian experience, we must first examine the many traces of Africa in Europe. Zemon (2001) argues that present-day Balkan Egyptians descend from Egyptians who arrived in southeastern Europe as blacksmiths and ironworkers during the Middle Ages, before Roma. According to Zemon, these numbers increased significantly during the Ottoman period. Throughout time the Balkan region has served as a crossroads of various migration waves and cultural intersections, and Balkan Egyptians trace their origins to this migratory nexus. During an interview Zemon explained to me that over time these Egyptian populations became more assimilated into majority Balkan populations, and most adopted the Albanian language, but they never fully integrated into majority society, nor did they practice much exogamy. He relies on the historical writings of Herodotus that speak to Egyptian presence in the Balkans, as well as artifacts and letters from areas like Ohrid, North Macedonia (near Southern Albania), to prove an early Egyptian presence in the Balkans. Zemon expressed that Egyptians were among the first Africans in Europe, but many Balkan Egyptians today are not yet conscious of their identity.

"What about you and your family's origin?" he asked me in 2020, a moment where the interviewee became the interviewer. "Where is your family from?" The question was somewhat unexpected but not unfamiliar, and I proceeded to explain my family's history in Mississippi and Texas but acknowledged my inability to trace that lineage beyond the US plantation. "This is similar for Balkan Egyptians," he said, noting that, like Black Americans, Egyptians in the Balkans may not be able to highlight their exact African origins. "We do not necessarily have any feelings or attachment for today's Egypt, but we are connected to ancient times." Here Zemon is further evoking shared sentiments with Black Americans who, for generations, have invoked ancient Egypt and Nubia to assert and reclaim heritage, whereby "Nubian" itself is a flexible term that at times is used in lieu of "Black" (Bonnet 2019). Like Roma, Egyptians in the Balkans are named as "black" but Egyptians also employ the language of blackness and Africanness to distinguish themselves from Roma. Referring to Albanians and Macedonians, Zemon says, "Roma and Egyptians are distinct. The so-called white people cannot make the distinctions between us—all the black people are the same to them." I previously noted that scholars have highlighted the ways that majority societies may differentiate between two different g---- groups, usually along the lines of those who are more assimilated or those who speak Romani versus those who do not. As it was with the name *jevg*, I have found that there are Albanians who do differentiate between Roma and Egyptians, often associating more positive attributes with Egyptians. Egyptians are at times described as "good businesspeople," like the two brothers who owned the store near my apartment. Or they may be referred to as "rule-followers" who send their kids to school, unlike Roma who may be described as living in umbrellas or always drinking alcohol and partying.

At the same time, I talked with numerous Albanians who had no idea how to differentiate Roma and Egyptians, or would not differentiate the two groups at all. "You know they are all *really* Roma g-----s, right?" a colleague of mine once asked me. Other Albanian interlocutors would use "Roma" and "Egyptian" (or *gabel* and *jevg*) interchangeably. Xheladin Taço, the leader of Rromani Baxt, said that he is often asked by Tirana lawmakers if his organization can, in their words, "do something about the Roma who beg on the main boulevard." These government officials were referring to the areas of town where Fatmir and Arben's family frequently begged and washed windows. Xheladin told me he repeatedly tells government leaders that those individuals are not Roma but rather Egyptian. "But they are *definitely* Roma," leaders often tell Xheladin. "Just look at their dress and their clothes! Look how they are in the street!" Egyptians are at times described as more socially integrated than Roma, and within the Egyptian community of Tirana you will find more business owners when compared with Roma. Still, there are numerous disparities between Albanians and Egyptians when it comes to education, health, and income. And areas of Tirana, such as the Braka neighborhood that has historically been home to many Egyptians, or Kinostudio for Roma, illustrate how even those Egyptians who have more income are still residentially segregated from Albanians.

It was in 2014 when Shpresa first took me to a meeting of a then newly emergent Egyptian political party in Albania. Prior to the meeting I had coffee with her and Allaman, another Egyptian who was serving as one of the party's first officers. "All the Albanian political parties eat [meaning "take"] our money [*hanë lekët*]," Allaman told me. "The white Albanians have political parties—they organize better than us. Roma and Egyptians, we only have *shoqata* [NGOs]. This is why we are forming a political force, a political party that will speak for the Egyptians, Roma, and all black people in Albania." Later at the meeting an older member of the political party told me, "Everyone in America should honor Martin Luther King Jr. day and night. That is the kind of movement we want here in Albania." This gentleman was not the first to express a connection to international Black movements for equality. Rubin Zemon's writings frequently refer to the global oppression of people of African descent, and he situates the plight of Balkan Egyptians alongside such experiences as the 1950s and 1960s civil rights movement in the United States. Further, in 2018, a coalition of Balkan Egyptians attended an event in Geneva for people of the African diaspora in Europe. Zemon told me that because of that gathering, an increased number of Balkan Egyptians have established connections and relationships through shared social media groups and chats. As Duijzings (2000) and Trubeta (2005) have pointed out, contemporary groups of Balkan Egyptians have begun to develop a newly emergent transnational and racial consciousness beyond local confines.

None of the names discussed thus far are fixed in meaning, and we know from scholars such as Stuart Hall (2002) that identity is unstable and conjectural. The identity of "Balkan Egyptian" is no different. I had another coffee with Shpresa and Allaman shortly after that initial political party meeting. "I just want to know about my history, my people," Allaman told me. He continued, "Who are we, the Egyptians? The Roma have a name, a status, and a flag. We do not have those things. And they [Albanians] call us Roma . . . I do not know about language. We speak Albanian but why do we not speak the Egyptian language? The Roma speak their language. What about customs and culture for us?" At first Allaman posed his questions to me, searching for expert insight. He was somewhat disappointed when I told him that not only did I not have answers, I was trying to learn about Balkan Egyptians from him. Allaman thought deeply about his questions as he tried to understand what it meant to be Egyptian. By contrast, interlocutors like Idi, a human rights organizer in Tirana and Durrës, completely rejected the name "Egyptian." "Do not call me Egyptian," he loudly proclaimed. "You know that I am *jevg*!" I asked him why he felt this way and he said, "Tell me, do I speak the Egyptian language?" He paused and I surmised that he was waiting on me to answer. "No," I replied, somewhere between a question and response. "Exactly, I do not," he continued. "What culture do I have from Egypt? What language? Where is the connection between us and Egypt? There is not one, so I am not Egyptian. I am a *jevg*."

Allaman's questions illuminate the precarious nature of "Egyptian," one that drives him to seek answers, whereas the same precarity is unsettling for Idi, who rejects "Egyptian" as a result. June 24 is now recognized as the International Day of Balkan Egyptians, and in addition to growing numbers of artistic and heritage celebrations that mark this day, scholars and community organizers have used this recognized holiday to facilitate increased dialogue about societal inequities. June 24 carries significant meaning for people like Allaman who have longed to have a day of recognition like Roma. Still, it can be argued that these recognitions and designations have not yet opened the door for local racial reckonings. Webs and entanglements of race, identity, and subjugation are produced by multilayered, dynamic, and messy social processes, and in the case of Roma and Egyptians, despite changes in Albania since the arrival of democracy, both groups are still seen as occupying a space of the g---- minority (ERRC 1997), a space shaped by racialized subject formation. These collective processes of race-making render both Roma and Egyptians as "black." In our interview Rubin Zemon referred to this type of grouping as *dora jonë*, meaning "our side" or "our kind," but in my research in Albania this most commonly gets expressed as *dorë e zezë*, or the "black side."

Dorë e zezë

I used to watch Sami's youngest son dash into the small door beneath the stairs of my friend Mira's apartment building. He was shy, always quickly running away when I approached the steps. Ten people lived in the basement, and as Mira told me, they were technically squatters. Sami was the head of the household. I often heard his name yelled from windows and would watch as he collected plastic jugs or aluminum cans from people in the alley. Sometimes he would meet people in the stairwell; other times they might drop materials from their windows.

Mira's and Sami's families shared a cordial if not friendly relationship as neighbors. Still, she warned me about getting too close. "Do not ever go inside *their* hallway if you are ever over *there*," Mira once told me. "You can smell that house from a hundred meters away." Sami's family collected recyclables that they would sell to a man who managed used materials in Tirana. This was their primary means of earning money, and on average the family of ten made roughly six dollars a day, eight if there was a really good yield. Because they kept most of their collections, much of which had come from waste bins, by the door, a distinct

FIGURE 13. Examples of vehicles to collect scrap material. Photo by author.

smell always lingered in the alley. Sometimes people walking by would yell out "romë" or "gabelë" in a derogatory manner, but Sami told me that he was not Roma. "I am *jevg*. We are not Roma," he said, clicking his tongue. "We do not speak that *gabezqe*," reminiscent of Fatmiri's response. "My family is Egyptian."

With time, Sami eventually agreed to do an interview with me over coffee. He remained somewhat reserved when our conversation began, but he soon relaxed as he told me about his childhood, his family, and his life in Tirana. At some point he looked downstairs at two people who walked inside and then suddenly back at me. "Wait, stop a minute," he said, waving his hand in front of me. "Turn off the recorder." I followed his instruction, unsure of what was happening. As he paced along the balcony his eyes were focused on the young couple that was now seated and drinking coffee. He called someone on his phone, but whoever it was did not answer. He returned to the table. "That is my niece and she is here with a boy who is *dorë e bardhë* [white] and I do not recognize him." Sami's phone rang and he quickly answered it. "Oh, ba [short for dad], niece is here with a boy. He is *dorë e bardhë*. Do you know about this?" I assumed that the niece lived with Sami's parents. "Oh, he is a colleague from work? I wanted to let you know that I saw her because I did not know who this was. Okay, good, good, *ciao, ciao* [*Mirë, mirë, ciao, ciao*]." Sami ended the call. "He is a colleague from work," he said to me, as though I did not hear him on the phone, and as though I too needed to be reassured about the man that was with his niece. "What is *dorë e bardhë*?" I asked him. He answered, "Them, shqiptarët [Albanians], they are *dorë e bardhë* and *we* are *dorë e zezë*."

As I noted in chapter 3, the Albanian word for black (*zezë*) can take on numerous meanings. The verb *zezoj* means to blacken, to ruin and destroy, to be defamed. The expression *me të zeza* refers to being in mourning; it speaks to misfortune, impurities, or calamity. *Zezë* is often used in opposition to *bardhë* (white), which connotes fair skin, happiness, fortune, purity, or honor. When it comes to racialization in Tirana, I was already familiar with the term *zezë* (black) because for years people had exclaimed *zezake* when they saw me. This word also has multiple English translations including "Black person," "African," "African American," or "Negro." My conversation with Sami, however, was one of the first times I heard someone use *dorë e zezë* to mean "black" or "blackness." To date, there is very little research on this subject, and some scholars like Tracy Koci have previously argued that racialized identities do not exist in post-communist Albania. "The Roma in Albania," she writes, "have no political concept of themselves as 'black' as opposed to 'white'" (2001, 391). Koci further adds that the general Albanian population does not polarize groups along lines of race, arguing that Enver Hoxha made great strides to abolish ethnicity and race. Koci's research and writing on race are limited, but she asserts that there is no political consciousness of blackness among Roma in Albania. Yet my long-term ethnographic research reveals otherwise. In one of my conversations with Rubin Zemon, he spoke to this notion explicitly: "You hear, 'We are all Albanians and we do not make distinctions between religion.' You know, you hear things like the religion of Albania is Albanianism . . . and the history of communists promoting a homogenous population and so on. But in society . . . it is totally divided. There are *dorë e bardhë* and *dorë e zezë*. And they do not mix."

This chapter thus far has shed light on racialization processes that have continually rendered Roma and Egyptians outside of whiteness, even when the limits of whiteness (Maghbouleh 2017) are not explicitly named or acknowledged. The broader understandings of whiteness (as good, clean, pure, honorable, superior) and blackness (as evil, impure, dirty, dishonorable, inferior) beyond phenotype have shaped everyday racial logics. Sami says that Egyptians have long used racialized articulations of *zezë* as dark-skinned or black, but perhaps contemporary formations draw attention to newly aligned and realigned understandings and expressions of blackness, thus capturing the varied experiences of feeling, claiming, and articulating what it means to be "black."

I talked with interlocutors in the Romani and Egyptian settlement at Kreshtë about the notion of *dorë e zezë*. "Egjiptianet dhe Romët të dy janë dorë e zezë" (Egyptians and Roma are both black). This is what Flutura, an Egyptian woman married to a Roma man, explained to me while we sat inside her shanty on top of thick blankets on the floor, a large pan of freshly cooked green peppers and bread next to us. The family members passed around the pan as we talked, eating pieces of the bread with the peppers on top. At that time in 2014 Flutura had lived in the Kreshtë settlement for nearly fifteen years. She and her siblings grew up in Tirana, and her family's home was in the Laprakë neighborhood in Tirana. But they were forced to flee in '97 when an Albanian family claimed that the property had been wrongly seized by Hoxha's regime and asserted that they were the rightful owners. The Albanian family was ultimately able to claim the home, resulting in the displacement of Flutura and her family. Sharing her thoughts about living in Kreshtë, she said, "It is difficult to live here—can you not look around and see this? Do you think it is normal for us, for black people, to be forced to live like this? Without food and without money? When our men have to go out, to spend all day in the trash, gathering cans, to steal . . . is this life? Life is supposed to be lived like everyone else, having a job, a house, your kids in school, that is life. But we live like animals. We are like animals compared to everyone else!" Flutura was often very animated in her speech. She was particularly vocal about racial discrimination (her wording), which she felt impacted every single Roma and Egyptian person in Albania: "There is a lot of racial difference and discrimination and our races are very segregated," she said. "The white [people] are preferred as employees over the black [people]. But they do not realize that the black [people], we work harder than the white ones [*jemi më shumë punëtorë*] . . . black [people] in Albania do the work that really makes you sweat."

As an analytical category, *dorë e zezë* speaks both to the ways that people self-identify and the ways that groups are collectively racialized and named. For Flutura, blackness was intimately tied to labor, segregation, and space. The exclusion of Roma and Egyptians, the relegation to the outskirts where they lacked resources and infrastructure, was enough to illustrate how race shaped livelihoods. "Can you not look around and see this?" she asked me. Her comments also echo similar sentiments from the section on *gabel*, those sentiments of marginalization and dehumanization. "Is this life? . . . We are like animals compared to everyone else!" Flutura was very direct in her speech, at times seemingly annoyed that I even asked some of my questions, as if to suggest that I could look around and observe the settlement myself without asking her what she thought about it.

Chunks of garbage and crumpled paper cluttered the muddy grounds of Kreshtë along the side of the river. There were two overflowing portable toilets, the only ones in an area of about fifty families. The smell of burning trash often lingered in the air. And as I previously noted, this settlement was towered over by six large apartment buildings that remained unoccupied for more than six years after their completion, completely empty and overlooking Romani and Egyptian families that struggled to maintain their shanties and shacks below. The municipality had used the same rhetoric employed by the taxi driver: Roma and Egyptians were not a good *fit* for the buildings.[11]

As illustrated by Flutura, Fatmir, Sami, and Arben's family, blackness is intimately tied to the space of the margins, to those spaces on the side of the road (Stewart 1996). The exclusion from whiteness is acutely felt in terms of where those racialized as black live as well as where they collect scrap materials or money from begging. I became even more aware of this connection to the road in conversations with Flora. I first mentioned Flora in chapter 2 when she invited me to her house to celebrate her birthday. She is Arben's aunt and a cousin of Fatmir, and she frequently begged on the main boulevard with her children. We spent numerous hours in and around the boulevard as she and her sister would ask passersby for money but more often received scorn and shame in return.

"Vajza ime e madhe është dorë e bardhë" (My oldest daughter is white), she told me one day. She leaned closer and whispered, "I am not really *dorë e zezë*. I am *dorë e bardhë*. My parents are *dorë e bardhë* but now I am married to a *jevg* and he is *dorë e zezë*." She paused for a minute or two, her face remaining pensive but her mouth still. She resumed by nodding her head toward her older daughter and said, "She is white. Her dad was white too, but he died. My current husband is black, and my daughter thinks that he is her father, though he is not." She continued, "People treat me like I am *dorë e zezë*. They yell at me from the road, saying dirty things like, '*Të dhjefsha racën!*' [May your people be destroyed!]. Or they may yell, '*Ik, moj jevgë!*' [Leave, *jevg*!]." She sighed, releasing burdened exhales. "They curse at us because they think that we are *dorë e zezë* but I am not. I am *dorë e bardhë*."

This was the first time I had heard this from Flora, and after that day I never heard her mention it again. She would continue to refer to her family as black people and would tell people that because I am Black, I, too, am her family. Her story illustrates the ways that *dorë e zezë* is a racial assemblage, an assemblage that can take multiple forms in race-making processes as shaped by spatial, occupational, or geographic positionality. I had previously observed that Flora's daughter had a much lighter skin tone than the rest of her children and their family, and she also had blond ringlets of bouncing hair, hair that many Albanian pedestrians would stop to touch and comment on as they walked the boulevard. But her different phenotypic markers do not necessarily indicate that someone is not Roma or Egyptian. It is these kinds of racial logics and assumptions, for example, that have led to accusations of Roma kidnapping children in Ireland and Greece (Labropoulou, McLaughlin, and Almasy 2013). What Flora's story does illustrate is how the racial logics of *dorë e zezë* operate: that *dorë e zezë* is an index of appearance and what it means to *look black* or what it means for someone to be called black. Her story demonstrates how *dorë e zezë* can be assigned even when it is not self-ascribed. This example also yields greater insight into what it means to *feel black* and be treated with ridicule, even if someone says that they are *really* white. As Flora understands it, this disdain and scorn might not happen if people knew that she was not *really* black. Yet it is her proximity to *dorë e zezë*, her begging, her space on the road, that make her and her daughter black.

Her story further reveals the ways that local racialized categories are shaped by space, labor, and proximity to blackness, such that Flora and her daughter would be racialized as black by marriage. In this way, all of those racialized as black are excluded from whiteness; they all become *gabel*, the stranger.

Multifaceted Meanings of "Blackness"

When it comes to understanding processes of race-making, it is important to analyze how local racial logics work to produce blackness as outsiderness. Those racialized as *dorë e zezë* are rendered outside of whiteness, criminalized as thieves, public health threats, tricksters, liars, untrustworthy. As was demonstrated in chapter 2, this blackness is at times seen as counter to the idea of *besa* (honor). In this way, blackness represents dishonor and impurity, and Roma and Egyptians fall outside of the borders of authentic belonging and honor. Dishonesty and dishonor are often associated with that which is uncivilized and unbecoming of authentic Albanianness. This is exemplified with people like Fatmir, who lied about his age, frequently begged restaurant patrons for money, and usually cunningly gave contradictory information about himself. For many Albanian people who worked in and dined in Blloku, this misrepresentation was only evidence of dishonor and shame (*turp*). But the more I got to know Fatmir, the more I came to understand some of his practices as protection strategies. He did tell lies and sometimes did so to collect more money, but he also lied as a means of concealing information about himself and his family. He was not in school and was often chased out of restaurants. He had to learn how to subvert the police and how to help relatives like his ailing mother. In his case, some of his secretive behavior stemmed from trickery and deception, but it also served as a defense mechanism. By contrast Shpresa, my research assistant whose story I shared in chapter 1, was regularly called by Albanians to *parë filxhan*, the practice of looking into coffee grinds and predicting a person's future. There is a perplexing mysticism where Roma and Egyptians are racialized as black untrustworthy outsiders and criminals, and at the same time are believed to possess a type of fortune-telling magic that Albanians do not have (an additional example derives from the supposed magic from the previously discussed Ponzi scheme company Sude). Both of these examples with Fatmir and Shpresa illustrate how racial logics operate in the local landscape. These local constructions of blackness point to the ways that those who are *gabel* and *jevg* are given certain innate and natural properties unique to those who are "black" but not necessarily those who are "white." In this way, race becomes one way in which difference is articulated, but the articulations of blackness are not necessarily straightforward.

"Balkan Egyptians to Homeland: We Belong to You." This was the title of a 2018 news story from an English language Egyptian newspaper, *Daily News Egypt*. The story's main image featured Balkan Egyptian leaders holding such as signs as:

"The Balkan-Egyptian community of Albania wants equality, dignity, and rights" "We want a strategy for national development"
"We want status"
"We want alleviation of poverty"

These signs do not differ significantly from demands of Romani activists and organizations seeking better housing and jobs in Tirana, and such overlap illuminates the intersecting forms of oppression and marginalization that shape both social groups. Yet I argue that the formation of Egyptianness and Egyptian articulations of blackness speak to processes that racialize Egyptians outside of the Albanian nation in particular ways. Balkan Egyptians assert a type of blackness that distinguishes them from Roma, that names their marginalization and exclusion in Albania, and blackness that expresses a desire for inclusion in their *real* homeland. Through the creation of a political party, the formal recognition of Balkan Egyptian holidays, and conferences of experts to study Egyptian heritage in the Balkans, this group demonstrates the ways that blackness is shaped by exclusion from Albanian whiteness. In these contemporary claims from Egyptians, we can see remnants of the letter from Korça that was highlighted in the *jevg* section, whereby residents from the Kulla e Hirit neighborhood demanded recognition and increased representation of their socioracial group. Egyptianness is about consciousness.

Both Roma and Egyptians articulate blackness to name what anthropologist Damani Partridge terms exclusionary incorporation (2012). In this way, claims to blackness can be seen as a vehicle or tool for emphasizing and enunciating the contradictions of liberal democracy's arrival (Partridge 2023). For Roma, however, the construction of blackness draws more attention to the processes of blackening, whereby they are racialized as black but do not necessarily articulate an African-descended transnational black identity. As I have shown, both Roma and Egyptians are collectively racialized as black in Tirana, and many Albanians struggle to differentiate the two groups. Roma in Tirana will express solidarities with black people and other global minoritized subjects, and as I have shown, they may say that words like *gabel* register in the same ways as terms like *n*gga*, but Roma do not necessarily claim blackness as a means of expressing their racial subjectivity. To return to the word *zezoj*, which means to blacken, to ruin, or to defame, I argue that Romani articulations align more with this idea of blackness, the idea of being made black through racialized marginalization. This occurs in multiple forms, through the parallel experiences of enslavement, to the long-held beliefs and articulations of Roma having "Negro-like characteristics" (Ozanne 1878), to the Porrajmos, to the intentional segregation of Roma and the denial of access and resources over time. Roma and Egyptians are both blackened, becoming social pariahs racialized outside of the Albanian national and European racial imaginary, and the language of *dorë e zezë* speaks to the commonly shared experiences and social formations. Yet the rhetoric of blackness and sociopolitical language of belonging emerges in unique and newly aligned ways for both groups, producing a multiplicity of blackness.

"The majority societies in the Balkans think of all of us as g-----s," Rubin Zemon tells me, "but Roma and Egyptians have a different habitus." Zemon, along with Rivelino Çuno and other members of the Egyptian political party in Albania, use the language of blackness to call attention to inequality and discrimination, and many Balkan Egyptians feel that their political cause is aligned with other "black" groups throughout the world. Balkan Egyptians assert a black identity and subject position in response to those social practices that render them outside of Albanianness, a blackness that intimately aligns them with other African-descended populations. Blackness is an articulation of how they have been racialized as inferior but also distinguishes them from Roma. In some ways the name "Egyptian" could be viewed as a way to distance from Roma, from *gabel*, and, to a further extent, from *jevg*. This subject area has received little attention and needs further inquiry, but some scholars have suggested that the proclamation of Egyptian identity is made by a group that was Roma but over time stopped speaking Romani and assimilated into majority Balkan cultures (for longer discussion, see Marushiakova and Popov 2000; Trubeta 2005). My aim in sharing this research has less to do with efforts to verify or authenticate Romaniness or Egyptianness, as much as I am interested in the forms of racialization that produce these varied and overlapping black identities and subjectivities.

It is important to note that many Roma in Albania may distance themselves from Egyptians whom they consider a people group without a language, without a flag, and, as one interlocutor told me, without a culture. Some Roma in Tirana show disdain for Egyptians, especially those who believe that Egyptians stem from previous generations of Roma who stopped speaking Romani to become more like Albanians (ERRC 1997). While those who are *jevg* and Egyptian distance themselves from Roma, Roma may also practice a similar distancing from Egyptians as they cling to what they consider *their* distinct cultural practices and symbols. Roma in Albania, and across Europe, experience interlocking and overlapping forms of racism and exclusion, yet they are an officially recognized European ethnic minority group, unlike Balkan Egyptians, who have only recently achieved ethnic minority status in countries such as Albania and Kosova. In the Balkans in particular, territorial claims and the boundaries of landownership, heritage, and language are distinctive markers of an authentic people group (Sula-Raxhimi 2018), and because of this, Egyptians are further excluded outside of the nation. As Sevasti Trubeta notes, "In each of the countries where [Egyptian] groups are present, they are not considered to be members of a titular nation.... [They] are socially positioned more or less on the margins of their respective societies" (2005, 77). Blackness, then, is not just indexed by phenotype and darker skin color but is also intimately tied to the racialized nation. These claims to blackness demonstrate how Egyptianness represents an authentic peoplehood and an authentic tie to a homeland. Egyptianness does not constitute Europeanness because of Egyptians' inability to trace their genesis to Europe temporally, spatially, and racially (Goldberg 2006). But black Egyptianness is an assertion of connection, of a linkage to a place elsewhere, where Balkan Egyptians are not racialized outside of white Europeanness. These claims to blackness are complex and elucidate how race becomes a counternarrative of self-identity, whereby claiming blackness is not just about affirming an authentic identity but also about the agency and possibility of blackness to mobilize and imagine a world otherwise (Khan 2019; Partridge 2023).

The Shaping of Social Worlds

What are some of the ways that race travels and shapes social worlds? This is the question that I asked in the beginning of this chapter. One of the key aims of this book has been to examine how discourses of racelessness shape everyday racial logics. By analyzing these six terms I have tried to highlight how blackness is produced and reproduced, both through rhetoric as well as through the racialization of space and the embodiment of race. To return to the discussion of race and embodiment from this book's introduction, race is about particular connections among bodies (Lemon 2002). The historical and ethnographic tracing of these six names sheds light on local constructions of racialized bodies, and the demarcations of whiteness and blackness that animate Tirana's social landscape, demonstrating how race, though often unnamed, unacknowledged, or rejected, is very present and active. In Ian Hancock's conceptualization of the pariah, he argues that the status of outcast is a result of a continuum of centuries of oppression (1987, 133). The tracing and naming of these six terms provides one way to map this continuum of outsiderness and nonbelonging that have shaped Romani and Egyptian livelihoods.

This chapter's focus on blackness reveals how *dorë e zezë* is produced and sustained through processes of antiblackness and anti-Romani racism. This is particularly salient in the racialization of space and spatialization of race. I do not mean to suggest that the boundaries of whiteness and blackness are always hardened; in fact, my research has revealed that there is much fluidity. In Tirana specifically, there are many neighborhoods with Roma and Egyptian settlements in closer proximity to Albanians, usually poorer Albanians from the northern region. During a conversation in the neighborhood of Bregu i Lumit, a Roma interlocutor once told me, "Këtu ka katunarë fare!" using an at times pejorative word, *katunarë*, to mean that her neighborhood was full of villagers from more rural regions. She told me that it was common for her and her neighbors to exchange words like *katunarë* or also *malokë* (hillbilly) and *gabel* in joking ways. "It is just something we do out here since we all live here together." Segregation is not fixed but rather is always ongoing and in process (Picker 2017), and this exchange demonstrates a certain kind of intimacy shaped by the spatialization of race and class in Tirana. While many of the Albanians racialized as white in areas like Bregu i Lumit would likely still articulate a distance from Roma and Egyptians, the relationships that exist in these spaces demonstrate how race creates and reconfigures boundaries that are slippery and smudged, and how people are constantly responding to them. At the same time, the ethnographic examples draw attention to convergences of antiblackness and anti-Romani racism that are present in Albania and across Europe. Blackness becomes what anthropologist Damani Partridge (2023) considers an articulation or envisioning of a different kind of future. Yet, as illustrated by my conversations with Flori at the Kreshtë settlement, there are many barriers that limit the possibilities of considering a different future; like others throughout the book, for Flori and Flutura, the textures of the communist afterlife have shaped an inability to imagine or envision otherwise.

This chapter has mapped key names to examine the constructions, formations, articulations, makings, and remakings of blackness as they shape social worlds. Throughout this book I have emphasized my focus on race, as opposed to racism, as my ethnographic object. But for the fifth chapter I do offer an analysis of racism as a means of further exploring the meanings of making of race. I now turn to the book's final chapter which maps sites of racism in three acts.

5

A QUESTION OF RACISM IN THREE ACTS

Racism. It animates marginality, inequality, and exclusion. Shaping all the fears and phobias: xenophobia, Islamophobia, Romaphobia, Albanophobia. Racism separates who is and who is not. It hierarchizes humanness and worth. Racism: often erased by the language of human rights in efforts to highlight harm inflicted on individuals rather than the racial logics that underpin everyday life. Racism: apparently identified by bones, the racist bones in some people's bodies, though no one seems to know which people or which bones these might in fact be. Racism is refuted, rejected, rebuffed. Racism is dismissed and disavowed, its potent proteins denatured by the fires of deep denial. Ethnic conflict, ethnic hatred, ethnic turmoil, ethnic unrest, ethnic strife, ethnic tension. Perhaps. Racially charged. Racially tinged. Racially sensitive. Racially insensitive. Racially divisive. Maybe. But racist? Racism? When the name of the game is racelessness, then there is no racism. When it comes to Europe and the Balkans, then, racism, like race, is Seussian: not here, not there, not anywhere.

I have previously said that one of the major issues with conducting ethnographic research about race is that people often assume I document racist acts or accounts, or my aim is to determine whether a person or a social group is *really* racist. The mention of race elicits an immediate defensiveness, as conversations collapse into accusations about racism, as was illustrated by my experiences on *Wake Up Tirana* chronicled in chapter 2. This of course is not limited to Albania or the Balkans. I have experienced multiple encounters in the United States in which Americans have shown caution or concern about my research on race. During graduate school I gave a conference presentation about identity and difference in Southeast Europe and was approached by a well-known white scholar in my field who was taken aback by my presentation. She leaned in to whisper to me, "But you are not saying that Albanians are racist, are you?" Another white American senior scholar attended one of my conference talks and during the Q&A session asked why I was not studying ethnicity instead of race, since, in his words, "Albanians are not a racist people." Racism has an accompanying anxiety especially in this moment of global interest in critical race theory, migration crises, ongoing wars, and conflicts over citizenship, belonging, and territory. So far in this book I have examined racialization in terms of racial logics and social processes that locally shape the constructions of whiteness, blackness, and otherness. In this final chapter of the book, I recall the letter from Romani activists in the last chapter, in which they said that racism is not just seen but also acts. I therefore ask what an inquiry of racism (that is, how it acts, operates, and is understood) can reveal about the meanings and makings of race.

In the beginning of this book, I discussed the racialized entanglements of the communist afterlife. Exploring these entanglements requires a mapping of certain sites, moments, and arrangements whereby racism is sometimes explicitly named, at times more tacit, and at other times refuted or refused. Racialization shapes the social landscape of the communist afterlife, and as I illustrate in this chapter, these racial logics serve as the building blocks of Europe's racial arrangements broadly. In thinking about the complexities of race in this current moment, in the often-articulated age of European color blindness, this chapter maps three different sites to explore the naming, contestation, categorization, determination, and rejection of racism. I examine how the word "racism" itself may not emerge in popular discourse, but racism is nevertheless active. The first act analyzes racism in the context of race, nation, and sport. The second act is an examination of race and representation on popular television. The third and final act draws attention to structural and everyday racism in the context of housing and evictions. The three acts and their stories focus on different subjects, and as such, it is best to read them as three mini chapters that are linked through the ethnographic tracing of race and racism.

Act 1: Race-Making on the Pitch

People just do not know how to properly behave. That is what many interlocutors say when we discuss racism in Tirana. Mimoza, for example, has told me numerous times that some people may lack a certain decorum, or they fail to demonstrate proper manners. As a result, offensive acts might occur—for example,

I might have an encounter with someone who makes a racist statement, but it is likely people that are from *rrethet* (districts other than Tirana but not *from* Tirana). This mirrors the language from the producers of *Wake Up Tirana*. For many of my interlocutors in Tirana, when it comes to discussions of racism specifically, the focus is usually about the outsiders who always cause trouble and make all Albanians *look bad*.

In the fall of 2008 Klubi i Futbollit Tirana (KF Tirana) played host to AC Milan in the first soccer match of the friendly Taçi Oil Cup. When I told Mira that I had purchased a ticket to the game, she was confused and asked why I wanted to go. "Because I love sports and I used to play football [soccer] in high school—in the US I have not had a chance to go to many professional games." "Yes, but," she responded, "why are *you*, a woman, going to the game alone? It is not really a place for women." Mira continued by saying that typically only men attended the matches, and she warned me that they do not know how to behave properly around women. "They use the worst profanity," she told me, adding that attendees provoke one another and are even encouraged to do so. "Besides, many of the people who come are not from Tirana." I considered her thoughts but ultimately decided to go to the match; after all, it would not be the first time I had witnessed inappropriate behavior and profanity.

I arrived a little early so that I could easily find a seat. The first thing I did was take out my notebook to jot down some fieldnotes. After about ten minutes a few young boys approached me and stared, saying nothing. One of them looked down to see what I was writing, though I was not sure if he could read English.

FIGURE 14. Football (soccer) match, Tirana. Photo by author.

After staring back for what seemed like an hour, likely only two to three minutes, he finally extended his hand for a sheet of paper. I was initially confused as I was not sure if he wanted to also take notes, but I gave him a sheet. Immediately the other three boys reached out their hands. Still perplexed, I handed them paper. I did not see anyone with pens and was worried they may ask for those next because I only had two. But then I saw all of them put the paper on the seats and sit down. For the remaining ten minutes before the game began, I handed out paper to roughly twenty people sitting near me, all of whom did not want to sit on the dirty stadium seats. And as a result I added a sheet of paper to my seat as well.

Tearing paper from my notebook may have been the most surprising part of the evening. I was prepared to hear profanity, and there was quite a bit, with fans reserving their worst obscenities for the referees. A significant number of fans were very drunk, and several were smoking, including the preteens next to me. Once some of the people near me realized that I understood Albanian, they asked me typical questions about why I was in Tirana and why I was attending a football match. Some even remarked about being surprised to see a woman at a game. As one of the attendees said, "This is not really a place for women because everyone behaves so terribly."

Everyone behaves so terribly. It is the type of language frequently used to describe sporting matches, especially football in Europe. Terms like "unsportsmanlike conduct," "spectator aggression," and "hooliganism" are regularly evoked to characterize inappropriate behavior at games. Officials, team organizations, and fans will all use this type of rhetoric to talk about offensive acts, and very often it is these terms that get used in lieu of "racist" or "racism." While researching the experiences of Black football players in Albania, for example, a member of the Albanian Football Federation (FFSh) once told a colleague and me that fans may behave inappropriately and may offend Black players but the association checks for racism and has never found any (Bickert and West Ohueri 2016). In 2013 the international governing organization of football, the Fédération Internationale de Football Association, better known as FIFA, assembled an anti-racism task force to address discrimination within its body of members. In 2016 FIFA determined that this task force had completed its work, and as a result the group was disbanded. In an online statement they noted: "FIFA is aware of the fact that the fight against racism and any other form of discrimination is a long term process, which is why the task force's recommendations [have] led to sustainable measures" (FIFA 2016). It should be noted that for a task force specifically named as anti-racist, only one of the group's eleven recommendations mentioned the word "racism."

As the previous chapters have highlighted, it can sometimes seem that terms like "ethnic conflict" and "ethnic hatred" have permanently marked the Balkan region. This is certainly the case as it pertains to relationships between Albanians and Serbians. An example derives from a key speech made by President Bill Clinton in 1999 during the Kosova-Serbia war. In this widely broadcast speech Clinton announced his decision for US troops to join NATO forces in a bombing campaign against Serbia, noting that there was an urgency for the US to become involved: "All the ingredients for a major war are there. Ancient grievances, struggling democracies and in the center of it all, a dictator in Serbia who has done nothing since the Cold War ended but start new wars and pour gasoline on the flames of ethnic and religious division" (Clinton 1999).

Ancient grievances. Gasoline on the flames of ethnic and religious division. In many ways these kinds of articulations have become almost predictable in any conversation about this region, illuminating the persistent Balkanism (Todorova 1997) that shapes the idea of permanent ethnic instability and frames the Balkans as the only European region where geopolitical conflict exists. I say this not to minimize social or geopolitical conflict in the region but rather to argue that an exploration of these so-called ethnic ancient hatreds can yield insight about racialization, despite race not always being named. My approach here is not to make hard distinctions between ethnicity and race as, to reiterate Hall, ethnicity and race often play hide-and-seek (2017, 100). As such, I use the following sections to explore how race and racism may be hiding, particularly in those moments where events or practices might even be considered racist but not necessarily named. These forms of racialization reveal how the Balkan region is not exceptional within Europe but rather illustrates the ongoing production and reproduction of racial projects across the continent.

The Match

Many people were surprised that the 2014 football match was scheduled at all. In the fall of that year Serbia was set to host Albania in a qualifying game for the 2016 Euro Cup. The organizing body, UEFA (the Union of European Football Associations), had a track record for preventing matchups between countries that had shared or were experiencing ongoing conflict, such as Armenia and Azerbaijan or Russia and Georgia. When Albania drew Serbia, officials from both countries suggested that the game should not take place due to significant tension between the two nations, particularly on the issue of Kosova's statehood and autonomy.[1] UEFA, however, maintained its position that the game would be played since from their standpoint, Albania and Serbia had not experienced direct conflict. The association did announce that the match would involve certain restrictions. It was scheduled to be played in Belgrade, at Partizan Stadium, and as recommended by Serbia, Albanian fans were not allowed to attend. UEFA upheld this condition, and while there was disagreement from Albanian supporters, the Albanian state did not submit an official challenge to the ban against its fans.

Game day arrived. Chants outside of the stadium grew loud in the early hours of the evening as a heavy police presence surrounded the area: "Kosovo is Serbia, Kosovo is Serbia!" The game had not yet begun, but fans, the overwhelming majority for Serbia, filled the stadium as the shouts intensified. "Kosovo is Serbia!" As instituted by UEFA, Albanian fans were prohibited from entering the stadium, and those who were present had to remain in grassy areas outside of the stadium walls. "Kill, kill the Albanians!" spectators collectively yelled. Pregame warmups began and more flags appeared in the air. One was a Serbian national flag with a large superimposed image of Veljko Radenović, commander of a special Serbian police unit in Prizren, Kosova, during the 1999 war. Closer to the field another group of fans waved a large flag that read "Glory to Putin," in reference to Russia's president, one of Serbia's biggest allies.

Each team sang their national anthem prior to kickoff, with the crowd booing and jeering during Albania's song. Shortly after the game began there were loud firecrackers and smoke flares set off in the stands. A group of spectators burned the NATO flag, a nod to the 1999 bombing and those who continue to burn NATO's flag in response at sporting events. As the game proceeded, fans continued to throw litter and flares onto the pitch. On more than one occasion the referee was forced to pause the game to clear objects to try to ensure player safety. With the exception of two or three aggressive plays, the players themselves appeared focused on the game despite the raucous setting. But at the thirty-five-minute mark, Albania was lined up for a corner kick when two large flares were thrown from the stands, one nearly hitting an Albanian player. This caused the referee to again pause the game and talk with players to regulate their fans. The stadium announcer could be heard asking fans to refrain from throwing anything onto the pitch. "Kill, kill the Albanians," spectators continued to shout. "Kill them, slaughter them, until no Albanian is left!"

Due to the increasing number of flares being thrown onto the pitch, the referees were forced to stop the game once again near the forty-one-minute mark. It was at this point that a drone carrying a flag appeared in the sky, and the shouting briefly quieted as players and fans alike fixated on the flying object. As the drone lowered closer to the ground, the images on the flag became clearer: in the center was a large map of what some call "Ethnic Albania." This map is sometimes also referred to as "Greater Albania," a term that denotes irredentist and nationalist beliefs about the territories that some believe constitute the true or real Albania, including Kosova and parts of Serbia, Montenegro, North Macedonia, and Greece. At the top of the flag was written November 28, 1912, the date of

FIGURE 15. Drone flag flying above the pitch. Photo by Reuters.

Albania's independence from the Ottoman Empire, and bracketing the map were the images of Ismail Qemali and Isa Boletini, two important figures from the late nineteenth- and early twentieth-century Albanian Rilindja (National Awakening). Beneath their images in large letters was the word AUTOCHTHONOUS.

As the drone hovered closer to the pitch, Serbian player Stefan Mitrović grabbed the flag and pulled it down, which immediately prompted loud cheers and applause from the stands. Albanian players Andi Lila and Taulant Xhaka rushed to grab the flag, shoving Serbian players out of their way. Members of the Albanian team surrounded their teammates with the flag as if to protect it. At this point Serbian players from the sideline charged the pitch, and the intensity of shoving and pushing increased. Well-known Serbian supporter Ivan Bogdanov, nicknamed "Ivan the Terrible," soon ran onto the pitch and started attacking players. Bogdanov is known for being a right-wing Serbian ultranationalist with an arrest record for disrupting football matches. In fact, many people at the time thought he was still in prison. The Albanian players tried to leave the field with the flag, but more fans poured from the stands, throwing everything from punches to kicks to plastic chairs. Serbian security guards tried to break up the fighting, but others of the guards even joined the attack against Albanian players. A group of fans broke through another fence and chaotically flooded the field, chanting, "Kill them, stab them, until no Albanians are left!"

Both Serbian and Albanian players could be seen trying to clear fans from the pitch but to little avail. The referees were eventually called inside as the fighting continued, buttressed by physical and verbal flares. As officials escorted the Albanian team to the locker rooms, spectators threw more objects and trash, including additional chairs. Many of the players could be seen trying to crouch and cover their heads as they rushed through the tunnel opening. One person from the stands jumped through the security fence and aggressively kicked the last of the Albanian players as they huddled inside.

Neither team nor the referees returned to the field. There was a discussion among UEFA officials who wanted to resume play. But in conversations between the referees and the Albanian team, team captain Lorik Cana expressed that his team was neither physically nor mentally ready to resume the match, and he signed a declaration attesting as such. The game was thus suspended. Before departing, local Serbian police arrived to search the visiting locker room for the drone or any other evidence that the players had been involved in the stunt. They found none.

The Aftermath

The Football Association of Serbia (FFS) issued a statement after the game accusing the Albanian team of orchestrating a political plot to force the game's abandonment. They further insinuated that Olsi Rama, the brother of Albanian prime minister Edi Rama, was the responsible party. The Albanian Football Federation (FFSh) released a statement of their own, in which they condemned Serbia's *racist* violence. It read in part: "The Serbian side seems unable to condemn the violence, extremism, and racism that was displayed in Belgrade, but rather, they seem too busy weaving political statements that do not serve any purpose but to defend the shameful acts of racist violence and the unsportsmanlike conduct of their players, fans, and security staff" (BBC Sport 2014).

Versions of the drone flag were soon available throughout Albania, and fans showed support for their team by wearing the flag on shirts. Local newspapers were littered with headlines and photos of fans cheering the drone and Albanian's national team. Despite Serbia's accusations that the Albanian government and football federation were responsible for the drone, Albanian prime minister Edi Rama adamantly denied any involvement and tweeted that the match was an "ugly demonstration." Rama had been scheduled to make a formal visit to Belgrade the week after the match, the first by an Albanian prime minister to Serbia in nearly seventy years. After the drone incident and subsequent brawl, many wondered whether the scheduled visit would still take place.[2]

In the days following the game many people still speculated that Olsi Rama was the responsible party, but it was eventually revealed that the drone pilot was actually Ismail "Ballist" Morina. Originally from Northern Albania, Morina at that time was living in southern Italy but traveled to Belgrade for the match. Like almost all the Albanian fans, Morina remained outside the stadium throughout the game, where he eventually flew the drone and flag. His nickname "Ballist" is in reference to Balli Kombëtar, the anti-communist resistance movement against Italian occupation during World War II. In the summer of 2015, Digitalb, an Albanian television network within the Top Media Group, released a documentary film about the game titled *Autochthonous*. "The Serbian fans did not arrive for a game," the film's director states in the beginning. "They came for war." Ismail Morina was the primary focus of the film, and filmmakers traveled to his home village near Kukës to interview him. Morina cited revenge as his main motivation for flying the flag; he had witnessed Serbian fans burn an Albanian flag in a 2012 match between Serbia and Italy. He said he decided to feature Isa Boletini and Ismail Qemali on the flag to emphasize unity between a Kosovar Albanian leader who fought against Ottoman and Serbian occupation as well as one of the most prominent leaders of the Albanian independence movement. In response to his motivations for flying the flag at a match in Belgrade, Morina responded, "I have to say to the Serbian people, I do not hate them. I really do not hate them. But the past, our past, it is very, umm . . . it has hurt us. I do not hate them."

Official Match Ruling

A spokesperson for then-UEFA president Michel Platini said that Platini was deeply saddened by the events at the match. They released the following statement: "Football is supposed to bring people together and our game should not be mixed with politics of any kind. The scenes in Belgrade last night were inexcusable" (Gibson 2014). The game was scoreless when the brawl began, and since it was a qualifying match, UEFA had to determine whether there would be a rematch or if a winner would be declared based on the first half of play. The initial UEFA ruling awarded Serbia a 3–0 win, with officials arguing that the Albanian team forfeited the game because they were the ones who abandoned the pitch. Serbia still faced scrutiny in the form of fines and overall tournament point deductions. After UEFA upheld its decision, both teams filed appeals with the Court of Arbitration for Sport (CAS). CAS eventually rejected Serbia's appeal in 2015 but partially upheld Albania's. The court concluded that Albania was forced to abandon the match due to the violence inflicted on them, therefore reversing the UEFA result and awarding a 3–0 victory to Albania. In its appeal, the Albanian association argued that the chants from Serbia's fans were not just political but racist, and further, that racist violence was perpetuated both by Serbian supporters and at least two security guards. Additionally, Professor Sébastien Besson, an outside sports arbitrator, noted that it was not sufficient to label the chants by Serbia as political and that they fell under the category of racism.

As previously mentioned, members of UEFA maintained that they initially allowed the game to be played because Serbia and Albania had never had direct conflict with one another. But this justification failed to acknowledge that while the present-day geopolitical nation-state of Albania had not had a direct war with the present-day geopolitical nation-state of Serbia, for many people Albania and Serbia had certainly long experienced conflict, particularly on the issue of Kosova's independence. In speaking with my interlocutors, many felt that the drone flag included the images of Isa Boletini and Ismail Qemali because they represent historical liberation movements of Albanians in Kosova and Albania against Ottoman and also Serbian occupation. For people like Morina, there is a direct line between those past movements and the present-day fight for Albanian (particularly Kosovar Albanian) autonomy. This is further underscored by the term "autochthonous," an implication that Albanians are the unquestioned, nonmigratory original inhabitants of this part of the Balkan region. Returning to chapter 3's analysis of peripheral whiteness, this notion of being autochthonous evokes nationalist sentiments about territory, religion, and race. These sentiments represent efforts of those racialized outside of "European" to claim authentic and real Europeanness.

These registers and attachments travel across sports and global arenas. They document the way that race is produced and reproduced, uninhibited by geographic bounds. An example derives from the 2018 FIFA World Cup in Moscow, which featured a game between Switzerland and Serbia in the group stage of the tournament. At that time Switzerland's national team featured four Albanian players, including three on its starting lineup. Switzerland is home to a sizable Albanian population, many of whom migrated to the area from Kosova during the post-Yugoslavia wars. Switzerland defeated Serbia in the match, and both of the team's goals were scored by Swiss Albanian players, Granit Xhaka and Xherdan Shaqiri, with the latter coming in dramatic form in the final minutes of the game. After each of their goals, both Xhaka and Shaqiri ran along the sidelines making the double-headed eagle hand gesture toward Serbia and their fans, a practice that resembles the eagle from the Albanian national flag. The Serbian team was outraged by these actions and filed formal complaints, resulting in nearly $10,000 unsportsmanlike conduct fines from FIFA for both Xhaka and Shaqiri. That Russia played host to that year's World Cup only escalated tensions between the two teams, due to Russia's allyship with Serbia and its continued refusal to recognize Kosova.

Football and Europe's Racial Arrangements

The analyses of football and socioracial and ethnic formations are not meant to imply a fixed, immutable ancient ethnic hatred construed within a web of never-ending hostility. The match between Albania and Serbia was certainly a spectacle, but I do not draw attention to it to frame the Balkans as barbaric, uncivilized, or exceptional. This in fact was insinuated in some stories published by news outlets following the game, suggesting that the game demonstrated why some Western Balkan countries were not "quite ready" or "fit" for Europe. In the weeks following the game, *The Conversation* published an article titled "Albania v Serbia Football Drone Farce Shows Balkan Nationalism Is Still a Dangerous Powder Keg" (Alpion 2014), echoing that often-used powder-keg moniker for the region. This game does not illustrate a distinctly Balkan inability to escape ethnicity and nationalism as much as it illuminates Europe's unwillingness to address the racial logics that continue to animate its social landscape, the continued insistence on the absence of race in the face of an active presence. The 2014 UEFA match and its aftermath reflect the ways that histories and local identity formations have shaped contemporary relationships between Albania and Serbia. And certainly, more recently, the contemporary moment has been significantly impacted by the sociopolitical fabric of the former Yugoslavia, its breakup, and the ensuing wars. But in the Western imagination, the Balkans are consumed by ethnic conflict, rife with ethnic tension that somehow is unique to this region despite persistent and widespread issues of ethnicity and race that shape everyday life in Western European countries or countries like the United States, where Black people can be killed for jogging in a neighborhood, playing in the park, or sleeping.[3] The ethnonational conflicts in the Balkans do inform us about regional conflict, but they also demonstrate the production and reproduction of whiteness across Europe.

To return to the discussion from the book's introduction, race, ethnicity, and nation are not distinct but rather are deeply intertwined, and significant anthropological scholarship has attested to this. Writing about this relationship, anthropologist Kimberly Simmons maintains that "nationness is expressed along racial and national terms as lines are drawn and distinctions are made about a sense of belonging to a particular place or community within or across borders" (2002, 18). In their pioneering work on this subject, Basch, Schiller, and Blanc further argue that "to talk about nation is to talk about race" (1994, 37). The discussion of ethnic conflict in the Balkans, therefore, is a discussion of racialization. As Dusan Bjelić notes, in many ways ethnicities in the Balkan region have been turned into racial enemies shaped by broader European racial projects (2021). One of these European racial projects is shaped by religion and the racialization of Muslims (Rana 2011). Though the match was played by Serbia and Albania, for many

Serbian fans, Albania is a symbol for Kosova and Islam. One of the signs at the game read, "Serbia's Orthodox candles will remain lit in Kosovo," highlighting the intersections of race and religion that are particularly salient in contemporary demarcations of who is and who is not European. To consider Edward Said's classic work on orientalism, the dynamic between Kosova and Serbia demonstrates how Islam in Europe continues to stand for "terror, devastation, the demonic, [and] hordes of hated barbarians" (Said 1979, 59).

The question then becomes, what does an analytical framework of race illuminate about the organization of social relationships in the Balkans and Europe largely? What can an interrogation about the perceptions and understandings of racism reveal about the construction of race? Racism and nationalism are not solely a football matter in the Balkans; this is fundamentally a problem of Europe. Organizations like UEFA and FIFA have declared aspirations to address racism but rarely name it when it occurs and often insist on its absence. There is seemingly a desire to create space for the expression or celebration of national pride at football matches but not to the extent that it becomes political, yet in many cases the line of demarcation is blurry. If there are episodes, encounters, and expressions that are thought to explicitly involve race, they are deemed inappropriate and characterized as an aberration. Yet, in the case of European football, racial logics are always present, and they must be acknowledged if there is going to be a path toward addressing them. As Bjelić states, "Nations are not imagined communities but racialized communities.... Rather than a nation imagining its state, it is a state imagining its population" (2021, 13). The football pitch in Europe is one of the primary sites where people are imagined as representatives of the nation-state or not. As European or not. As white or not. What is needed is a more expansive, and historically and locally contextualized, understanding of racialization to trace how these sites of race-making illuminate the reproduction of race and racism even in the so-called post-racial, color-blind age.

Act 2: On Racial Mockery and Sketchy Comedy

An Albanian joke I have frequently heard goes something like this: A police officer walks into a store and asks the saleswoman, "How much is this refrigerator?" "You cannot buy it," she responds. "Why?" he asks. "Because you are a police officer." The officer is taken aback but then leaves the store. He soon returns in different clothes, this time in athletic gear. He proceeds to tell the saleswoman, "I want to buy this refrigerator." "You cannot buy it," she again responds. "Why not?" the man asks. "Because you are a police officer," she answers. The man is once again confused and leaves the store empty-handed. He returns home and puts on the best suit he owns and visits the store once more. When he arrives, he says to the saleswoman, "I want to buy this refrigerator. How much is it?" "You cannot buy it, she says, "because you are a police officer." "But how do you know that I am a police officer?" the man exclaims. "I have come multiple times in different outfits. How do you know that I am a police officer?" he demands to know. "Because," she says, "this is not a refrigerator—it is a washing machine."

This joke elicits a lot of giggles and laughs, but like many jokes, it can also prompt eye rolling and hand waving, as if to say playfully, "Just stop." I have been drawn to this joke ever since Besa first shared it with me. I like to ask my interlocutors about it because of what the joke communicates about police perception and the ways that many of my interlocutors love to share their feelings about local police as inept or *kot* (useless). But this joke is also a way to explore cultural contexts of humor that shape that which is deemed funny, not funny, and what is *just* lighthearted fun. Consider the following fieldnote from 2013:

> It was early evening, between five and six o'clock. I walked along Sami Frasheri Road, heading to meet a friend for a drink. Out of the corner of my eye I saw three teenage boys approaching, feeling them walk closer behind me with each step. Rather than pass me on the sidewalk, they slowed their pace, aligning their gait with mine. One of them reached out to grab my hair and said to his friends, in Albanian, "Hey, look here, her name is Jamaica! Oh, Jamaica, what's going on, Jamaica?" They snickered loudly, trying to keep grabbing my hair. Frustrated and annoyed, I turned to face all three of them. Though this encounter was seemingly more benign than others, I felt that familiar tension in my jawline when people mocked me on the street. But before I could say anything they stopped laughing and one of them said, "Është thjeshtë shaka" [It's simply a joke]. "It's not a funny one," I retorted. The same young man then remarked, "I am not racist."

Throughout my nearly twenty years of conducting ethnographic fieldwork in Albania, I cannot count the number of times that people in the street have made fun of my Black skin, my Black hair, my Black hips, the size of my Black buttocks.[4] Friends and interlocutors have likened the remarks to teasing, those quips that are made in jest. They have often encouraged me to ignore the insults, at times demanding that I not read too much into them as the comments are not necessarily offensive, or that they reflect broader cultural practices of commenting on bodies. I have frequently heard such statements as "People do it to bother [*për të ngacmuar*] someone but it does not *mean* anything," and because people so often comment on my body, I have experienced numerous times when my Albanian interlocutors explain them away. As an anthropologist I have observed times in which people have made jokes in passing about others, whether they make fun of someone's beard or their style of dress. I have also collected extensive fieldnotes about the body in public, and how criticism of a person's body can animate even the shortest of conversations as people greet one another and then immediately mention someone's weight loss or gain, hairstyle, or clothes. Such occurrences are by no means unique to Albania's social landscape; at the same time, these comments and so-called simple jokes, especially those about race and the body, provide an opening to critically explore how race is locally imagined in public realms and popular culture.

The above-highlighted ethnographic encounter was one of the few times whereby someone teased me about my body but then added that they were not racist. This moment has stood out in terms of how the young men perceived my reaction as well as how they then understood what *counts* as or *really* is racist. One of my neighbors once shared with me, "Here in Albania we do not have any racism, just jokes about people." Articulations of racelessness remain persistent, as the measures of what *counts* as racist continually shift, particularly when the object of analysis is humor. Humor is the primary focus of this chapter's act 2, which explores blackface and brownface on a popular Albanian variety television show. I interrogate local forms of humor by asking what they can illuminate about the logics of racism embedded within and produced by humor.

The weekly Albanian variety sketch show *Portokalli* (Orange) features two characters known as Drumba and Skrapi. Both characters are played by Albanian actors who use blackface and brownface in their portrayals. Drumba is a caricature of South African Black football players who have been recruited to play for Albanian teams and live in various Albanian local towns, usually outside of Tirana.[5] The actor who plays Drumba "blackens" his face with paint and makeup and wears a large black afro and mouthpiece with missing teeth. He speaks Albanian poorly and dances rambunctiously, singing loudly across the stage while his coach uses various tactics to calm him. Skrapi is a caricature of Roma people, and many of his sketches further entrench stereotypes of Romani family size, style of dress, language, and criminality. The sketches featuring Skrapi usually include exchanges between him and Albanians (whom he refers to as *dorë e bardhë*) where they talk about his life and his family. Skrapi's scenes also include political commentary and regularly conclude with moral lessons, thereby serving as a kind of teachable moment for Albanian audiences. The continued use of blackface and brownface in popular culture offers an opportunity to interrogate race and racism as they travel and produce forms of whiteness, blackness, and otherness. Like other sections in this chapter, I continue to probe how race and racism disappear once named.

Blackface and Brownface: Historical Formations, National Implications

The most well-known practices of modern blackface are traced back to mid- to late nineteenth-century minstrel shows in the United States, though exhibits and spectacles of Black bodies, including human zoos, have a much longer history in Europe.[6] Minstrel shows featured white performers who would blacken their faces with ash or shoe polish and then perform exaggerated portrayals of enslaved Black people that were intended to be comical and entertaining. Performances usually featured song and dance, and one of the more well-known characters of this time period is Jim Crow, who was depicted as lazy, criminal, and ignorant. Such performances not only made caricatures out of Black people but also reinforced the idea of slavery as "amusing, right, and natural" (Lott 2018). Similar to blackface, though lesser known, brownface speaks to the practice of white actors using paint to brown their faces to stereotypically portray people of color, for example, minstrel performances of Latinos in the mid-twentieth century. Such caricatures include that of José Jiménez from the *Bill Dana Show*, which aired in the United States in the 1960s and included the use of brownface to mock Latinos, especially regarding language and accents. These performances often relied on similar tropes from minstrel performances of the nineteenth century (Raúl 2016).

While Albania does not share this same history of transatlantic slavery or minstrel performances, the present-day use of blackface in popular culture is similarly shaped by white supremacy, the ridicule of blackness, and the racial logics that shape ideas about certain bodies and how they perform for certain audiences. The characters of Drumba and Skrapi call attention to these centuries-long practices that deride those racialized outside of whiteness. For those who are racialized as white and perform blackface, race itself becomes a "wearable commodity" (Velayutham and Somaiah 2021). Though blackface performances have significantly declined globally since the nineteenth and early twentieth centuries, in many places the continued use of blackface is considered harmless fun (Howard 2018), or as many Albanians might say, "thjeshtë shaka" (simply a joke). These dismissals are most adamant when the person criticizing blackface or brownface is a person of color (Velayutham and Somaiah 2021; Wekker 2016). In these instances, and in the case of Albania in particular, my Albanian interlocutors may reiterate harmlessness while also emphasizing that there is no intended malice—that these portrayals do not have any *real* meaning but are solely intended for comedic purposes. "Kaq!" (That's it!), an interlocutor once emphatically told me while we were watching an episode of *Portokalli* and I asked about Drumba and blackface.

While there are overlapping and shared experiences of racism between Roma and Balkan Egyptians with Black people of African descent in the West (Chang and Rucker-Chang 2020; West Ohueri 2021), I want to reiterate that these experiences are not necessarily analogous. At the same time, a focus on blackface and brownface enables scholars to study race relationally, and not just comparatively. As such, I maintain a distinction between blackface, which speaks specifically to the experiences of Black African-descended people, and brownface, which I use to refer to the practice of white performers darkening their skin to stereotypically portray people of color broadly, including Roma and Balkan Egyptians. Scholars have documented Romani representation in films and television through blackface, calling attention to long-standing practices of objectification and cultural appropriation (Rucker-Chang 2018; Moscaliuc 2019). Writing about the representation of Roma in Yugoslav film, Radmila Mladenova argues that Roma are presented as culturally other and racially different from Yugoslavs, and also from Europeans broadly. The bodies of Roma people are contrasted with those from dominant groups, with Roma viewed as "deviant creatures [whose] bodies and identities [provide] a symbolic space on which the boundary of Europeanness is inscribed" (Mladenova 2016). Relatedly, Sunnie Rucker-Chang (2018) maintains that Roma are continually objectified in post-Yugoslav film, noting that depictions of Roma as unable to conform to cultural and social norms mirror the ways that Balkan states have been othered as Europe's internal outsiders. On the use of non-Roma actors to play Roma in Balkan films, Mladenova additionally notes: "By donning the mask of the denigrated Other, [socioracial] groups who are considered ambivalently white go through a kind of initiation rite into white 'civilized' society, confirming and conforming to its symbolic order. By projecting their less desired features onto g-----s, the inhabitants of the Balkan states can prove to be true Europeans" (2016, 27).

There are few, if any, studies on contemporary blackface and brownface in Albania. In her book *Race and the Yugoslav Region*, Catherine Baker (2018) explores popular culture in the former Yugoslavia, noting the ways that musicians like Genta Ismajli, a Kosovar Albanian, appropriates blackness in her performances. In her 2009 song "Si panter i zi" (Like a black panther), Ismajli says lines such as "Now do it like a Black girl," and in the video she is seen in blackface with an Afro ponytail and revealing clothing, as she and the dancers around her seem to imitate what they consider Black dancing. Ismajli goes on to also sing "do it like a white girl," "do it like a Latina," and she concludes this segment of the video by "doing it like an Albanian girl," wearing traditional Albanian clothes and performing Albanian folk dancing known as *valle*. Ismajli's performance has received little scrutiny as it pertains to donning blackface and brownface, but analyses such as Baker's have shed light on racialization and representation in

Balkan popular culture. Related discussions of blackface include social media conversations about the ways that hip-hop artists in Kosova make claims to blackness in their music and videos, including the use of "n*gger" in lyrics. Albanian singer Rita Ora has recently come under scrutiny in the media for engaging in what is known as blackfishing, a term that refers to white celebrities who intentionally use hairstyles, makeup, and fashion to enhance their features and create ambiguity so that they appear as if they are Black or have Black heritage (Cherid 2021). Many people online have criticized Ora for trying to appear to be Black through the use of box braids and cornrows, and in a 2016 interview with television host Wendy Williams, Ora was asked about her background and whether she was Black, to which she stated that she "might as well be." Such an articulation draws attention to the discussion from chapter 3, whereby Ora sees herself as both peripherally white as well as approximate to blackness. This chapter's discussion of blackface provides another opportunity to explore what these performances reveal about how Albanians understand their own racialized identities.

Blackface and brownface performances reveal the textures of a nation's racial imagination and, in this case, what it means to *really* be European. To return to Gloria Wekker (2016), these depictions are not harmless amusement; rather, they illustrate racial hierarchies and are deeply rooted in the silent ordering practices that rank humanness. Writing about the figure of Zwarte Piet (Black Pete) in the Dutch imagination, Wekker notes, "Dutch audience(s) need to be convinced of the happiness of the black character; that blacks were naturally funny, carefree, frolicking, without a worry in the world" (2016, 165). For Wekker, Zwarte Piet solidifies the white/black boundary between "us" and "them," illuminating how race configures national belonging as well as European whiteness that is reaffirmed as superior to blackness. Considering this, how do the characters of Drumba and Skrapi produce and reproduce ideas of blackness and otherness, and what do these portrayals reveal about the ways that blackface and brownface cement racial logics of European whiteness as superior to blackness?

On Fantasy, Desire, and Eating the Other

The caricatures of Drumba and Skrapi are underpinned by layers of fantasy and desire, whereby the bodies of those marked as others are consumed; blackness and brownness become commodified. One of my own ethnographic encounters provides an example of this objectification and desire of the black body. A research colleague once invited me to speak to students at a local university in Tirana, and while walking upstairs to the classroom, I heard a student say about me, "Wow, what a huge ass, I would just love to eat it!" When I turned around, she had her hands near her mouth like she was eating, but as her eyes met mine, she realized that I understood Albanian and looked ashamed. I said to her, "No, please do not do that." My colleague rolled her eyes and made a comment about college students and immaturity, but more than immaturity, this encounter spoke to objectification of the black body and the desire to consume it.

Race and racial difference in Albania are commodified and devoured by audiences for enjoyment, with the dominant group eating the body of the other (hooks 2015). As bell hooks notes, "When race and ethnicity become commodified as resources for pleasure, the culture of specific groups, as well as the bodies of individuals, can be seen as constituting an alternative playground where members of dominating races . . . affirm their power-over in intimate relations with the Other" (2015, 367). In this case the intimacy does not necessarily stem from the sexual encounter but from the pleasure of consuming the other's exoticism. The other is objectified for amusement, enjoyment, becoming the site for playing black and brown to assert whiteness. In the following section I discuss two different episodes from *Portokalli*, one featuring the character of Drumba and a second episode with Skrapi. I provide an in-depth description about the episodes that includes details about their on-stage performances and interactions with other personalities from the show. I then offer an analytical discussion about racialization, humor, and othering.

Mockery and Mozambique

Produced by Top Channel, a subset of Top Media Group, the variety show *Portokalli* has been in syndication in Albania since 2005. Sketches with the character of Drumba, played by actor Salsano Rrapi, were most popular in the mid-2000s and early 2010s, though the character is still one of the most recognizable from the show. In addition to *Portokalli*, Drumba has also been featured on commercials for Digitalb, the satellite television company also owned by Top Media Group. As previously mentioned, Drumba's character is supposed to represent sub-Saharan African football players who have been recruited to live in Albania and play for local teams. In an episode from 2008, two football coaches travel to Mozambique, which audiences are led to believe is Drumba's home country, and the coaches recount their experiences there.

The clip begins with Drumba riding in the back of a car with his head coach, who is always dressed in a black suit, in contrast to Drumba, who either wears a jersey or mismatched clothing.[7] Drumba is not in a seat but rather is crouched into the trunk of the SUV. When they stop on the red carpet Drumba jumps out of the car to flashing lights and confetti from paparazzi and supporters welcoming them back to Tirana. Drumba is visibly upset with his coach, who at this point returns to the vehicle to retrieve a small bag. Drumba begins dancing around, moving his forearms under his armpits to imitate a dancing monkey. We then see the coach return from the car and give Drumba a piece of *byrek*, which he immediately eats on the red carpet. The camera then returns to the main stage where show host Amarda Toska, wearing a formal red dress, announces that the audience will now see what the African adventure was like.

The scene turns to four Albanian actors wearing blackface and various Afro wigs and medusa-style hair as they dance around a coconut tree in what we are to presume is Mozambique. All four characters wear long-sleeved black shirts and black tights, with white necklaces and bracelets, which we are to assume imitate an African style. The character imagined as Drumba's father wears a gold toga over the black clothes and has what appears to be a white animal bone above his beard. Drumba's mother wears an animal print skirt on top of black clothes. Only Drumba wears shoes while the rest of the family is barefoot. Drumba has a feather protruding from his hair. The characters loudly speak gibberish, which the audience is supposed to perceive as an African language—but it is a language that only the four characters on stage can understand. As Drumba finishes dancing he bumps into the coaches who are walking on stage with their suitcases. We then hear the four characters in blackface speaking, and one of the discernable words is *makalena*, which they repeat multiple times. Drumba then says to the coach, "Mirëseerdhe [Welcome] . . . it is me, Drumba . . . This is mama, father, sister." The manager recognizes Drumba but then shows confusion as he tries to ascertain who is Drumba's mother and who is Drumba's father. He begins to introduce himself to the person who he thinks is Drumba's father, but this character is actually Drumba's mother. The audience roars with laughter at the mistake. The assistant coach makes fun of him for making such a gaffe. Drumba's father then starts yelling the word *jumanji* as the characters continue to speak a nonsensical language.

The head coach brings out a bag of gifts for the family, and Drumba has to calm his family's excitement. Drumba's father says "Hakuna matata" (the familiar line from the movie *The Lion King*), which elicits more laughs from the audience. The gifts turn out to be different types of *byrek*, which makes the audience laugh even harder. After the gifts are distributed, Drumba's father becomes very animated and starts to wave his club and yell. He sends Drumba over to the head coach, and Drumba tells him, "Baba thotë, ti marton motra ime"[8] (My father says that you marry my sister), a suggestion that makes the audience hoot and clap with amusement. The coach is astonished and says, "Tell me again what they are saying," looking stunned at the thought. He then turns to the other coach to clarify that Drumba's family is in fact proposing that he marry Drumba's sister. The head coach then asks Drumba, "Which one is your sister again?" The camera then turns to the character imagined as Drumba's sister, who is played by an Albanian male actor in blackface wearing multiple necklaces and bracelets. The audience continues to shriek at the idea of Drumba's coach and sister getting married. At this point the manager starts to debate with the family, emphasizing why he cannot marry Drumba's sister. Drumba says this is a tradition in Mozambique, and Drumba's family tries to convince the coach that this is what he is obligated to do. The coach then asks to speak to Drumba's sister privately, and the two move away from the others and closer to the front of the stage. He tells her that he is a really bad guy, someone she should not want to marry. Whatever bad things there are in this world, he tells her, those things describe him. He then says that in fact he is gay. This prompts tumultuous laughter from the audience. The head coach then looks to the other coach and asks him to give him more words that will scare away Drumba's sister, to which the assistant coach replies, "What do you mean, words that will scare her? They eat dinner with tigers and lions!" The audience continues to laugh as the character of Drumba's sister forcefully grabs the manager and pulls him closer while making kissing sounds. The petrified coach starts asking loudly, "What is she saying? What is she doing?" "My dad says you need to kiss your wife," Drumba replies. At this point there are multiple roars and howls from the audience. The assistant coach warns the head coach that he must marry Drumba's sister, or their family might come after him with a tiger, and then they may even add the tiger and a little spice to a pot to eat it. The coach says that he hopes the family is eaten by the tiger, arousing more laughter in the studio. The band begins to play slow music, indicating the end of the sketch, as Drumba's family carries the manager off stage, suggesting that he is going to stay with them.

Caricatures, Carriages, and Collections

The character of Skrapi, played by Albanian actor Florian Binaj, first appeared on *Portokalli* in the mid-2010s.[9] Skrapi is imagined as a Roma man who makes a living by collecting scrap material, hence his name. Skrapi typically appears on stage with his carriage in tow. Binaj uses makeup or paint to darken his face and wears a wig with dark, curly hair. He additionally wears gold and silver crowns over some of his teeth and has an accentuated unibrow.

In a more recent episode of *Portokalli* from 2020, Skrapi arrives on stage with his carriage to meet one of the show's cohosts, Xhemi Shehu. He is wearing a Phat Farm jacket, seemingly a nod to Black American fashion, also suggesting that he likely found the jacket or it was given to him to resell. Skrapi and Xhemi casually exchange greetings, and when she asks about his children, he responds, "They are growing up and also increasing." This makes the audience laugh, and Xhemi asks, "Increasing, huh?" and Skrapi affirms this. She tells Skrapi that the last time they met, he had eleven kids and asks if that is still correct, to which he replies, "There are 13.5." When Xhemi asks why 13.5, Skrapi says that his wife is currently pregnant. This is meant to be amusing as it reiterates the widely held belief that Roma families in Albania have too many kids. They continue to joke about the large size of Roma families, and Skrapi makes fun of how fast they reproduce. He then asks, "But what about you all? How many kids do you have?" With this question he is distinguishing himself from Albanians, and Xhemi responds that her family only has two kids. Skrapi is confused by this. He clarifies to ask if they have two older kids or two kids in total, to which Xhemi confirms that she has two kids. "That is so bad—I feel so bad about this," Skrapi says. The audience laughter ensues.

Xhemi continues, "I feel bad for all of this stuff you are carrying in your carriage, collecting iron." Skrapi responds by asking what else they (meaning Roma) can do;[10] he says they receive empty promises from the government and unfortunately, everyone knows how the Albanian government acts. This political banter prompts further laughing and clapping from the audience, because in Albania political humor is almost always in style. Skrapi continues by saying that his people are obligated to collect scraps from waste, to work with torn and shredded materials—what else are they supposed to do? "Mos u mërzit" (Do not worry), Xhemi says. "Do not worry because things will get better." "What are you saying to me?" Skrapi asks cheekily. "What they [the government] do not do for *you* that are white, are they going to do for *us* who are black?" Skrapi goes on to tell Xhemi that many generations of people in Albania have heard that the state would do it, that Albania would provide for its people. "And now three generations have passed,[11] and when will things change?" The two continue back and forth, and Xhemi says she thinks that the government's visions for change will only exacerbate the world's problems, to which Skrapi laughs and agrees. Xhemi tells Skrapi that despite the issues he has remained an upstanding person and that the world is just a bit distorted right now but can get better. Skrapi tells her that the aspirations she is talking about are very difficult but that she has described the issues in a nice way.

Skrapi then looks around and somewhat nervously asks Xhemi if she has any unwanted aluminum cans. Xhemi seems taken aback, telling Skrapi that she does not have any cans with her on stage, which draws more laughter from the audience. Xhemi then realizes that she has not asked Skrapi how he has been doing throughout the pandemic, and then asks what it has been like to venture out during this time. Skrapi responds by joking, "We are going *in*, not *out*, because no one is allowed out right now." The audience laughs once again, a nod to Albania's strict policies during earlier stages of the COVID-19 pandemic when most people were not allowed outside of their homes without documented permission. Skrapi adds that during the thirty-day restriction, the government promised they would take care of people, but their commitments proved hollow. Xhemi and Skrapi then discuss how politicians and famous people did not adhere to travel restrictions while others in Albania were subjugated to different and far stricter rules. They are especially critical of politicians who vote for policies to which they themselves do not follow. Xhemi says, "The government is made up of animals, not people," to which Skrapi retorts, "No, do not refer to them as animals because that would be a compliment." To this audience members snicker and chuckle.

The pair continues discussing the sad state of the world. Skrapi asks Xhemi if she knows who the biggest villain is, and when she asks who, he says it is the financial market. Xhemi is initially confused, but Skrapi explains his thought, arguing that the market tells people that they will be millionaires if they buy certain clothes, certain cars, certain houses. "And as a result what do we have now throughout the world? We unfortunately have very sad generations of people with very beautiful photos." At this point Skrapi's phone rings and his face lights up in response. "Who is it?" Xhemi asks, and Skrapi lets her know that it is Qeli, his seventeen-year-old son. The audience laughs at the mention of this because the word *qeli*, which is not a typical name, means "prison cell" in Albanian, suggesting a natural link between Roma and crime. Skrapi tells Xhemi that he must leave because he and his son have a lot of work to do. She asks if he is going to take a few moments to catch some air, but he reiterates that he must begin working immediately. She wishes him well and they part ways, ending the scene.

Spectacles of Blackness, Scenes of Ridicule

The portrayal of Drumba becomes pleasure for *Portokalli*'s audiences, as their appetites for amusement are satiated by degrading and ridiculing performances of the feral and wild character. In many other sketches Drumba sings loudly and dances across the stage, as his coach tries to calm him and teach proper decorum. His character is always missing teeth and communicates in broken or derogatory Albanian that is meant to be comical. An example comes from an episode in which Drumba tries to say Mamurras, the name of an Albanian city, but instead he says, "Mua m'a rras," a derogatory expression implying forced sex. When Drumba says this, his coach is shocked and confused, and he asks Drumba to say it again, which elicits howls of laughter from the audience. Drumba is imagined to be Black, but also as barbaric, foreign to whiteness and humanness. His attempts to speak and behave in a socially appropriate manner serve as comedic relief but also confirm his inability to be or become civilized or European. To reiterate Wekker (2016) and Rucker-Chang (2018), those amused by blackface tend to believe that such performances are simply comedic as opposed to reflective of those ordering practices and hierarchies that shape global and local racial logics. In the case of Drumba, even if Albania's own relationship to whiteness is peripheral, the contrast with Drumba serves to demonstrate Albania's closer proximity to Europeanness and whiteness.

Like nineteenth- and early twentieth-century blackface performances, the depiction of Drumba's black body demonstrates inferiority in relationship to the white body (Howard 2018). Black bodies are deformed, not fully human, or to a greater extent not human at all (Wynter 1994). The exaggerated physical features and the representation of blackness as viewed through the bodies of Drumba and his family elucidate how the Black body is imagined as amusing and absurd. As Howard (2018) notes, there is a kind of common-sense-ness about the comedic nature of the Black body, one that suggests that because Black bodies are so innately different from white bodies, and therefore nonnormative, Black bodies are therefore humorous and naturally funny. These depictions become what Stuart Hall referred to as "ritualized degradation," a representation so normalized that it does not need any explanation (Hall 1997). Such representations do not need to be questioned or scrutinized because they are thought to be widely accepted and innocuous.

You will recall from chapter 2 my preshow conversation with Enon, the host of *Wake Up Tirana*, in which he refused to engage in a conversation about Drumba and race, arguing that the portrayal was rooted in Albania's history and that by bringing up race, I was taking the character out of context. A possible element of this history stems from Albanian television during the communist period. Radio Televizioni Shqiptar (Albanian Radio and Television) was the only channel broadcast in the country during the regime, and the show *Vende dhe Popuj* (Places and People) was a regularly scheduled program. The show focused on various world regions, often highlighting what were thought to be exotic societies that Albanians may not otherwise know about. Episodes aired in the 1970s featured segments about famine in African countries like Ethiopia. Many of my interlocutors have discussed how the show focused on these issues of hunger in other places to convince Albanian viewers that they were better off, despite widespread food shortages in Albania at that time. What these episodes also did, however, was shape the now widespread beliefs that Africans generally do not have food, and as such, they must really desire even the most basic staples of Albanian cuisine, such as *byrek*. Black football players in Albania have observed the ways that some people are enamored when they eat *byrek*. As a further example, a 2015 article from *Opinion*, an Albanian news website, profiled a Black Brazilian player who was compared to Drumba because he seemed more content with *byrek* than a full salary (Opinion 2015). While these logics might be thought to be raceless, they in fact illuminate the ways that Blackness (and Africanness) are racially imagined, shaped by these histories of representation and consumption.

Admiration amid Mockery?

The character of Skrapi is not the first representation of Roma and Egyptians on *Portokalli*. An episode from 2006, for example, features two men imagined to be Egyptians who ride around town in a carriage led by a donkey. They wear flamboyant clothing as they sing what we are led to believe are Romani wedding songs. In the sketch the two men are mocked for their fashion, their gold and silver teeth, and the misspelled words written on the side of their carriage, with some words written with backward letters. They also carry around large bags of trash. Another example includes a sketch from circa 2006 that features two Albanian actors wearing blackface to depict those considered *jevg*. They wake up inside trash bins on the street, and one has a banana in her hair. These two actors argue about the country's economic and political climate, but they do so while reinforcing the same degrading ideas about Roma and Egyptians as degenerate.

While these characterizations parallel that of Skrapi, there are multiple ways in which they diverge. Skrapi's character is mocked as he is intimately tied to waste, but amid the mockery he provides insightful political commentary and pearls of wisdom for Albanian audiences. He critiques the government and is mindful of the socioeconomic challenges faced by Roma. This resonates with Albanian viewers who are also quite frustrated with the current political milieu. Skrapi's insights are welcomed by audience members who laugh but also likely very much agree with at least parts of his perspective.

Similar sentiments emerge from a different episode where Skrapi is a professor for three Albanian students. The skit is thought to be humorous as many viewers would find it absurd to have a Roma man teaching Albanian students. One of the students is visibly upset and crying because of relationship woes. Skrapi consoles her by reminding her that people fight and breakup, but they also experience joy. The student continues to cry, saying that she thought the relationship was wonderful but now she does not think it was, to which Skrapi replies, "Do not forget that you are the wonder." This elicits loud audience enthusiasm evidenced through whistling and applause. Skrapi then quotes Aristotle, saying that people cannot learn without pain, adding, "Perhaps our problems do not lie in how much love is given to people but which people we love." This observation is immediately followed by resounding claps and cheers.

Skrapi has gained significant notoriety as a *Portokalli* character. Not only is Florian Binaj, who plays Skrapi, one of the show's most beloved actors, but Skrapi himself has become somewhat iconic. He appears on stage for sketches about his life and also performs musical numbers, such as Guns N' Roses's "Sweet Child o' Mine," accompanied by the show's live band. In recent years Skrapi has gone viral on platforms like YouTube and TikTok, with users sharing many of his life lessons. An example comes from a widely shared social media clip in which Skrapi says, "Life is like a bow and arrow. If you want to move forward, you first have to bring the arrow back. And when the difficulties of life bring you back, it means that you are about to go to something bigger." Comments on this clip include those such as "Të lumtë goja," a wish that Skrapi's mouth, and therefore his words, will be blessed.

Though Skrapi's character is presented as a bridge between Albanians and Roma, this framing actually highlights how brownface is tied to fantasy and desire. As I illustrated in chapter 4, there are some Albanians who do have closer relationships with Roma in Tirana, but these relationships are largely between poorer Albanians and Roma, who may live in closer proximity to one another on the outskirts of the city. But these kinds of interactions and social familiarity between middle- or upper-class Albanians and Roma are rare. As such, regular conversations between Skrapi and someone like Xhemi Shehu would not likely occur in Tirana. Further, the likelihood that Skrapi could be a professor that is well received by white Albanian students is fantastical, as a significant number of Roma and Egyptians experience many educational barriers as well as high unemployment in Albania. Numerous Roma interlocutors have shared with me about the constant racism they have faced as students in the classroom, let alone instructors. For Roma in Tirana that do secure formal employment, the jobs usually involve street cleaning or local waste management. I have interviewed multiple Romani interlocutors about their struggles to obtain jobs in other sectors, and for the small number who do become educators, very few teach in classrooms where Albanian kids make up the majority of the population. Skrapi's performance reiterates the distance between white Albanians and Roma as the use of brownface demonstrates that there is not even the possibility that a Roma actor could play the role of Skrapi. The white actor in brownface could be understood as a performance that illuminates future friendship possibilities, but what emerges from Skrapi's character is a glimpse into a racial imagination that is myopic to the racism of blackface and brownface as well as the everyday racism experienced by Roma and Egyptians in Albania.

The scripted representation of Skrapi, like that of Drumba, additionally underscores the role of pleasure and what it means for audiences to delight in the consumption of those marked as other, even if the character of Skrapi brings forth lessons and moral takeaways. The *Portokalli* stage is the playground where white Albanians take delight in pleasures: amusement, the fantasy of embodying blackness and otherness, the illusion of a closer proximity with those marked as other. Unlike many Western countries, Albania does not have a history of serving as a colonial empire, and this consideration is key when using theoretical frameworks to analyze these racialized performances in the contexts of fantasy and desire. At the same time, the practices of brownface and blackface do serve a similar purpose, but instead of evoking colonial fantasies or imperialist nostalgia (hooks 2015), these performances superiorly situate Albanians alongside those deemed even more other and primitive, thus affirming European whiteness that is otherwise peripheral and precarious.

"You do not understand *our* humor." This is an often-expressed sentiment in response to critiques of Drumba and Skrapi, as well as *Portokalli* sketches in general. In my case, as a sociocultural anthropologist who is not Albanian nor a native Albanian speaker, I do not easily dismiss this sentiment. The subject of humor and language is complex, and social and historical context are necessary for understanding comedic performances. Further, it is true that *Portokalli*, like other variety shows, features numerous characters designed to make fun of people throughout Albanian society, not just Roma, Egyptians, and Black people. For many viewers the show provides an opportunity for collective enjoyment, a time for people to savor jokes and what they view as innocuous portrayals about daily life for many different types of people in Albania. In many ways the show itself represents a creative liberty and opportunity previously thought to be impossible.

It is difficult to understate Top Media's reach and influence in Albania. Founded in 2001 by businessman Dritan Hoxha, Top Channel, part of Top Media Group, is a powerful news and media production network in Albania. Dritan Hoxha played a significant role in rethinking the Albania mediascape following the collapse of the regime, and two of his creations, Albania Top Radio and Top Channel, have stood in stark contrast to the state-run media of the communist period. Since its inception Top Channel has represented possibility, particularly the possibility of expressing and imagining without confinement. Since 2005 *Portokalli* has represented this possibility. But it is precisely this domain of imagination that highlights how racialization operates even when racial meaning and racial logics are disputed.

In her analysis of Zwarte Piet and blackface in the Netherlands, Wekker similarly notes that many Dutch people are very sensitive to foreigners who criticize the practice and consider it racist, believing that outsiders do not have the right to determine what is racist. Several of my interlocutors assert that because Albania is small, a place where the communist regime publicly proclaimed solidarity and antiracism, and where people are ignorant because of past isolation, accusations of racism ring hollow because anything that might be considered racist is in fact innocent since people do not know better. This positionality of "not-knowing" thus enables Albanians to disavow racism (Wekker 2016; see also Mills 1997). Yet such standpoints further elucidate how global whiteness, anti-Romani racism, and antiblackness shape local contexts, because even in Albania, a small country that experienced significant global dislocation under during its communist period, the European white body is configured against those who are Black or Roma, and Black and Roma bodies are racialized as other for pleasure and consumption by those racialized as white.

Act 3: A Matter of Health and Safety or Racism?

I first met Agim and Elira in the informal Roma settlement at Breg Lumi (shorthand for Bregu i Lumit [Riverbank]) in the fall of 2013.[12] The couple had arrived at the neighborhood only a few weeks prior with their older son and young baby. They were living in a shack that previously belonged to a family who had relocated to a new settlement. A group of American and British missionaries had recently begun helping them with some of their needs like diapers and meals, and one missionary was trying to help Agim secure a job. Elira was born in Tirana, but her family moved to Greece when she was very young, though she does not remember at what age. She attended school for only four years and does not know how to read or write well in Greek, Albanian, or Romani, though she speaks all three languages. She met her husband Agim in Greece. Because he finished grade eight, he knows how to read and write in Greek, and like Elira, he additionally speaks Albanian and Romani. At some point there was an issue with their Greek residency registration, and while Elira said she did not know the full details as to why, the couple and their children had to return to Albania while her family stayed in Greece. Their primary form of income derived from Agim's scrap collections, though around the time we first met, Agim had recently gotten a *motorr* (small motorbike), which the family hoped would make it easier to look for work.

Elira and Agim did not stay long at Breg Lumi. In late winter they moved to the small settlement at Paskuqan and then briefly returned to Breg Lumi. By early spring they had relocated to the larger Romani settlement at Liqeni (the Lake). Elira said she had some distant relatives there who had space for them to potentially stay for a longer period. Two friends and I went to visit Elira at the lake one evening, and as we made our way into the settlement, we passed a group of men cooking something over an open flame. They greeted us, and my friend asked if they were making *qofte* (meatballs) and one of the men joked back, "Oh yes, we are making donkey meatballs," as they all erupted with contagious laughter that soon found me giggling as well. The same guy also tried to convince us on our way out that he was indeed cooking donkey meatballs.

There was still some daylight out, so like most of the other families, Elira's shanty was open with a makeshift door of hanging blankets pushed to the side. She was inside with her baby boy. Agim and Elira's oldest son were out collecting scraps. There was no power at the settlement because residents were not allowed to use electricity until 7:00 p.m. Elira told us that the electricity came from a generator, but she did not know how long it would last as the community did not have much money. Despite this, her barrack was warm inside from the wood-burning stove. We sat not far from the stove, on a bench covered with a blanket. A small board with two or three photos hung near us. Elira's baby had recently been sick, perhaps with an ear infection, but they did not know for sure. As she held him and patted his back, I noticed that she had names tattooed on her hand: Agim's near her wrist, and what I learned was her brother's name closer to her thumb. Elira was not very talkative; her words came in spurts, but she formed her staccato thoughts as though her sentences were continuous. "I wish my son could go to school," she said. I asked her how long her family had been looking for a more permanent place to stay and she looked despondent. "Ne duam një shtëpi në tokë," she later responded. "We want a house in the ground." This was a phrase I had grown accustomed to hearing from Romani and Egyptian interlocutors who did not want to live in tents in informal settlements, who did not want to have to move around frequently in search of a job or house. Elira wanted a house in the ground.

That many Roma families in Albania do not have a place to live is rarely understood as a problem of racism, social exclusion, and marginalization. That a significant number of Roma and Egyptian families in the Balkans remain suspended in temporary relocation settlements is thought to reflect their cultural values and practices. "You cannot do anything to help *them*," my Albanian neighbor would say. "This is what *they* want to do and how they want to live."

Fire at the Train Station

I return to the conversation I highlighted in chapter 4, where an Albanian taxi driver became upset about my research because in his mind, Roma and Egyptians in Tirana were at fault for their own experiences of marginalization; their homelessness, joblessness, and outsiderness were their own making. When I asked him how he knew this, he looked baffled and replied, "I have never done any readings or studies—I just know these things. Everyone knows them."

Everyone knows what they need to know or what they already know. Even the police in Tirana already know. So when the reports first came in February 2011, the police did not yet have a full story, but one thing they already knew: the Roma families were at fault. On the evening of February 20, families of the

Roma community near Stacioni i Trenit (the train station) gathered to celebrate the wedding of Elis Hysenaj. As is tradition with many Romani weddings, most of the residents from the neighborhood (between thirty and forty families) joined the pre-ceremony festivities that included a night of music, dance, and celebration before the formal ceremony, which was to take place the following day. Around midnight two Albanian men who lived near the community, Besmir and Klodian Vladi, arrived at the celebration. This was not necessarily unexpected as it was sometimes common in some communities for non-Romani neighbors to visit and join wedding festivities (Likmeta 2011b). These two cousins, however, did not arrive to celebrate but rather to cause commotion. According to the families present, the two Albanian men shouted numerous insults and obscenities, as they verbally harassed wedding attendees, destroyed decorations, and violently assaulted Xhevrije Hysenaj, the mother of the groom. They then set fire to part of the Roma settlement and, according to witnesses, threatened to burn all the shanties and ravage the entire community if the families did not relocate elsewhere: "Do t'ju djegim barakat, do t'ju heqim që këtu, do t'i zhdukim gabelët!" (We will burn all of your barracks [shanties] and force you out of here—we will destroy the *gabel*!") Many of the Roma families went to local police for help, but the police did not provide protection or implement any sanctions. In fact, the police later claimed that they believed the Roma families were responsible for initiating the conflict, and they found no fault with Besmir and Klodian Vladi (Likmeta 2011b). Following this, members of the Romani community at the train station feared for their lives, and many felt they could no longer remain at their settlement because of the violent threats. As such, most of the residents, around forty families, decided to leave the settlement and soon found themselves without housing. The Vladi cousins returned to the area shortly thereafter and destroyed the remnants of the camp.

Word of the fire and violent encounter eventually spread to other Romani and Egyptian communities in Tirana, and various human rights activists and media representatives became involved in the matter. This prompted an investigation by the Organization for Security and Co-operation in Europe (OSCE) and ambassadors from the United States and the European Union (Likmeta 2011a). A joint statement was released that in part called on the Albanian government to probe what happened and provide social assistance to the displaced Roma families. The ambassadors additionally called attention to Albania's participation in the Decade of Roma Inclusion, a pan-European coalition of twelve countries who had committed to improving the socioeconomic conditions of Romani populations.

Due to this outside pressure and demands for further inquiry, the Tirana prosecutors' office began a formal investigation. The Vladi cousins were arrested later that spring and charged with "damage to private property through arson" and "incident of ethnic and racial conflict," the latter of which falls under Article

256 of Albania's Penal Code. In its entirety Article 265 states: "Inciting hate or disputes on the ground of race, ethnicity, religion, or sexual orientation, as well as intentional preparation, dissemination, or preservation for purposes of distributing writings with such content, by any means or forms, shall be punishable by imprisonment from two to ten years" (Republic of Albania 1995). Besmir and Klodian Vladi were brought to trial under these charges. The trial judge, Shkelqim Mustafa, ruled that the two defendants were guilty of the arson attack but not guilty of inciting racial or ethnic hatred. Judge Mustafa claimed that the defendants' actions were not motivated by racism; rather, in his opinion, the Vladi cousins were simply upset at the loud wedding music that was disturbing them in their homes. According to Mustafa's interpretation of the law, the crime of racial hatred can only be proven on the basis of "active actions that produce hatred between ethnicities or races through words or writing." The judge further added, "This [type of] crime can only happen by disseminating pamphlets or holding public rallies that lead to hatred between races and ethnicities" (Likmeta 2011a). For the charges of arson, Besmir Vladi was sentenced to six months in prison, while Klodian received a sentence of four months.

Local prosecutors and human rights attorneys later appealed the initial ruling. In August 2012, nearly one and a half years after the attack on the Roma camp, the Court of Appeals ruled that Article 265 did in fact apply to this case. At this point, however, the defendants had been out of jail for quite some time, and rather than receiving new sentences, they were credited with time served. The local prosecutor's office decided not to pursue a further appeal with the High Court, and as such the case was eventually dismissed. Two years later many of the surrounding areas near the train station were also demolished to pave the way for a new project, led by the Democratic Party, that would extend Tirana's main boulevard and add new apartment complexes. The boulevard project was completed in early 2019, at which point Tirana was led by Socialist Party mayor Erion Veliaj. Veliaj spoke at the grand opening about the benefits of the road extension, particularly in easing traffic in the area. In his speech he additionally highlighted the significance of the road project for the city of Tirana:

> In a few days we are preparing to celebrate the ninety-ninth anniversary of Tirana being [designated as] Albania's capital city. We have been continuing for ninety-nine years to finish the project started by the Italians, as it pertains to the boulevard and its original axis, which was conceived by the Italians, remained unfinished with the communists, and has now become our thirty-year struggle. Therefore, for all those who want to see an eloquent Tirana, they will have to support the working Tirana, the clean Tirana, the right Tirana, the Tirana that is not blocked by a noisy minority, but is empowered by a silent majority.

FIGURE 16. Road that was built years after the 2011 fire at the train station. Photo by author.

I want to note that when Veliaj uses the term "minority" here, it does not seem that he is referencing ethnic and racial minorities such as Roma; rather, he is calling out those people who hold different or critical political viewpoints about beautification and expansion projects in Tirana. In this case he appears to be speaking to those who oppose the urban development changes in Tirana, changes that he argues make Tirana better. His remarks about the "clean" and "right" Tirana, however, do draw attention to racialized understandings of cleanliness. It is not insignificant that the new road extends through an area that previously housed the large Roma settlement as well as some smaller used clothing shops mostly run by Roma and Egyptian families. A few of the families in this area were experiencing housing transitions, but most of the families had been settled in this Roma camp since the early 1990s. Though the Roma families from the train station community largely relocated in response to the attack by the Vladi cousins, it is significant that their community was set afire and demolished, after which the municipality proceeded with its renewal projects. And this Roma community, like others throughout the region, had likely already been threatened with eviction, as many Roma settlements are deemed unlawful by the municipality. In this case, however, it was not the municipality that directly forced the Roma families out but rather a result of racist violence inflicted on them. And once the area was reconstructed, the mayor described it as beautiful, cleaner, and better.

Unjust Uprooting

Anti-Romani racism is entrenched in Central and Eastern Europe. It is pervasive. Roma and Egyptians often speak of racism as a muzzle that impedes their ability to fully exist. As discussed in chapter 4, Rigers would yell throughout my neighborhood, "They treat me like an animal here!" "We are animals here!" Flutura from Kreshtë would repeatedly assert. Archival documents highlighted in chapter 4 unearth historical attempts of the Albanian government to relocate Roma and Egyptian families, yet the party regularly racialized these unwanted strangers as social pariahs. The racial logics of exclusion and marginalization have taken different forms in the communist afterlife, yet a throughline remains. The subject of housing is once again central for understanding the racial arrangements of the contemporary moment.

It was 2015 and the site was the Liqeni Roma and Egyptian community. This was the same community where Elira and Agim sought refuge the previous year, and the site where many Roma families from the train station community had made their new home. In the early months of the year Tirana's municipality indicated that they had developed a plan to relocate the families from the lake to build a new development on the area that was under local jurisdiction. The Liqeni residents, however, informed the Office of the Ombudsman that they never heard about the plan for their relocation. The ombudsman's office, alongside various civil society organizations, tried to propose a long-term relocation plan with the municipality, arguing that a forced eviction was not in alignment with international human rights standards nor the Decade of Roma Inclusion. This plan for the Liqeni community, many organizations argued, did not align with the goals of inclusion and improving Romani and Egyptian livelihoods.

The community was not relocated in the spring of 2015, but later that fall the residents reported that they received a sudden visit from local police. The officers did not provide detailed information, but they mandated the families to flee the area. Several of the Liqeni residents reported that they were confused, but officers said that the municipality had already spoken with the residents and that the decision for new development was final. There had been additional reports about tensions between the Roma and Egyptian families and their Albanian neighbors near the lake, and a story was circulating that a German tourist had recently been physically assaulted by Roma and Egyptian men in that area, though the residents disputed this version of events. Nearby Albanian neighbors were featured on local news segments where they complained about the hygiene of the camp residents and said that they thought the area was unsafe for children.

Following this abrupt visit from police officers, the municipality arrived with bulldozers the very next day. Most of the families at Liqeni did not have the chance to gather their belongings. Many would later tell reporters that they were bewildered about the situation and noted that despite claims from the municipality that they had other places to live in cities like Elbasan, these families said they did not have anywhere else to go. The nearby civil emergency centers that currently housed people from other forced displacements and relocations were full. In the middle of the EU-sponsored Decade of Roma Inclusion, the municipality demolished the Liqeni neighborhood. "Politicians in Albania are just celebrities," a Roma friend once said to me. "Oh you know, all of the black people in Albania, we just move them out . . . Let us focus more on technology and let us build more trees! This is how the government works."

Days after the demolition, Tirana's Mayor Veliaj held a press conference at the site to discuss the master plan for the artificial lake. Numerous people were in attendance, and there was a display with pictures showcasing plans for greener development. "We are here to make a promise today," Veliaj began. "To restore the lake back to a place where city dwellers can gather, and not a lake where invaders gather." As Mayor Veliaj continued his speech, he was interrupted by Leonard Olli, a local journalist and politician. Olli angrily admonished Veliaj, telling him that he should be ashamed about what happened with the families who lived at the lake:

> OLLI: Look at this site of violence!
> VELIAJ: Where is the violence? We cleaned up this area. To clean up the city is violence? To make the city greener is violence? *Qyteti do gjelbërohet!* [The city will be greener!] People will be able to come here with their children—this will be a place people can enjoy with their children. *Your* children will be able to play here.
> OLLI: But you have discriminated against the families who lived here!

Veliaj pointed to the area where the ruins of the Roma and Egyptian families' homes remained. He told Olli to see the vision of the future, where the artificial lake will be greener and cleaner, free from scum and grime. Several of the attendees responded with applause. Olli was escorted from the podium as Veliaj told the attendees that they were awaiting something more beautiful, something different. Veliaj closed by saying that the former primitivity of Tirana cannot be forgotten, but he was looking forward to a better future. "I cannot wait for your children and future generations to come and enjoy the atmosphere of a greener Tirana."

Writing about forced evictions and racial segregation, Giovanni Picker emphasizes that while local media may document the displacement of Roma communities throughout Europe, this only yields "chronicles [but] not explanations"

(2017, 2). Racism is an underlying social force that drives this displacement, but it is rarely named. "Racelessness," Picker notes, "is one of the most crucial conditions under which race can silently drive segregation and maintain it largely undisturbed" (18). As was illustrated by the aftermath of the 2011 fire and eventual destruction of the Roma train station camp, the judge framed racism as individual animus and personal hatred toward a group, and ultimately he ruled that the fighting and fire caused by the Vladi cousins were not racist. But this event, as well as the subsequent displacement and the forced eviction and demolition at the lake, draw attention to the simultaneous negation and normalization of racism. These violent acts are not aberrations; they are shaped by the racial logics and rhythms that regularly dehumanize Roma and Egyptians in Tirana. Racism is denied; one camp was thought to have been destroyed because of disagreements and the other because of public health. The persistent inequality of the social landscape is natural, and any difficulties experienced by Roma and Egyptian families are the result of their *own* cultural practices deemed to be immutable traits. Further, in both cases, what ultimately results from the unjust uprooting is the promise of betterment: better roads, better parks, a better future. The erasure and removal of Roma and Egyptians is thus beneficial for making Tirana greener and better.

Though it is often considered a permanent fixture, segregation is not a fixed state of being. It is etched into the local landscape by ordinary processes (Picker 2017). Even for those former residents of demolished communities that were supposed to receive new housing, many are still indeterminately suspended in relocation zones in the outskirts of the city. These forms of segregation and displacement speak not only to Tirana but also Albania and Europe broadly. Displacement is both material and symbolic, highlighting the relocation of Roma and Egyptians, "beyond the . . . boundaries of the nation and at times . . . beyond the realm of humanity" (Picker 2017, 48). While displacement at an earlier period of the regime may have been framed as social upscaling, contemporary forms "are an outcome of policies that intentionally or involuntarily violate the rights of some citizens and contribute to their abandonment and further isolation in places of exclusion, places produced by social and political abandonment" (Sula-Raxhimi 2021, 24).

Numerous politicians in Tirana have argued that the forced relocation of Romani and Egyptian settlements is in their best interest, because these are matters of public health, public safety, and public good. But as American writer James Baldwin once argued, urban renewal is just another way of saying Negro removal (Baldwin 1963). While Baldwin's statement refers to the experiences of Black Americans, the structural and global forces of white supremacy, anti-Romani racism, and antiblackness shape local relations, and as such I argue we can map both points of conversion and diversion when it comes to relational analyses of those racialized as "black." Black Americans and Roma and Balkan Egyptians in Albania share parallel experiences with structural racism, and it is structural racism, bolstered by racial logics that hierarchize human worth, that makes these targeted and forced evictions possible. Racism shapes the everyday social landscape of Tirana, revealed not just in events or encounters but, as Philomena Essed (1991) argues, in the intricacies of relationships, acts, and attitudes. The everyday racism experienced by Roma and Egyptians themselves illuminate Europe's racial arrangements, as their lives are regularly rearranged for the benefit of those believed to be of more worth—for those who *really* belong and *really* are European.

Racism and Europe's Racial Arrangements

I began this chapter with a discussion of how conversations about race oftentimes collapse into accusations and defensiveness of who or what is racist or not. And one of the more persistent misconceptions about racism in Albania, and across Europe and globally, is that racism is singularly about hatred, malice, or interpersonal dislike of a person or group. When I first began writing this chapter, I contemplated naming it something along the lines of "Racial Understandings and Misunderstandings." I wanted to explore what people understand to be racist or what qualifies as racism, and how often racism itself is framed as a misunderstanding. I believe scholars can learn a great deal about race from public discourse and lay understandings of what is considered racist and what is deemed not to be. The logics of what counts as racist, and how racism is named, disguised, or ignored, can yield insight into how race is made.

Like the preceding chapters, the three acts of this chapter have continued to trace race as an ethnographic object. Taken together, these arenas of sport and geopolitics, media and representation, and space and place, speak to the multiscalar and multimodal nature of race and racism. These sites underscore how processes of racialization are not siloed but overlapping, imbricated, and deeply embedded within societal fabrics. In this chapter I have examined the registers of racism in the context of ancient hatreds and national enemies, the practices of blackface and brownface, and the subjects of housing, segregation, and displacement. All three sites demonstrate how race and racism are denied while at the same time racial logics are quotidian. The three modes further reveal how ordinary logics of whiteness, blackness, and otherness animate Albania and Europe, and continue to demarcate the boundaries of Europeanness.

Race frequently gets obscured while racism is licensed, operating with impunity, shielded by assertions of racelessness. Examples such as the football match between Albania and Serbia reveal how assertions of "autochthonous" are often framed singularly as ethnic conflict typical of the Balkan region. Yet, as I have argued, race also organizes social relationships within this region, and through the analytic of football, we can locate race's active presence in the Balkan region and Europe broadly. Mapping racialization processes and examining how people grapple with racism in the Balkans offers a window to trace Europe's racial arrangements, arrangements that are not easily reducible to ethnic hatred. Moreover, critical inquiries into race shed light on the ways that aspirational Europeanness is buoyed by antiblackness and anti-Romani racism. Though Albanians are peripherally white, as demonstrated by previous chapters and the second and third acts of this chapter, the desire for European whiteness, inclusion, and authenticity are shaped by racialized exclusion whereby Black people, Roma, and Egyptians are racialized as outside of Europeanness while Albanians seek and long for white inclusion.

These racialization processes are complex. Albania does not share the same histories of colonialism and transatlantic slavery as Western Europe or the United States, yet, as I have shown in this chapter, practices of blackface and brownface, as well as racial segregation and forced displacement, are rooted in and shaped by the same racial logics and racial imaginations of white supremacy and superiority. In our scholarly inquiry of racialization, it is important to explore how racism operates, and as I have shown in this chapter, these analyses must be globally and locally situated. Examining the rhythms and tempos of racism provide a way to expand our studies of how race is made, and continually produced and reproduced, perhaps kindling necessary reckonings that can uproot racial logics.

CONCLUSION

I write this conclusion as an opening rather than a closing. As an anthropologist, taking an ethnographic approach has allowed me to trace race as a method of writing against assumed racelessness, to further examine *why* race, *how* race, and *where* race. In the introduction I told you, the reader, that I would be a very present ethnographer throughout this text. This is due in part to my commitment to ethnographic reflexivity but also because many of my initial questions about race stemmed from those first encounters in Albania in the summers of 2006 and 2007. It was the responses to my Black body, the subsequent conversations that followed, the ways blackness was named in the local language, and the disavowals of race as a social category of analysis that prompted my research inquiries. As Patricia Hills Collins (2000) has argued, Black women's experiences and scholarship are frequently dismissed or not counted as knowledge, yet it is my ethnographic standpoint that has allowed me to theorize about the complexities of race and challenge dominant epistemologies. Scholarship in Central and Eastern Europe tends to be dominated by fields such as history, political science, and cultural studies, but I argue that there is a need for increased anthropological and ethnographic analyses. Ethnography asks questions that require deeply engaged and in-depth fieldwork, methodological approaches that strengthen scholarly examinations of social phenomena. I rely on many of my personal encounters to ask how race is understood, but as an ethnographer I have a responsibility to my interlocutors to try to authentically and ethically engage this research. This is especially key in the context of southeastern Europe, as my Albanian, Romani, and Egyptian interlocutors, and interlocutors in the Eastern European and Eurasian region broadly, are constantly responding to what American and Western scholars think about them. Ethnography can be absurd, invasive, and extractive, but ethnography can also provide an opportunity to produce richly detailed and generative research built on dialogue and accountability (Collins 2000), authentic relationships, and continual questioning of our own positionalities as we carry out this work and produce scholarship.

Race is about people, and ethnography is about people too. Long-term research with people can tell us a lot, and the research for this book has significantly derived from conversation, from talk, from everyday exchange. But people are also confusing. They might say one thing one day, a different thing the next. A person could articulate a thought or sentiment but then maintain that they meant something else. Interpretations may change. Responses, reactions, recountings are not always predictable. A colleague once told me that she likes researching texts written by dead people because the words have already been written, and further, she does not have to worry what these authors might think of what she writes about them. Such is not the case with present people. People are fickle, and emotions and sentiments can be slippery, often requiring multiple modalities to actively map and trace. Anthropologists rely on in-depth and interrogative ethnography to study human behavior, but of course there are still limits to ethnography, chief among them the reliance on the anthropologist, in this case me, as the key narrator. Still, despite these limits, it is my hope that ethnographic fieldwork can yield greater insight into the ways that racialization shapes all people, delineating the local emergences of race and race-making as shaped by global structures. And as I have argued throughout this book, a slowed ethnographic attunement can prove beneficial for probing the routes of race and racial logics, and the sites of racialization processes and their reckonings, as shaped temporally, geographically, socially, and politically.

I hope that this book expands conversations and dialogue regarding race, paving the way for further inquiry into racialization and how race operates. I lacked the tools to study or even name racialization and race-making during my first fieldwork encounters, and was often encouraged to limit my analysis to nationalism or ethnicity. I was told that there was no race in Albania or the Balkans. Yet, as I developed a more critical and analytical lens, I focused my anthropological spyglass (Hurston 1935) to locate and trace race. Race became the ethnographic object and not just because my interlocutors asked me about it. My locally situated examinations shed light on local racial grammars, racial logics, and formations in Albania's historical record, and interlocutors who both named race as a force that organized their social lives, including local forms of segregation, marginalization, and inequality. I started to map how Europe's racial arrangements shaped the social fabric of its margins, discovering how the global shapes the local and the local the global. Albania, it turns out, can teach us a great deal about race globally.

At the 2023 annual meeting of the Association of Slavic, East European, and Eurasian Studies I attended multiple sessions about race in the broader region of Central and Eastern Europe and Eurasia. Some panelists in these sessions posed questions about the applicability of race frameworks for the study of Eastern Europe, and while there were questions shaped by persistent investments in race-lessness, others asked whether frameworks largely developed in Western academia were suitable for studying localities outside of the West. I do believe that these tensions can be productive and generative ground for deeper inquiry into the study of race. Racialization is operative, but race is contoured by nation, class, gender, religion, and language; there remains a need for more work that examines these contours. The study of race in Central and Eastern Europe and Eurasia must be historically contextualized, but we also need to continually question and interrogate those dominate narratives of history. At the same time, it is imperative that we attend to and take the lead from the field of critical Romani studies. Racialization processes are layered, and the story of race is more complicated than we may often approach it, but any discussion of race and racialization in Europe remains vastly incomplete without the analysis of Romani subjectivities (Costache 2023; Kóczé 2018). The racial anxieties and angst tied to European aspiration reveal how European whiteness is underpinned by antiblackness and anti-Romani racism. We need to interrogate the messiness and unevenness of race and racial logics, to pose complex questions and engage in scholarly dialogue about racialization while also attending to the everyday and ongoing lived realities of racialization and race-making that shape white supremacy, antiblackness, and anti-Romani racism. Now is the time to return to questions posed by Black feminist scholars such as Patricia Hill Collins (2000) and bell hooks (2014): As researchers, what questions do we ask? How do we interpret our findings? And what do we do with the knowledge that we obtain?

This book represents an effort to engage race in novel ways. Global processes of racialization are significant for understanding social relationships, the production and criminalization of difference, power, inequality, and space. In scholarly analyses of such concepts as whiteness, blackness, and otherness, we must contend with the complexities and multilayered understandings. I have argued that processes of racialization and race-making are sustained by racial logics, and each of the book's chapters has illuminated how those logics operate and produce race. The first chapter's analysis of the communist afterlife underscores the importance of understanding the rhythms, patterns, and textures of the contemporary, emphasizing the necessity of historically and locally contextualizing the study of race. This local contextualization, further analyzed in the book's second chapter, prompted me to consider what it means to publicly discuss race, and how to address such questions as racism versus ignorance. This question has long remained with me, and I return to it later in this conclusion. Chapter 3's focus on peripheral whiteness reveals how the global racial orders shape paradoxical local landscapes where Albanians are racialized both inside and outside of whiteness, an inquiry that opens the question of how race travels and shapes social worlds. Chapter 4 answers that question through its interrogation of six names. Discussions of whiteness and blackness must be expanded beyond racist hatred or conflict (Painter 2015), and chapters 3 and 4 are instrumental for complicating and stretching our approaches to whiteness and blackness. Extending the analysis of race to considerations of racism, chapter 5 analyzes three sites of racism, asking how they yield insight into racialization and race-making. This chapter ultimately demonstrates the need for new ways to examine Europe's racial arrangements and how people negotiate them. In this moment of intense migration and relocation in Europe, as Ruth Wilson Gilmore argues, scholars must focus on the geographies of racial capitalism (Card 2020) and whiteness that configure European inclusion and exclusion.

Just as race operates, so does racelessness. In the post–World War II landscape race is often publicly understood as only a problem of the Americas and the West, and racism is further framed only in terms of malevolence and animus stemmed by superficial notions of phenotype. All the while claims to racelessness continue to obscure and disguise whiteness and white supremacy, further entrenching everyday forms of socioracial inequality and violence. Fields such as Eastern European and Eurasian studies, and European studies broadly, must challenge how we study and approach race. This must include analyses that destabilize racelessness, interrogate the conceptualizations of race in Europe, and consider relational analyses of racialization (instead of privileging comparative analyses) that shape incorporation and exclusion. There is a need to ask about the actions, doing, and mechanisms by which people are racializing and being racialized, by which race is imagined, is made, and operates. Racial ideas have shifted from the early modern ideas of the eighteenth and nineteenth centuries, but the concept remains durable, and scholars need a new hermeneutics of the idea of race (Turda and Quine 2018) and its continual manifestations. We need to develop more historicized and contextualized frameworks that can disrupt and destabilize ongoing racial hierarchies and systems of meaning (Hall 2017) that shape social life.

From Racelessness to Naturalizing Race

I have encountered numerous discourses in my research and teaching experience that treat race and racism as natural, which has prompted me to critically examine the imaginaries and foundational logics that perpetuate the idea of race and racial hierarchies as inherent, biological, and immutable. Examples of approaching race and racism as natural include moments where students, colleagues, or friends have told me that societies instinctively divide themselves by race and color,[1] and that due to an innate human propensity for making enemies, for creating an us-versus-them, it must only be natural that race and racism exist. Though some people may offer this as a seemingly simple and straightforward explanation about how to contend with societal group dynamics, such an understanding of race is frequently used to impede collective response to white supremacy and racial inequality, to absolve any guilt about racism and racial disparities, and ultimately to iterate why there is nothing that can be done to address racism. If race and racism are natural, then there is little that humans can do to change so-called natural groupings, disparities, or marginalization.

I have argued that Albania provides an ideal case for studying race, for probing the history and historiography of race, and for understanding the malleability of race and ongoing local and global racialization processes. An additional reason that Albania is a case study that yields insight into the study of race stems from the ways that the larger Balkan region is positioned as raceless yet simultaneously framed by the West, broadly defined, as a region of naturalized conflict and ancient ethnic hatred. This so-called natural, at times even referred to as tribal, ethnic division is frequently accentuated as innate, perpetual, and always enduring. At the same time these conflicts seemingly exist in a vacuum, detached from global formations and social processes, as counter to Europe, and as *only* about ethnicity and not race. Like imaginations of race, Balkan ethnic hatred is framed as natural, marked by fixed socialities, fixed identities, and fixed hierarchies. It is my hope that this work can push back against these ideas of fixity—that this book can serve as an opening to think through the complexities of racialization and its intersections and overlaps with ethnicity, nation, class, and religion. Racialization is operative but not singular; even in those areas deemed raceless, critical analyses can disrupt and debunk ideas of natural hatred and hierarchical social ordering.

The racialization of the Balkans has been constitutive to the formation of European whiteness. Albania and the Balkan region occupy a marginal space on the edges of whiteness, and European whiteness has been constructed against this periphery. But these race-making processes and the production of peripheral whiteness have not been uniform, and one of the goals of this book has been to examine the processes by which race is made—how race happens. Scholars must move beyond race disavowal because assertions of racelessness facilitate racialization's momentum (Heng 2018) across various spatial and geopolitical contexts but without the ability to name or address it.

Racism or Ignorance?

Because I see this book as an intellectual contribution to conversations beyond the academy and into the public sphere, I want to return to my appearance on the show *Wake Up Tirana*, discussed in chapter 2. You may recall that the segment was titled "Racism or Ignorance?"—a title that initially caught me off-guard but has now become a question with which I am well acquainted. In some ways I do think this framing of racism versus ignorance represents an emic response to my research inquiries, as my interlocutors may invoke it as a means of emphasizing Albania's unique history when it comes to the subject of race. I teach a graduate course on global race and racism, and one of my students recently referred to the class as a history course. As an anthropologist I immediately responded with confusion and told her that I was not a historian, to which she replied that she had learned so much history in the course that, to her, it indeed felt like a history course. History is key for understanding race, and while the *Wake Up Tirana* segment's discussion of ignorance at times felt like an attempt to minimize or justify my racial encounters in fieldwork, I think it could also be seen as a plea to understand Albania's particular history. This is an ethnographic book, but this research has required a significant amount of historical and archival study, revealing the necessity of historically contextualizing the study of race. In the case of Albania, this history of the Ottoman Empire, the communist revolution, the history of Roma and Balkan Egyptians, the history of blackface, and the more recent history of the communist afterlife—all of these must be locally situated and contextualized. Eastern Europe and Eurasia is not a raceless region, but history is key to tracing the region's racial complexities and ambiguities (Baker et al. 2024).

I also reflect on this question of racism versus ignorance because it is a question to which I find myself continually responding. As I have said throughout this book, whether in fieldwork in Albania or in conversations in the United States, discussions of race regularly collapse into debates about whether someone or something is *really* racist or not. I have argued that Albania and the Balkan region are positioned as raceless, and therefore, to the extent that a Black scholar like me might encounter anything tangentially related to race, such actions or behaviors may immediately be named as ignorant or unintentional, or blamed on a history of isolation, improper decorum, or curiosity at best. And in the landscape after World War II, the US civil rights movement, and South African apartheid, race and racism are intimately tied to morality, and ultimately the angst produced by the insinuation of potential immorality. No one wants to be accused of racial discrimination, racial thinking, racial bias, racial tinging, or racism because no one wants to be seen as a bad person.

The discussion of sincerity, informed in part by John Jackson's conceptualization (2005), remains important for the unpacking the notion of racism versus ignorance. You may remember my friend Pavli from the section titled "The Hunger Games," which included the story of language barriers and how Pavli and I could not communicate when we first met. Still now, more than fifteen years later, and with my ability to now speak and comprehend Albanian, I regularly reflect on this story with Pavli and his family as we fondly remember that summer we met. We have since shared coffees, lunches, dinners, celebrations, and weeklong stays where Pavli's parents hosted me in their home in the village. I once described my friendship with Pavli to my friend Niku in Tirana and he said, "Eh, see, you are researching race in Albania, and look at that—that story proves to you that we are not racist."

Niku's takeaway illustrates what I believe is another widely held sentiment about race: an attachment to the belief that sincere connection between people is indicative of racelessness, and further, that sincerity shared between differently racialized people is the antidote to racism and ongoing racial logics that structure societal fabrics of inequality, marginalization, and exclusion. That when it comes to race, if people *knew* better, then they might *do* better. If people *really* or *genuinely* knew one another, then there would be no need to contend with race. Or if people committed themselves to color-blindness, then they would eliminate race and change social relationships. As the book has demonstrated, this framing of race is superficial and hollow but remains stubbornly persistent. And as I have reiterated multiple times throughout this book, such beliefs are not unique to Albania and are representative of broader global discussions of race and racialization. There is a need for new paradigms that move beyond race and morality, paradigms that include those regions thought to be raceless.

Can Race Be Unmade?

The subject of race-making has been a key focus of this book, and this focus prompts the question as to whether race can be unmade, undone, or dismantled. In the era where declarations of color blindness and proliferation of post-racial desires abound, it can be tempting to think that race is not meaningful and that somehow racialization will just undo itself. But to the extent that the unmaking of race is even possible, we must collectively reckon with race and the racial logics that continue to organize societies. I think, for example, about chapter 3 and findings shared from the European Values Survey about how people felt about neighbors of another race. What are such measures really telling us about our societies? They may offer revelations about attitudes, interpersonal feelings, and sentiment, but how do we address the underpinnings of how race is imagined? How do we study and name the histories that shape these racial logics, to ultimately move toward a recognition that race is both past and present? These measures may be able to show how people's values change over time, but there is a need for sharper tools and multipronged approaches to disrupt the racialization processes that systemically and systematically shape societal fabrics worldwide.

Racial reckonings are not easy, but race denial, race avoidance, and race refusal only fertilize the soil whereby white supremacy, antiblackness, and anti-Romaniness are reproduced in newly aligned forms. Current debates about race and efforts to prevent the teaching of it have only underscored the need for greater attention to the subject, particularly in a global context. Analyses of the Balkan region provide a way to probe whiteness and blackness in ways that remain underexplored. This book has shown that studying race in Europe's periphery can yield greater insight into ongoing and overlapping social hierarchies, intersections of race, class, nation, migration, interconnected geographies, globalization, and racialization. Doing so underlines that race is deeply embedded, and the nature of its undoing may require more than is at times estimated.

Yet the idea of undoing and unmaking remains key. Global studies of race and racialization draw our attention to how race organizes social life, providing the opportunity to think about the doings and makings of race as well as the *un*doings and *un*makings of race; the imagination and the *re*imagination. This first begins with reckoning. Continued refusal and rejection will not erase the impacts of actively present racial logics as shaped by a centuries-long legacy of hierarchical ranking of humanness; it will only impede our ability to recognize and remedy them.

Notes

INTRODUCTION

1. Similar to a minivan, *furgons* are a commonly used form of transportation to cities. Whereas buses tend to have a formalized system including monitored operations, set prices, and timetables, furgons are a more informal mode of transportation often run by the owner of the vehicle, who sets his own prices. Travelers can often catch furgons at set locations throughout the city or can hail them from the side of the road. Furgons are particularly popular with people traveling to smaller villages outside of cities.

2. I do not suggest that Albania's communist history is inescapable or always deterministic. In fact, some of my interlocutors would reveal this notion, as they passionately long to rid Albania of Hoxha and Ottoman residues (explained more in chapter 3). The idea of entanglement is one that allows me to consider the behaviors, sentiments, and stories that foreground social life as shaped by a sociopolitical and economic system that changed the world. Its legacies and memories shape the ways in which people continue to map that which has yet to happen (Amy 2010). This calls attention to the forms of longing, nostalgia, and angst that are particularly salient in the current moment. Svetlana Boym (2001) writes about a nostalgia that rebels, one that yearns for a different time, and Kathleen Stewart (1988) writes about a nostalgia that erupts. Influenced by such understandings, I use ethnography to trace how *mall* ("longing" or "yearning") and *merak* ("worry" or "angst") unfold in everyday life through actions, protests, feelings, articulations, and responses. These forms of yearning and angst call attention to disillusionment, disenchantment, memory, and also rememory, as Toni Morrison (1987) termed the processes of remembering and recalling even those things once forgotten or buried. Ultimately, I ask, what does it mean to long for a past when unable to imagine a future?

3. Historical context is key for any study of race and racialization (see Baker 2018; Goldberg 2006 and 2009; Rexhepi 2023). This book focuses on the communist afterlife, but Albania could be framed in terms of an Ottoman afterlife.

4. Previous census counts in Albania did document national and linguistic populations, but these did not include information for race and ethnicity, as the nation was the primary organizer of social relations, and further, Roma were formally considered a linguistic minority in Albania until ca. 2005 but were not formally recognized as a national minority until 2017.

5. See the note on language in the front matter. I further discuss names, race, and Roma in chapter 4.

6. Blumenbach, like Linnaeus, never used the term "race" in his writing, but by the third edition of his text, he began to rank humans along lines of skin color and skull measurement, believing the white variety, what he eventually termed "Caucasian," to be superior. I frequently tell my students that if they get nothing at all from my courses on race, they should not use the term "Caucasian" as a formal designation for white people, as it only reiterates a false scientific and biological notion of race. This is my same hope for you as a reader of this book.

7. *Byrek* is a pastry dish made of flaky dough and filled with cheese, meat, spinach, or other vegetables such as leeks. As in other Balkan countries, *byrek* is very popular

throughout Albania, available as cheap street food but also often served in more formal capacities at family meals.

8. I have chosen to use the Albanian spelling of Kosova throughout except in quotations.

9. For many years I have been told that *zezak/zezake* is an Albanian word that means "Black person." Many of the conversations have stemmed from moments wherein I was called the word, perhaps on the street or in a restaurant, and those around me would grow concerned that I might be offended. It was one of the first words I learned in Albanian because I was described this way by numerous people, often hearing someone exclaim it as soon as they saw me. Deriving from the Albanian word for the color black (*e zezë*), *zezake*, I have been told, "*simply* means 'black.'" Yet Pavi Qesku, one of Albania's leading translators, notes that the word could mean "black," "negro," or "darkie." I include this note not to definitively define the term but to provide background and destabilize its assumed simplicity in meaning. I discuss the naming of blackness further in chapter 4.

10. Often considered a type of moonshine, raki is a common alcoholic drink in the Balkans, made with distilled fruits such as grapes or plums.

11. This book examines the racialized experiences of Roma and Balkan Egyptians in Albania. This book is not a cultural history of the Roma, nor would I consider it a source for comprehensive knowledge about Romani culture, language, or history in Albania. For more on these subjects see Kurtiade 1995; Sula-Raxhimi 2021; Silverman 2012; Hancock 2002; Kolsti 1991; Trubeta 2005; Dalipaj 2012; De Soto, Beddies, and Gedeshi 2005.

12. I use the European term "football" throughout the book to denote soccer.

13. This is how the expression is pronounced in spoken Albanian. Standard written Albanian would be "Sa do të rrojmë, do të mësojmë."

1. THE COMMUNIST AFTERLIFE

1. This speech was found in the Marxists Internet Archive. The original source is *Selected Works*, vol. 1 (Tirana: Nëntori, 1974), 399–40; first published in the *Bulletin of the National Liberation War*, no. 52, November 30, 1944; transcription/translation by Ismail Badiou, at https://www.marxists.org/reference/archive/hoxha/works/1944/11/28.htm.

2. Chapter 4 includes an extended discussion about Romani and Egyptian housing, including during the communist period.

3. According to Musaraj (2011, 2021), in both pyramid and Ponzi schemes, investors are promised high yields and returns, but whereas pyramid scheme investors make their money by helping recruit new investors, participants in Ponzi schemes are lured by the promise of high returns on lucrative assets or reassurances of state bailout. Musaraj argues that the prominent investment companies in Albania represented the latter.

4. Rendered phonetically in English, this would be pronounced along the lines of "ch-fah doh tuh bey-meh" or "ch-doh bey-meh." I am grateful to Ajkuna Tafa for her assistance with this transliteration.

5. "How far behind we are, how far!" An expression I hear commonly, reflecting a sentiment of being delayed or lagging behind, referring to time, progress, and/or development.

6. The word *gjynah* can be translated in multiple ways, including "sin," "transgression," "pity," or even "crime." In this case, when Mimoza uses the term, she is calling attention to the awful nature of the transgressions and wrongdoing.

7. A *shanti* is a makeshift nonsupported dwelling, akin to a tent outdoors. The Albanian word for it would be *barakë*, meaning "barrack."

8. Chapter 2 provides a longer discussion of what it means to be *mërzitur*.

9. This understanding is similar to the idea of nesting orientalisms in the former Yugoslavia as examined by Milica-Bakic Hayden (1995).

3. PERIPHERAL WHITENESS

1. I introduce chapters 3, 4, and 5 with a framing exposition that speaks to the multiplicity of meaning of whiteness, blackness, and racism. My writing style here illustrates aspects of the ethnographic research and writing process whereby I trace and map the elements and fragments of race-making.

2. Here I return to both Wekker (2011) and Frankenberg (1993) regarding whiteness as often unmarked, unnamed, and invisibilized. In this case, whiteness is associated with the need to feel European and be recognized as such.

3. Because processes of nation-building and identity formation involve various complexities, scholarly examinations must nuance analyses of nationalism. As such, this example of contrasting viewpoints does not necessarily illustrate a clear dichotomy between those Albanian nationalist leaders in New England and those based in Albania.

4. Over the years, Othello's racial identity has been one of the play's key analytical themes. As Patrick C. Hogan (1998) has noted, Othello is a character that has experienced racism and is the victim of racial despair. Such ideas have been debated by numerous scholars, but according to Golemi (2020), it was this interpretation of Othello's character that prompted Noli to translate the play into Albanian.

5. Deriving from the Ottoman term Toskalik, Tosk is a term that refers to one of Albania's two major dialectal and cultural subgroups. The other major group, Gheg Albanians, reside in Northern Albania, north of the Shkumbin River, and they primarily speak the Gheg dialect of Albanian. It is important to note that many of the party's leaders were Tosk and that Hoxha himself was from the southern city of Gjirokastër. See Blumi (1997) for more on the distinctions between Gheg and Tosk and how these manifested during state socialism.

6. My research assistants reported that while administering the survey they were repeatedly asked about the question, with multiple respondents voicing that they experienced anxiety (*ankth*) when trying to decide how to answer.

7. May 5th is a day honoring martyrs of World War II, particularly the assassination of Qemal Stafa by the Italian fascists.

8. Commonly thought to be a slur as it is an intentional mispronunciation of the term *Shqiptar*, which means "Albanian" in the Albanian language.

9. King and Mai (2008) document similar sentiments, noting the ways that Albanian migrants in Italy believe that the Italian media creates a "stereotypical construction of the Albanian migrant as the embodiment of all the features characterizing *uncivilization*" (188).

10. These sentiments mirror anthropologist Sarah Green's (2005) discussion of an expression she often encountered: "This is the Balkans—what do you expect?" Though Greece's positionality within the Balkans may be ambiguous and uncertain, the belief that Greeks possessed a Balkan mentality is often reiterated with greater certainty.

4. ON BLACKNESS

1. I have changed the names of some of the settlements where I conducted long-term fieldwork in an effort to protect the identities of people with whom I have worked. Excluding those leaders who are public figures, names have been changed to protect the privacy of individuals.

2. This name is also written as *arrixhi*.

3. Following World War I, Roma were segregated from Albanians in many aspects of everyday life (for example housing, cemeteries, mosques) but were allowed to live on the outskirts of town and sell their goods and crafts in the cities (Crowe 2007).

4. A 2015 study estimated that more than one-third of Roma school-aged children do not regularly attend school, compared to 97 percent of Albanian children that do (Meçe 2015).

5. Launched in 2005 and sponsored by multiple international organizations such as the World Bank, the United Nations Development Program, and the Council of Europe, the Decade of Roma Inclusion was designed to be a pan-European initiative to address racial discrimination and improve the socioeconomic status and inclusion of Romani people across the continent. Participating countries included Albania, Bulgaria, Croatia, Czechia, Hungary, Montenegro, North Macedonia, Romania, Serbia, and Slovakia.

6. Letter from Pellumb Fortuna and Romani organizations in Tirana, May 21, 2010.

7. At that time 100 lekë, Albania's form of currency, was worth close to one dollar.

8. The area of Tirana known as Bllok/Blloku served as the primary residence for Hoxha and party leaders during the communist regime. It was a secluded area, and local residents needed permission to enter the premises. Today Blloku consists of numerous bars, cafés, and dance clubs, and is popular with tourists as well as Tirana's elite. Though it is vacant, Hoxha's villa remains largely intact.

9. I thank Daviola Ndoja for helping with this translation of an older form of Albanian writing.

10. Scholars like Ger Duijzings (2000) and Eben Friedman (2007) subscribe to the idea that Egyptian identity became popular in the former Yugoslavia once the authorities provided an option for Albanian-speaking Roma to gain more political clout if they were not considered Albanian. The Yugoslavian census was used to set ethnic quotas for jobs, housing, and political appointments. Some argue that due to the various interethnic conflicts and competition within the former Yugoslavia, Albanian-speaking Roma had an incentive to identify as Egyptian and thus receive more access to resources if they were not considered Albanian or Roma (Duijzings 2000; Friedman 2007).

11. After a deadly fire in 2015 the municipality constructed more stable housing for Roma and Egyptian families, but they were not allowed to be tenants in the vacant buildings. As of 2018 the apartment buildings were no longer vacant, but the buildings' residents often complain about the bothersome *gabelët* (plural form of *gabelë*).

5. A QUESTION OF RACISM IN THREE ACTS

1. For a brief background, Kosova declared independence from Serbia in 2008, but to this day, nearly half of the United Nations member states still do not recognize Kosova as a country, including Serbia. Just over 90 percent of Kosova's population is Albanian, and the majority of Kosovar Albanians are Muslim. These dynamics heavily shape Albanian-Serb relations. For more on this subject and its impact on social relations in the region, see Luci and Marković (2009); Petrovic (2008).

2. Edi Rama did eventually visit Belgrade in November 2015, though the subject of Kosova's independence remained very tense.

3. Referencing the killings of Ahmaud Arbery, Tamir Rice, and Aiyana Stanley-Jones.

4. For this book I have chosen to limit my discussion of negative fieldwork encounters, but I want to note that this encounter was benign compared to those that featured greater mental, sexual, and physical harassment. These violent encounters were thankfully rare, but nevertheless, as a woman ethnographer, I have experienced numerous difficulties because of harassment. This is the subject of forthcoming research about ethnography and ethnographic methods.

5. For more on this see Bickert and West Ohueri (2016).

6. Examples include human zoos and human freak shows in Western Europe that featured exhibits where Black bodies were presented, like the case with Sarah Baartman, who was referred to by the demeaning nickname "Hottentot Venus." For more see Holmes (2007).

7. Permissions were not granted to reprint copyrighted images, but as of June 2024 this clip and others can be found at https://www.youtube.com/watch?v=0SmhZQPWs-s&t=134s.

8. It is important to note that this sentence is willfully constructed to sound grammatically incorrect, further infantilizing Drumba's character.

9. Similar to copyright images of Drumba, the author was unable to attain permission to reprint images of Skrapi, but as of June 2024 images and clips of Skrapi can be found on YouTube, such as the following: https://www.youtube.com/watch?v=1fgKNGyxPxI.

10. Here I return to chapter 1's discussion of "ç'farë do të bëjmë?" as a way of expressing a type of dejection about Albania's contemporary sociopolitical landscape.

11. Three generations including that of Skrapi and Xhemi, their parents, and their grandparents.

12. Here I have chosen to use the actual name of this settlement as well as that of Liqeni as I am drawing attention to public displacements and relocations that occurred between the years 2011 and 2018.

CONCLUSION

1. The work of scientists in the nineteenth and early twentieth centuries on race contamination played a pivotal role in shaping societal ideas about innate and distinctly defined racial groups and racial purity. Though they are widely discredited today, the residues of such notions continue to shape contemporary ideas of race. For more, see Fredrickson (2009) and Roberts (2011).

References

Abrahams, Fred. 2015. *Modern Albania: From Dictatorship to Democracy in Europe.* New York: New York University Press.

Abu-Lughod, Lila. 1991. "Writing against Culture." In *Recapturing Anthropology: Working in the Present*, 466–77. Santa Fe: School of Advanced Research.

Alim, H. Samy. 2009. "Racing Language, Languaging Race." CLIC 2009 Symposium on Race and Ethnicity in Language, Interaction, and Culture. University of California Los Angeles.

Alim, H. Samy, Paul V. Kroskrity, and Angela Reyes. 2020. "The Field of Language and Race: A Linguistic Anthropological Approach to Race, Racism, and Racialization." In *The Oxford Handbook of Language and Race*, edited by H. Samy Alim, Angela Reyes, and Paul V. Kroskrity. Oxford: Oxford University Press.

Alim, H. Sami, John R. Rickford, and Arnetha F. Ball. 2016. "Introducing Raciolinguistics." In *Raciolinguistics: How Language Shapes Our Ideas about Race*, edited by H. Sami Alim, John R. Rickford, and Arnetha F. Ball. Oxford: Oxford University Press.

Alpion, Gëzim. 2014. "Albania v Serbia Football Drone Farce Shows Balkan Nationalism Is Still a Dangerous Powder Keg." *The Conversation*, accessed February 5, 2023. https://theconversation.com/albania-v-serbia-football-drone-farce-shows-balkan-nationalism-is-still-a-dangerous-powder-keg-33101.

Amy, Lori E. 2010. "Re-Membering in Transition: The Trans-national Stakes of Violence and Denial in Post-Communist Albania." *History of Communism in Europe* 1:207–24.

Anzaldúa, Gloria. 1987. *Borderlands/La Frontera: The New Mestiza*. San Francisco: Aunt Lute.

Attewell, Nadine. 2014. *Better Britons: Reproduction, National Identity, and the Afterlife of Empire*. Toronto: University of Toronto Press.

Baker, Catherine. 2018. *Race and the Yugoslav Region: Postsocialist, Post-Conflict, Postcolonial?* Manchester: Manchester University Press.

Baker, Catherine, Bogdan Iacob, Aniko Imre, and James Mark, eds. 2024. *Off White: Central and Eastern Europe and the Global History of Race*. Manchester: Manchester University Press.

Bakic-Hayden, Milica. 1995. "Nesting Orientalisms: The Case of Former Yugoslavia." *Slavic Review* 54(4): 917–31.

Baldwin, James. 1963. "James Baldwin Confronts the Realities of Race in America." *PBS*, April 1. https://www.pbs.org/video/james-baldwin-confronts-realities-race-america-tmpwbs/.

Baldwin, Kate A. 2002. *Beyond the Color Line and the Iron Curtain: Reading Encounters between Black and Red, 1922–1963*. Durham, NC: Duke University Press.

Basch, Linda G., Nina Glick Schiller, and Cristina Szanton Blanc. 1994. *Nations Unbound: Transnational Projects, Postcolonial Predicaments, and Deterritorialized Nation-States*. London: Routledge.

BBC Sport. 2014. "Albania Players 'Bruised and Bloodied' by Serbia Violence." October 16. https://www.bbc.com/sport/football/29642545.

Bego, Fabio. 2023. "Race and Exclusion in State Socialism: African Students in Communist Albania." *Balkan Insight*, accessed March 31, 2024. https://balkaninsight.com/2023/03/22/race-and-exclusion-in-state-socialism-african-students-in-communist-albania/.

Behar, Ruth, and Deborah A. Gordon. 1995. *Women Writing Culture*. Berkeley: University of California Press.

Bejko, Julian. 2021. "The Age of Understanding the Past." In *Remitting, Restoring and Building Contemporary Albania*, edited by Nataša Gregorič Bon and Smoki Musaraj. Cham, Switzerland: Springer.

Bengtsson, Ingemar, and Karol Życzkowski. 2017. *Geometry of Quantum States: An Introduction to Quantum Entanglement*. 2nd ed. Cambridge: Cambridge University Press.

Berdahl, Daphne. 1999. *Where the World Ended: Re-unification and Identity in the German Borderland*. Berkeley: University of California Press.

Berlant, Lauren Gail. 2011. *Cruel Optimism*. Durham, NC: Duke University Press.

Bezemer, D. J. 2001. "Post-socialist Financial Fragility: The Case of Albania." *Cambridge Journal of Economics* 25(1): 1–23. https://doi.org/10.1093/cje/25.1.1.

Bickert, Matthias, and Chelsi West Ohueri. 2016. "Football on the Fringes of Europe: Black African Players and Their Livelihoods in Albania." In *Diversity of Migration in Southeast Europe*, edited by Mirjam Zbinden, Janine Dahinden, and Adnan Efendic. Berne: Peter Lang.

Bjelić, Dušan I. 2018. "Toward a Genealogy of the Balkan Discourses on Race." *Interventions* 20(6): 906–29. https://doi.org/10.1080/1369801X.2018.1492955.

Bjelić, Dušan I. 2021. "Abolition of a National Paradigm: The Case against Benedict Anderson and Maria Todorova's Raceless Imaginaries." *Interventions* 24(2): 1–24. https://doi.org/10.1080/1369801X.2020.1863842.

Blumenbach, Johann. 1795. *De generis humani varietate nativa*. Göttingen: Vandenhoek & Ruprecht.

Blumi, Isa. 1997. "The Politics of Culture and Power: The Roots of Hoxha's Postwar State." *East European Quarterly* 31(3): 379–98.

Blumi, Isa. 1998. "The Commodification of Otherness and the Ethnic Unit in the Balkans: How to Think about Albanians." *East European Politics and Society* 12(3): 527–69.

Blunt, Wilfrid, and William T. Stearn. 1971. *The Compleat Naturalist: A Life of Linnaeus*. London: Collins.

Boatcă, Manuela. 2006. "No Race to the Swift: Negotiating Racial Identity in Past and Present Eastern Europe." *Human Architecture: Journal of the Sociology of Self-Knowledge* 1 (Fall 2006): 91–104.

Boatcă, Manuela. 2010. "Multiple Europes and the Politics of Difference Within." In *The Study of Europe*, edited by Hauke Brunkhorst and Gerd Grözinger. Baden-Baden: Nomos Verlagsgesellschaft.

Bon, Natasha Gregoric. 2008. "Storytelling as a Spatial Practice in Dhërmi/Drimades of Southern Albania." *Anthropological Notebooks* 14(2): 7–30.

Bonilla-Silva, Eduardo. 2018. *Racism without Racists: Color-Blind Racism and the Persistence of Racial Inequality in America*. 5th ed. Lanham, MD: Rowman & Littlefield.

Bonnet, Charles. 2019. *The Black Kingdom of the Nile*. Foreword by Henry Louis Gates Jr. Cambridge, MA: Harvard University Press.

Böröcz, József. 2021. "'Eurowhite' Conceit, 'Dirty White' Resentment: 'Race' in Europe." *Sociological Forum* 36(4): 1116–34. https://doi.org/10.1111/socf.12752.
Boym, Svetlana. 2001. *The Future of Nostalgia*. New York: Basic Books.
Briggs, Charles L. 2005. "Communicability, Racial Discourse, and Disease." *Annual Review of Anthropology* 34(1): 269–91. https://doi.org/10.1146/annurev.anthro.34.081804.120618.
Bucur, Maria. 2010. *Eugenics in Eastern Europe, 1870s–1945*. Oxford: Oxford University Press.
Bunzl, Matti. 2005. "Between Anti-Semitism and Islamophobia: Some Thoughts on the New Europe." *American Ethnologist* 32(4): 499–508. https://doi.org/10.1525/ae.2005.32.4.499.
Burawoy, Michael, and Katherine Verdery. 1999. *Uncertain Transition: Ethnographies of Change in the Postsocialist World*. Lanham, MD: Rowman & Littlefield.
Card, Kenton, dir. 2020. *Geographies of Racial Capitalism with Ruth Wilson Gilmore*. https://antipodeonline.org/geographies-of-racial-capitalism/.
Carew, Joy Gleason. 2015. "Black in the USSR: African Diasporan Pilgrims, Expatriates and Students in Russia, from the 1920s to the First Decade of the Twenty-First Century." *African and Black Diaspora* 8(2): 202–15. https://doi.org/10.1080/17528631.2015.1027324.
Casciani, Dominic. 2022. "Don't Blame Us for UK Border Problems, Says Albanian PM." BBC News. Accessed January 2023. https://www.bbc.com/news/uk-politics-63489276.
Cela, Xhenson. 2021. "Blackface, Stereotypes, and Prejudice: Albania's Racist Comedy Shows." European Roma Rights Centre, August 13. http://www.errc.org/news/blackface-stereotypes-and-prejudice-albanias-racist-comedy-shows.
Chang, Felix B., and Sunnie Rucker-Chang. 2020. *Roma Rights and Civil Rights: A Transatlantic Comparison*. Cambridge: Cambridge University Press.
Cherid, Maha Ikram. 2021. "'Ain't Got Enough Money to Pay Me Respect': Blackfishing, Cultural Appropriation, and the Commodification of Blackness." *Cultural Studies, Critical Methodologies* 21(5): 359–64. https://doi.org/10.1177/15327086211029357.
Clinton, Bill. 1999. "Address to the Nation on Airstrikes against Serbian Targets in the Federal Republic of Yugoslavia (Serbia and Montenegro)." Office of the Press Secretary. Washington, DC, January 5. https://www.clintonlibrary.gov/sites/default/files/documents/kosovo-press-1999.pdf.
Collins, Patricia Hill. 2000. *Black Feminist Thought: Knowledge, Consciousness, and the Politics of Empowerment*. 2nd ed. New York: Routledge.
Cornell, Stephen, and Douglas Hartmann. 2007. *Ethnicity and Race: Making Identities in a Changing World*. 2nd ed. Thousand Oaks, CA: Pine Forge Press.
Costache, Ioanida. 2018. "Reclaiming Romani-ness." *Critical Romani Studies* 1(1): 30–43. https://doi.org/10.29098/crs.v1i1.11.
Costache, Ioanida. 2023. "Roma as 'Ontological Other': Decoloniality, Whiteness, and Race-making in the European Space." Association for Slavic, East European, and Eurasian Studies annual convention, Philadelphia, December 3, 2023.
Council of Europe. 2017. "Roma Recognised as a National Minority in Albania." Council of Europe: Newsroom, November 17. Accessed September 28, 2022. https://www.coe.int/en/web/tirana/news/-/asset_publisher/SENehJ2ESZrW/content/roma-recognized-as-a-national-minority-in-alban-1.
Craven, Christa, and Dána-Ain Davis, eds. 2013. *Feminist Activist Ethnography: Counterpoints to Neoliberalism in North America*. Lanham, MD: Lexington.

Crowe, David. 2007. *A History of the Gypsies of Eastern Europe and Russia*. 2nd ed. New York: Palgrave Macmillan.
Dalakoglou, Dimitris. 2017. *The Road: An Ethnography of (Im)mobility, Space, and Cross-Border Infrastructures in the Balkans*. Manchester: Manchester University Press.
Dalipaj, Gerda. 2012. "Roma Communities in Elbasan." In *Albania: Family, Society and Culture in the 20th Century*, edited by Andreas Hemming, Gentiana Kera, and Enriketa Pandelejmoni. Zurich: LIT.
Dedijer, Vladimir. 1945. *Beleškee iz Amerike*. Beograd: Kultura.
De Soto, Hermine, Sabine Beddies, and Ilir Gedeshi. 2005. *Roma and Egyptians in Albania: From Social Exclusion to Social Inclusion*. Washington, DC: World Bank.
Drakulić, Slavenka. 1999. "We Are All Albanians." *The Nation*, May 20. https://www.thenation.com/article/archive/we-are-all-albanians/.
Duijzings, Gerlachlus. 2000. "The Making of Egyptians in Kosovo and Macedonia." In *Religion and the Politics of Identity in Kosovo*, edited by Cora Govers and Hans Vermeulen. New York, NY: Columbia University Press.
Durham, M. E. 1909. *High Albania*. London: E. Arnold.
Ebron, Paulla. 2001. "Contingent Stories of Anthropology, Race, and Feminism." In *Black Feminist Anthropology*, edited by Irma McClaurin. New Brunswick, NJ: Rutgers University Press.
Elia, Peter. 2023. "The Peak of the Balkans Trail: Europe's Last True Wilderness." BBC, January 4. https://www.bbc.com/travel/article/20230103-the-peak-of-the-balkans-trail-europes-last-true-wilderness.
El-Tayeb, Fatima. 2011. *European Others: Queering Ethnicity in Postnational Europe*. Minneapolis: University of Minnesota Press.
Erebara, Gjergj. 2020. "Organizatat dënojnë dhunën e policisë bashkiake ndaj ricikluesit [Organizations Condemn Municipal Police Violence Against Recycler]." *Reporter.al*, May 26. https://www.reporter.al/2020/05/26/organizatat-denojne-dhunen-e-policise-bashkiake-ndaj-ricikluesit/.
ERRC (European Roma Rights Centre). 1997. *No Record of the Case: Roma in Albania*. Budapest: European Roma Rights Centre.
Essed, Philomena. 1991. *Understanding Everyday Racism: An Interdisciplinary Theory*. Newbury Park, CA: Sage.
Essed, Philomena, and Sandra Trienekens. 2008. "'Who Wants to Feel White?' Race, Dutch Culture and Contested Identities." *Ethnic and Racial Studies* 31(1): 52–72. https://doi.org/10.1080/01419870701538885.
Fassin, Didier. 2011. "Racialization: How to Do Races with Bodies." In *A Companion to the Anthropology of the Body and Embodiment*, edited by Frances E. Mascia-Lees. Oxford: Wiley-Blackwell.
Federal Writers' Project. 1939. *The Albanian Struggle in the Old World and New*. Boston: The Writer, Inc.
Fevziu, Blendi. 2016. *Enver Hoxha: The Iron Fist of Albania*. Edited by Robert Elsie; translated by Majlinda Nishku. London: I. B. Tauris.
FIFA (International Federation of Association Football). 2016. "Clarification on FIFA Task Force against Racism and Discrimination." Inside FIFA, September 29. https://www.fifa.com/about-fifa/organisation/news/clarification-on-fifa-task-force-against-racism-and-discrimination-2837757.
Fisher, Max. 2013. "A Fascinating Map of the World's Most and Least Racially Tolerant Countries." *Washington Post*, May 15. https://www.washingtonpost.com/news/worldviews/wp/2013/05/15/a-fascinating-map-of-the-worlds-most-and-least-racially-tolerant-countries/.

Fishta, Iljazz, and Michael Schmidt-Neke. 1997. "Nationalism and National Myth: Skanderbeg and the Twentieth-Century Albanian Regimes." *European Legacy* 2(1): 1–7. https://doi.org/10.1080/10848779708579680.
Fleming, Crystal Marie. 2017. *Resurrecting Slavery: Racial Legacies and White Supremacy in France*. Philadelphia: Temple University Press.
Fonseca, Isabel. 1995. *Bury Me Standing: The Gypsies and Their Journey*. 1st ed. New York: Knopf.
Frankenberg, Ruth. 1993. *White Women, Race Matters: The Social Construction of Whiteness*. Minneapolis: University of Minnesota Press.
Fredrickson, George M. 2009. *Racism: A Short History*. Princeton, NJ: Princeton University Press.
Frey, William. 2020. "Even as Metropolitan Areas Diversify, White Americans Still Live in Mostly White Neighborhoods." Brookings Institution, March 23. https://www.brookings.edu/research/even-as-metropolitan-areas-diversify-white-americans-still-live-in-mostly-white-neighborhoods/.
Friedman, Eben. 2007. "The Politics of the Census: Of Gypsies, Roms, and Egyptians." *Anthropology of East Europe Review* 25(2): 67–77.
Galaty, Michael. 2018. *Memory and Nation Building: From Ancient Times to the Islamic State*. Lanham, MD: Rowman & Littlefield.
Garner, Steve. 2007. "The European Union and the Racialization of Immigration, 1985–2006." *Race/Ethnicity: Multidisciplinary Global Contexts* 1(1): 61–87.
Gates, Henry Louis, and Andrew S. Curran, eds. 2022. *Who's Black and Why? A Hidden Chapter from the Eighteenth-Century Invention of Race*. Cambridge, MA: Belknap Press of Harvard University Press.
Ghodsee, Kristen Rogheh. 2010. *Muslim Lives in Eastern Europe: Gender, Ethnicity, and the Transformation of Islam in Postsocialist Bulgaria*. Princeton, NJ: Princeton University Press.
Gibson, Owen. 2014. "Serbia v Albania Violence: UEFA Opens Inquiry into 'Inexcusable' Clashes." *The Guardian*, October 15. https://www.theguardian.com/football/2014/oct/15/serbia-albania-violence-uefa-inquiry-drone.
Gjermeni, Eglantina, and Lori E. Amy. 2016. "The Dissidence of Daily Life." In *Dissident Friendships: Feminism, Imperialism, and Transnational Solidarity*, edited by Elora Halim Chowdhury and Liz Philipose, 180–94. Champaign: University of Illinois Press.
Gobineau, Arthur. 1915. *Essay on the Inequality of Human Races (1853)*. London: William Heinemann.
Goldberg, David Theo. 2002. *The Racial State*. Malden, MA: Blackwell.
Goldberg, David Theo. 2006. "Racial Europeanization." *Ethnic and Racial Studies* 29(2): 331–64.
Goldberg, David Theo. 2009a. "Racial Comparisons, Relational Racisms: Some Thoughts on Method." *Ethnic and Racial Studies* 32(7): 1271–82.
Goldberg, David Theo. 2009b. *The Threat of Race: Reflections on Racial Neoliberalism*. Malden, MA: Wiley-Blackwell.
Golemi, Marinela. 2020. "Othello in the Balkans: Performing Race Rhetoric on the Albanian Stage." *Multicultural Shakespeare: Translation, Appropriation and Performance* 22(37): 125–38.
Green, Sarah. 2005. *Notes from the Balkans: Locating Marginality and Ambiguity on the Greek-Albanian Border*. Princeton, NJ: Princeton University Press.
Hall, Stuart. 2017. *The Fateful Triangle: Race, Ethnicity, Nation*. Cambridge, MA: Harvard University Press.
Hall, Stuart. 2021. *Selected Writings on Race and Difference*. Edited by Paul Gilroy and Ruth Wilson Gilmore. Durham, NC: Duke University Press.

Hancock, Ian. 1987. *The Pariah Syndrome: An Account of Gypsy Slavery and Persecution*. Ann Arbor, MI: Karoma.

Hancock, Ian. 2002. *We Are the Romani People = Ame sam e Rromane d*zene*. Paris: Centre de recherches tsiganes; Hatfield, UK: University of Hertfordshire Press.

Hancock, Ian. 2010. *Danger! Educated Gypsy: Select Essays*. Hatfield, UK: University of Hertfordshire Press.

Hann, C. M. 2002. *Postsocialism: Ideals, Ideologies and Practices in Eurasia*. London: Routledge.

Haraway, Donna. 1988. "Situated Knowledges: The Science Question in Feminism and the Privilege of Partial Perspective." *Feminist Studies* 14(3): 575–99.

Hartigan, John. 1999. *Racial Situations: Class Predicaments of Whiteness in Detroit*. Princeton, NJ: Princeton University Press.

Hartman, Saidiya. 2007. *Lose Your Mother: A Journey along the Atlantic Slave Route*. New York: Farrar, Straus & Giroux.

Hazili, Qemal, and Nexhip Myftar. 1930. Letter to the Premier of the Albanian Government. Kryeminister. Albanian National Archive, Tirana, Albania.

Heng, Geraldine. 2018. *The Invention of Race in the European Middle Ages*. Cambridge: Cambridge University Press.

Hogan, Patrick C. 1998. "'Othello,' Racism, and Despair." *CLA Journal* 41(4): 431–51.

Holmes, R. 2007. *The Hottentot Venus: The Life and Death of Saartjie Baartman*. London: Bloomsbury.

hooks, bell. 2014. *Talking back: thinking feminist, thinking black*. 2nd ed. New York: Routledge.

hooks, bell. 2015. "Eating the Other: Desire and resistance." In *Black looks: race and representation*. New York: Routledge.

Howard, Philip S.S. 2018. "A laugh for the national project: Contemporary Canadian blackface humour and its constitution through Canadian anti-blackness." *Ethnicities* 18 (6): 843-868.

Humphrey, Caroline. 2002. *The Unmaking of Soviet Life: Everyday Economies after Socialism*. Ithaca, NY: Cornell University Press.

Hurston, Zora Neale. 1935. *Mules and Men*. Illustrated by Miguel Covarrubias. Philadelphia: J. B. Lippincott.

Hysa, Armanda. 2010. Ethnography in Communist Albania: Nationalist Discourse and Relations with History. *In Historični seminar 8*, edited by Katarina Keber and Luka Vidmar. Ljubljana, Slovenia: Založba ZRC.

Jackson, John L. 2005. *Real Black: Adventures in Racial Sincerity*. Chicago: University of Chicago Press.

Jarvis, Christopher. 2000. "The Rise and Fall of Albania's Pyramid Schemes." *Finance and Development* 37(1). https://www.imf.org/external/pubs/ft/fandd/2000/03/jarvis.htm.

Jezernik, Božidar. 2004. *Wild Europe:The Balkans in the Gaze of Western Travellers*. London: Saqi.

Jhally, Sut. 2002. *Race the Floating Signifier: Stuart Hall in Lecture*. Northampton, MA: Media Education Foundation.

Jodi, Melamed. 2015. "Racial Capitalism." *Critical Ethnic Studies* 1(1): 76–85.

Junker, Thomas. 2018. "Blumenbach's Theory of Human Races and the Natural Unity of Humankind." In *Johann Friedrich Blumenbach: Race and Natural History, 1750–1850*, edited by Nicholaas A. Rupke and Gerhard Lauer. Boca Raton, FL: Routledge.

Kaçiu, Ervin. 2022. "Trajektore të skajimit të Romëve gjatë periudhës së qeverisjes së Mbretit Zog dhe regjimit Nazi-Fashist." *Antropologji* 5(1): 5–25.

Kajsiu, Blendi. 2011. *Albanian Democratization between Europeanization and Neoliberalism*. Tirana: Albanian Institute for International Studies.

Kalmar, Ivan Davidson. 2022. *White but Not Quite: Central Europe's Illiberal Revolt*. Bristol, UK: Bristol University Press.

Kapllani, Gazmend, and Nicola Mai. 2005. "'Greece Belongs to Greeks!' The Case of the Greek Flag in the Hand of an Albanian Student." In *The New Albanian Migration*, edited by Russell King, Nicola Mai, and Stephanie Schwandner-Sievers. Brighton, UK: Sussex Academic Press.

Kettler, Andrew. 2020. *The Smell of Slavery: Olfactory Racism and the Atlantic World*. Cambridge: Cambridge University Press.

Khan, Aisha. 2019. "Race and Racial Thinking: A View from the Atlantic World." In *Ideologies of Race: Imperial Russia and the Soviet Union in Global Context*, edited by David Rainbow. Montreal: McGill–Queen's University Press.

King, Russell, and Nicola Mai. 2008. *Out of Albania: From Crisis Migration to Social Inclusion in Italy*. Oxford: Berghahn.

Koci, Tracy. 2001. "Albania: Awakening from a Long Sleep." In *Between Future: The Roma of Central and Eastern Europe*, edited by Will Guy. Hatfield, UK: University of Hertfordshire Press.

Kóczé, Angela. 2018. "Race, Migration, and Neoliberalism: Distorted Notions of Romani Migration in European Public Discourses." *Social Identities* 24(4): 459–73.

Kóczé, Angéla, Violetta Zentai, Jelena Jovanović, and Enikő Vincze. 2018. *The Romani Women's Movement: Struggles and Debates in Central and Eastern Europe*. Boca Raton, FL: Routledge.

Koinova, Maria. 2000. *Roma of Albania*. Athens: Center for Documentation and Information on Minorities in Europe—Southeast Europe.

Kolsti, John. 1991. "Albanian Gypsies: The Silent Survivors." In *The Gypsies of Eastern Europe*, edited by David Crowe, John Kolsti, and Ian Hancock. New York: Routledge.

Kurtiade, Marcel. 1995. "Between Conviviality and Antagonism: The Ambiguous Position of the Romanies in Albania." *Patrin* 3:10–15.

Labropoulou, Elinda, Erin McLaughlin, and Steve Almasy. 2013. "Roma Family in Ireland Reunited with Daughter after DNA Test." CNN, October 24. https://www.cnn.com/2013/10/23/world/europe/europe-mystery-girls.

Lame, Artan. 2005. "Shqipni e harrume." *Klan*, February 24, 54–55.

Lemon, Alaina. 2000. *Between Two Fires: Gypsy Performance and Romani Memory from Pushkin to Post-socialism*. Durham, NC: Duke University Press.

Lemon, Alaina. 2002. "Without a 'Concept'? Race as Discursive Practice." *Slavic Review* 61(1): 54–61.

Lemon, Alaina. 2019. "The Matter of Race." In *Ideologies of Race: Imperial Russia and the Soviet Union in Global Context*, edited by David Rainbow. Montreal: McGill–Queen's University Press.

Likmeta, Besar. 2011a. "Albania Absolves Roma Camp Arsonists of Racism." *Balkan Insight*, November 18. https://balkaninsight.com/2011/11/18/albania-absolves-roma-camp-arsonists-of-racism/.

Likmeta, Besar. 2011b. "Albania Police Criticised after Attack on Roma Camp." *Balkan Insight*, March 11. https://balkaninsight.com/2011/03/11/albania-police-under-fire-after-attack-against-roma-camp/.

Likmeta, Besar. 2011c. "Rightists and Greeks Denounce Albania Census." *Balkan Insight*, October 5. https://balkaninsight.com/2011/10/05/albania-population-census-stirs-calls-for-boycott/.

Linné, Carl von. 1964. *Systema naturae*. Reproduced from the 10th ed., 1759. Vol. 34, *Historiae naturalis classica*. Weinheim: J. Kramer.

Lott, Eric. 2018. *Black Mirror: The Cultural Contradictions of American Racism*. Cambridge, MA: Harvard University Press.

Loyd, Thomas R. 2021. "Black in the USSR: African Students, Soviet Empire, and the Politics of Global Education during the Cold War." PhD diss., Georgetown University.

Luci, Nita, and Predrag Marković. 2009. "Events and Sites of Difference: Mark-ing Self and Other in Kosovo." In *Media Discourse and the Yugoslav Conflicts: Representations of Self and Other*, edited by Pål Kolstø. New York: Routledge.

Luku, Esilda. 2019. "Why Did Albanians and Their Collaborationist Governments Rescue Jews during the Holocaust?" *Revista Hiperboreea* 6(2): 33–49. https://doi.org/10.3406/hiper.2019.953.

Maghbouleh, Neda. 2017. *The Limits of Whiteness: Iranian Americans and the Everyday Politics of Race*. Stanford, CA: Stanford University Press.

Malcolm, Noel. 2002. "Myths of Albanian National Identity: Some Key Elements, as Expressed in the Works of Albanian Writers in America in the Early Twentieth Century." In *Albanians Identities: Myth and History*, edited by Stephanie Schwandner-Sievers and Bernd Jürgen Fischer. Bloomington: Indiana University Press.

Mann, Stuart E. 1933. "Albanian Romani: Introduction." *Journal of the Gypsy Lore Society* 12(1): 1–32.

Mark, James. 2022. "Race." In *Socialism Goes Global: The Soviet Union and Eastern Europe in the Age of Deolonisation*, edited by James Mark and Paul Betts, 221–54. Oxford: Oxford University Press.

Marushiakova, Elena, and Veselin Popov. 2001a. *Gypsies in the Ottoman Empire: A Contribution to the History of the Balkans*. Translated by Olga Apostolova; edited by Donald Kenrick. Hatfield, UK: University of Hertfordshire Press.

Marushiakova, Elena, and Veselin Popov. 2001b. "New Ethnic Identities in the Balkans: The Case of the Egyptians." *Philosophy and Sociology* 2(8): 465–77.

Marushiakova, Elena, and Veselin Popov. 2013. "'Gypsy' Groups in Eastern Europe: Ethnonyms vs. Professionyms." *Romani Studies* 23(1): 61–81.

Massey, Douglas S. 2020. "Still the Linchpin: Segregation and Stratification in the USA." *Race and Social Problems* 12(1): 1–12. https://doi.org/10.1007/s12552-019-09280-1.

Matache, Margareta. 2017. "Biased Elites, Unfit Policies: Reflections on the Lacunae of Roma Integration Strategies." *European Review* 25(4): 588–607. https://doi.org/10.1017/S1062798717000254.

Matras, Y. 2004. "The Role of Language in Mystifying and Demystifying Gypsy Identity." In *The Role of the Romanies: Images and Counter-Images of "Gypsies"/Romanies in European Cultures*, edited by Nicholas Saul and Susan Tebbutt. Liverpool: Liverpool University Press.

Mbembe, Achille. 2001. *On the Postcolony*. Berkeley: University of California Press.

Mbembe, Achille. 2017. *Critique of Black Reason*. Translated by Laurent Dubois. Durham, NC: Duke University Press.

Mbretnija Shqiptare Ministria te Brendëshme [Kingdom of Albania, Ministry of the Interior]. 1943a. *Mbi Arixhijt* [On the Arixhijt]. Tirana: Directorate of Correspondence.

Mbretnija Shqiptare Ministria te Brendëshme [Kingdom of Albania, Ministry of the Interior]. 1943b. Mbi Arixhijt. Pergjigjet. [Response about Arixhij]. Tirana: Directorate of Correspondence.

McClaurin, Irma, ed. 2001. *Black Feminist Anthropology: Theory, Politics, Praxis, and Poetics.* Piscataway, NJ: Rutgers University Press.

Meçe, Merita. 2015. *Inclusion of Roma Children in Albania's Education System: Rhetoric or Reality?* Flensburg, Germany: European Centre for Minority Issues.

Mëhilli, Elidor. 2017. *From Stalin to Mao: Albania and the Socialist World.* Ithaca, NY: Cornell University Press.

Mernacaj, Nosh. 2021. *Growing Up in Communist Albania.* Self-published.

Mills, Charles W. 1997. *The Racial Contract.* Ithaca, NY: Cornell University Press.

Misha, Piro. 2002. "Invention of a Nationalism: Myth and Amnesia." In *Albanian Identities: Myth and History,* edited by Stephanie Schwandner-Sievers and Bernd Jürgen Fischer, 33–48. Bloomington: Indiana University Press.

Mladenova, Radmila. 2016. "The Figure of the Imaginary Gypsy in Film: I Even Met Happy Gypsies (1967)." *Romani Studies* 26(1): 1–30. https://doi.org/10.3828/rs.2016.1.

Morrison, Toni. 1987. *Beloved.* New York: Knopf.

Moscaliuc, Mihaela. 2019. "Accessorizing (with) 'Gypsyness' in the Twenty-first Century." *Critical Romani Studies* 2(1): 92–114.

Mudure, Mihaela. 2003. "Blackening Europe: The African American Presence." In *Blackening Europe: The African American Presence,* edited by Heike Raphael-Hernandez. London: Taylor & Francis.

Musaraj, Smoki. 2021. *Tales from Albarado: Ponzi Logics of Accumulation in Postsocialist Albania.* Ithaca, NY: Cornell University Press.

Mwaria, Cheryl. 2001. "Biomedical Ethics, Gender, and Ethnicity: Implications for Black Feminist Anthropology." In *Black Feminist Anthropology: Theory, Politics, Praxis, and Poetics,* edited by Irma McClaurin. New Brunswick, NJ: Rutgers University Press.

Neuburger, Mary. 2004. *The Orient Within: Muslim Minorities and the Negotiation of Nationhood in Modern Bulgaria.* Ithaca, NY: Cornell University Press.

Newkirk, Pamela. 2015. *Spectacle: The Astonishing Life of Ota Benga.* New York: Amistad.

Nishku, Genta. 2020. "The Wretched on the Walls: A Fanonian Reading of a Revolutionary Albanian Orphanage." *Feminist Critique* 3: 39–63.

Nixon, Nicola. 2009. "'You Can't Eat Shame with Bread': Gender and Collective Shame in Albanian Society." *Journal of Southeast European and Black Sea Studies* 9(1–2): 105–21. https://doi.org/10.1080/14683850902723447.

Nixon, Nicola. 2010. "Always Already European: The Figure of Skënderbeg in Contemporary Albanian Nationalism." *National Identities* 12(1): 1–20. https://doi.org/10.1080/14608940903542540.

Omi, Michael, and Howard Winant. 1994. *Racial Formation in the United States: From the 1960s to the 1990s.* 2nd ed. New York: Routledge.

Opinion. 2015. "Historia e çuditshme: Ushqehet me byrek dhe vishet me firmato. Njihuni me futbollistin që ka zëvendësuar "Drumban" në kampionatin shqiptar të futbollit?" [A strange history: Eats byrek and has the signature look. Have you met the football player that has replaced Drumba in the Albanian championship?] December 25. https://opinion.al/historia-e-cuditshme-ushqehet-me-byrek-dhe-vishet-me-firmato-njihuni-me-futbollistin-qe-ka-zevendesuar-drumban-ne-kampionatin-shqiptar-te-futbollit/.

Osei-Opare, Nana. 2019. "Uneasy Comrades: Postcolonial Statecraft, Race, and Citizenship, Ghana-Soviet Relations, 1957–1966." *Journal of West African History* 5(2): 85–111. https://doi.org/10.14321/jwestafrihist.5.2.0085.

Ozanne, James William. 1878. *Three Years in Roumania.* Whitefish, MT: Kessinger.

Painter, Nell Irvin. 2010. *The History of White People*. New York: W. W. Norton.
Painter, Nell Irvin. 2015. "What Is Whiteness?" *New York Times*, June 20.
Papa-Pandelejmoni, Enriketa. 2021. "Legitimization vs. Delegitimization of Terror: Controversies on Transitional Justice and Communist Past in Albania." Balkan Circle (virtual conference), UT Austin, October 1.
Partridge, Damani James. 2012. *Hypersexuality and Headscarves: Race, Sex, and Citizenship in the New Germany*. Edited by Matti Bunzl and Michael Herzfeld. Bloomington: Indiana University Press.
Partridge, Damani James. 2023. *Blackness as a Universal Claim: Holocaust Heritage, Noncitizen Futures, and Black Power in Berlin*. Oakland: University of California Press.
Parvulescu, Anca, and Manuela Boatcă. 2020. "The *Longue Durée* of Enslavement: Extracting Labor from Romani Music in Liviu Rebreanu's *Ion*." *Literature Compass* 17(1–2): n.p. https://doi.org/10.1111/lic3.12559.
Peshkopia, Ridvan, and Konstantinos Giakoumis. 2021. "Nationalistic Education and Its Colourful Role in Intergroup Prejudice Reduction: Lessons from Albania." *Journal of Southeast European and Black Sea Studies* 21(3): 457–80. https://doi.org/10.1080/14683857.2021.1932161.
Petcut, Petre. n.d. *Wallachia and Moldavia*. Istanbul: Council of Europe.
Petrovic, Tanja. 2008. "Serbs, Albanians, and Those in Between: The Gradation of Otherness and Identity Management in the Nation-Building Process." *Two Homelands* 27: 67–80.
Picker, Giovanni. 2017. *Racial Cities: Governance and the Spatial Segregation of Roma in Urban Europe*. London: Routledge.
Pierre, Jemima. 2008. "Activist Groundings or Groundings for Activism? The Study of Racialization as a Site of Political Engagement." In *Engaging Contradictions: Theory, Politics, and Methods of Activist Scholarship*, edited by Charles R. Hale. Berkeley: University of California Press.
Pierre, Jemima. 2012. *The Predicament of Blackness: Postcolonial Ghana and the Politics of Race*. Chicago: University of Chicago Press.
Pojani, Dorina. 2010. "Tirana." *Cities* 27 (6): 483–95.
Qejvanaj, Gentian. 2021. "Albanian National Action Plan for Roma Inclusion, 2016–2020: A Study on the Program Achievements at the Halfway Mark." *SAGE Open* 11(3): n.p. https://doi.org/10.1177/21582440211036107.
Qesku, Pavli. 2004. *Fjalor Shqip-Anglisht*. Edited by Fatmir Xhaferi. Tirana: Botime EDFA.
Qirici, Mina. 2004. *Romët e Shqipërisë në Folklor/Romet of Albania in Folklore*. Tirana: Open Society Institute (Roma Culture Initiative).
Rana, Junaid. 2011. *Terrifying Muslims: Race and Labor in the South Asian Diaspora*. Durham, NC: Duke University Press.
Raúl, Pérez. 2016. "Brownface Minstrelsy: José Jiménez, the Civil Rights Movement, and the Legacy of Racist Comedy." *Ethnicities* 16(1): 40–67.
Reinhartz, Dennis. 1999. "Unmarked Graves: The Destruction of the Yugoslav Roma in the Balkan Holocaust, 1941–1945." *Journal of Genocide Research* 1(1): 81–89. https://doi.org/10.1080/14623529908413936.
Republic of Albania. 1995. *Kodi Penal i Republikës Së Shqipërisë* [Criminal Code of the Republic of Albania]. Tirana: Ministria e Drejtësisë [Ministry of Justice].
Republika Popullore e Shqipërisë [People's Republic of Albania]. 1947. *Dega Për Zhdukjen e Krimeve* [Branch for the Elimination of Crime]. Tirana: Ministrija e Puneve të Mbrëndëshme [Ministry of Internal Affairs]. Tirana.

Republika Popullore Socialiste e Shqipërisë [People's Socialist Republic of Albania]. 1979. *Për disa probleme lidhur me stabilizimin e shtetasve arixhinj* [About several problems related to the stabilization of Arixhi Nationals]. Tirana: Ministria e Puneve të Brendshme, Drejtoria e Policisë Popullore [Ministry of Internal Affairs, Director of the People's Police].

Republika Popullore Socialiste e Shqipërisë [People's Socialist Republic of Albania]. 1981. *Për stabilizimin e Harxhinjve* [About the stabilization of the Arixhi]. Tirana: Ministria e Puneve të Brendshme, Drejtoria e Policisë Popullore [Ministry of Internal Affairs, Director of the People's Police].

Rexhepi, Piro. 2023. *White Enclosures: Racial Capitalism and Coloniality along the Balkan Route*. Edited by Walter D. Mignolo and Catherine E. Walsh. Durham, NC: Duke University Press.

Roberts, Dorothy. 2011. *Fatal Invention: How Science, Politics, and Big Business Recreate Race in the Twenty-first Century*. New York: New York University Press.

Robinson, Cedric J. 2000. *Black Marxism: The Making of the Black Radical Tradition*. Foreword by Robin D. G. Kelley, with a new preface by the author. Chapel Hill: University of North Carolina Press.

Roediger, David R. 2005. *Working toward Whiteness. How America's Immigrants Became White: The Strange Journey from Ellis Island to the Suburbs*. New York: Basic Books.

Roland, L. Kaifa. 2013. "T/Racing Belonging through Cuban Tourism." *Cultural Anthropology* 28(3): 396–419. https://doi.org/10.1111/cuan.12011.

Rosa, Jonathan, and Nelson Flores. 2020. "Reimagining Race and Language: From Raciolinguistic Ideologies to a Raciolinguistic Perspective." In *The Oxford Handbook of Language and Race*, edited by H. Samy Alim, Angela Reyes, and Paul V. Kroskrity. Oxford: Oxford University Press.

Rucker-Chang, Sunnie. 2018. "Roma Filmic Representation as Postcolonial "Object."" *Interventions* 20(6): 853–67. https://doi.org/10.1080/1369801X.2018.1492951.

Rucker-Chang, Sunnie, and Chelsi West Ohueri. 2021. "A Moment of Reckoning: Transcending Bias, Engaging Race and Racial Formations in Slavic and East European Studies." *Slavic Review* 80(2): 216–23. https://doi.org/10.1017/slr.2021.75.

Said, Edward W. 1979. *Orientalism*. New York: Vintage.

Saideman, Stephen. 2013. "Comparative Xenophobia, Parts I and II." *Saideman's Semi-Spew* (blog), May 16. http://saideman.blogspot.com/2013/05/comparative-xenophobia-part-i.html.

Seeman, Sonia T. 2023. "Creating White Out of Dark: The Ethno-National Racialization Project for Defining Turkishness by Hyper-Nominating Roma." Association of Slavic, East European, and Eurasian Studies annual convention, Philadelphia, December 3, 2023.

Shevchenko, Olga. 2008. *Crisis and the Everyday in Postsocialist Moscow*. Bloomington: Indiana University Press.

Silverman, Carol. 2012. *Romani Routes: Cultural Politics and Balkan Music in Diaspora*. New York: Oxford University Press.

Simmons, Kimberly Eison. 2002. "Reconfiguring Dominicanness: Competing Discourses Surrounding Race, Nation, and Identity in the Dominican Republic." PhD diss., Michigan State University.

Sinoruka, Fjori. 2024. "Albania's Statistics Institute Declines to Publish Preliminary Census Data." *Balkan Insight*, January 29. https://balkaninsight.com/2024/01/29/albanias-statistics-institute-declines-to-publish-preliminary-census-data/.

Smedley, Audrey. 1998. "'Race' and the Construction of Human Identity." *American Anthropologist* 100(3): 690–702. https://doi.org/10.1525/aa.1998.100.3.690.
Stephen, Lynn. 2007. *Transborder Lives: Indigenous Oaxacans in Mexico, California, and Oregon*. Durham, NC: Duke University Press.
Stewart, Kathleen. 1988. "Nostalgia—a Polemic." *Cultural Anthropology* 3(3): 227–41.
Stewart, Kathleen. 1996. *A Space on the Side of the Road: Cultural Poetics in an "Other" America*. Princeton, NJ: Princeton University Press.
Stoler, Ann. 1997. "Racial Histories and Their Regimes of Truth." *Political Power and Social Theory* 11: 183–206.
Sula-Raxhimi, Enkelejda. 2021. "Heterotopias of Displacement: The Production of Space in Postsocialist Albania." In *Remitting, Restoring and Building Contemporary Albania*, edited by Nataša Gregorič Bon and Smoki Musaraj. Cham: Springer International Publishing.
Susser, Ida. 2009. *AIDS, Sex, and Culture Global Politics and Survival in Southern Africa*. Hoboken, NJ: Wiley.
Taylor, Alice. 2020. "Albanian Ombudsman Launches Investigation into Police Violence against Roma Youth." *EXit News*, May 27. https://exit.al/en/albanian-ombudsman-launches-investigation-into-police-violence-against-roma-youth/.
Tochka, Nicholas. 2015. "To 'Enlighten and Beautify': Western Music and the Modern Project of Personhood in Albania, c. 1906–1924." *Ethnomusicology* 59(3): 398–420. https://doi.org/10.5406/ethnomusicology.59.3.0398.
Todorova, Maria Nikolaeva. 1997. *Imagining the Balkans*. New York: Oxford University Press.
Trehan, Nidhi, and Angela Kocze. 2009. "Racism, (Neo)Colonialism, and Social Justice: The Struggle for the Soul of the Romani Movement in Post-Socialist Europe." In *Racism Postcolonialism Europe*, edited by Graham Huggan and Ian Law, 50–74. Liverpool: Liverpool University Press.
Trouillot, Michel-Rolph. 1995. *Silencing the Past: Power and the Reproduction of History*. Boston: Beacon.
Trounstine, Jessica. 2018. *Segregation by Design: Local Politics and Inequality in American Cities*. Cambridge: Cambridge University Press.
Trubeta, Sevasti. 2003. "'Gypsiness,' Racial Discourse and Persecution: Balkan Roma during the Second World War." *Nationalities Papers* 31(4): 495–514.
Trubeta, Sevasti. 2005. "Balkan Egyptians and Gypsy/Roma Discourse." *Nationalities Papers* 33(1): 71–95.
Turda, Marius. 2010. *Modernism and Eugenics*. New York: Palgrave Macmillan.
Turda, Marius. 2021. "The Location of 'Race': Conversation between Marius Turda and Marina Mogilner." *Ab Imperio* 2021(1): 32–49. https://doi.org/10.1353/imp.2021.0002.
Turda, Marius, and Maria Sophia Quine. 2018. *Historicizing Race*. London: Bloomsbury Academic.
Turda, Marius, and Paul Weindling, eds. 2007. *"Blood and Homeland": Eugenics and Racial Nationalism in Central and Southeast Europe, 1900–1940*. Budapest: Central European University Press.
Turnbull, Colin. 1962. *The Forest People*. New York: American Museum of Natural History.
Vargas, João Helion Costa. 2018. *The Denial of Antiblackness: Multiracial Redemption and Black Suffering*. Minneapolis: University of Minnesota Press.
Velayutham, Selvaraj, and Bittiandra Chand Somaiah. 2021. "Rap against Brownface and the Politics of Racism in Singapore." *Ethnic and Racial Studies* 47(7): 1–22.

Verdery, Katherine. 1996. *What Was Socialism and What Comes Next?* Princeton, NJ: Princeton University Press.

Vincze, Enikő. 2014. "Faces and Causes of Roma Marginalization: Experiences from Romania." In *Faces and Causes of Roma Marginalization in Local Contexts: Hungary, Romania, Serbia*, edited by Violetta Zentai, Julia Szalai, and Enikő Vincze. Budapest: Central European University Press.

Visweswaran, Kamala. 1994. *Fictions of Feminist Ethnography*. Minneapolis: University of Minnesota Press.

Vrăbiescu, Ioana. 2014. "The Subtlety of Racism: From Antiziganism to Romaphobia." In *When Stereotype Meets Prejudice: Antiziganism in European Societies*, edited by Timofey Agarin. Stuttgart: ibidem.

Vukanovic, T. P. 1959. "Gypsy Bear-Leaders in the Balkan Peninsula." *Journal of the Gypsy Lore Society* 38(3): 106–26.

Wekker, Gloria. 2016. *White Innocence: Paradoxes of Colonialism and Race*. Durham, NC: Duke University Press.

West Ohueri, Chelsi. 2021. "On Living and Moving with Zor: Exploring Racism, Embodiment, and Health in Albania." *Medical Anthropology* 40(3): 241–53. https://doi.org/10.1080/01459740.2020.1807539.

Winant, Howard. 2000. "Race and Race Theory." *Annual Review of Sociology* 26: 169–85. http://www.jstor.org/stable/223441.

Winant, Howard. 2001. *The World Is a Ghetto: Race and Democracy since World War II*. New York: Basic Books.

Woodcock, Shannon. 2016. *Life Is War: Surviving Dictatorship in Communist Albania*. Bristol, UK: Hammeron.

Wright, Michelle M. 2015. *Physics of Blackness: Beyond the Middle Passage Epistemology*. Minneapolis: University of Minnesota Press.

Wynter, Sylvia. 1994. "'No Humans Involved': An Open Letter to My Colleagues." *Forum NHI: Knowledge for the 21st Century* 1(1): 42–73.

Wynter, Sylvia. 2003. "Unsettling the Coloniality of Being/Power/Truth/Freedom: Towards the Human, After Man, Its Overrepresentation—An Argument." *CR: The New Centennial Review* 3(3): 257–337. https://doi.org/10.1353/ncr.2004.0015.

Ypi, Lea. 2022. *Free: A Child and a Country at the End of History*. New York: W. W. Norton.

Yuval-Davis, Nira. 2006. "Belonging and the Politics of Belonging." *Patterns of Prejudice* 40(3): 197–214.

Yuval-Davis, Nira, Georgie Wemyss, and Kathryn Cassidy. 2017. "Introduction to the Special Issue: Racialized Bordering Discourses on European Roma." *Ethnic and Racial Studies* 40(7): 1047–57.

Zakharov, Nikolay, and Ian Law. 2017. *Post-Soviet Racisms*. London: Palgrave Macmillan.

Zemon, Rubin. 2001. *History of the Balkan Egyptians*. Council of Europe. Accessed August 27, 2024. https://www.coe.int/t/dg4/education/ibp/source/fs_1_10.5.pdf.

Index

African leaders and students, 93–94
afterlives, 5. *See also* communist afterlife
Albania
  arrival of democracy in, 35–36
  assertion of racelessness/denial of race/racism in, 1–2, 7–8, 10, 11, 58–61, 105–6, 139–40, 161, 187, 189, 190
  as case study, 188
  as constructed by external nationalist leaders, 88–89
  demographic composition of, 6
  following Hoxha's death, 34
  under Hoxha, 29–34
  Italian occupation of, 116–17
  liberation of, 30
  map of, 3f
  market reforms in, 36
  migration from, 15, 35–36, 37, 50–51, 66, 97
  Penal Code, Article 256, 176–77
  peripheral whiteness and socialist period of, 92–94
  and qualifying game for 2016 Euro Cup, 152–57, 158–59
  relations between Greece and, 95–96
  reordering and restructuring in, 26–27
  return migrants in, 98–103
  westernization of, 90–91
  See also communist afterlife
Albanian Football Federation (FFSh), 151, 155
Albanian identity, 77, 78–79, 89–91, 101
Albanian migration and diaspora, 15, 35–36, 37, 50–51, 66, 97, 98–103
Albanians
  and differentiation between Roma and Egyptians, 135–36, 144
  marginalization of, 12–14, 15–16, 79, 83–84, 102–3
  perception of, 102
  performance and assertion of whiteness, 103–8
  as perpetual outsiders, 82, 83–84, 87–88
  racialization of, outside of whiteness, 13–14, 80, 103
  relationship between Greeks and, 61
  relationship between Northern and Southern, 93
  self-definition of, as Europeans, 83–86
Alia, Ramiz, 34, 35
anti-miscegenation laws, 115
antiracialism, 10
anti-racism, 93–94, 151
Appadurai, Arjun, 56
arixhi, 114–17, 120, 121
Association of Slavic, East European, and Eurasian Studies, 186
Attewell, Nadine, 5
authenticity, 78
autochthonous, 157, 182–83
Autochthonous (2015), 156

Baartman, Sarah, 197n6
Baldwin, James, 181
Basch, Linda G., 158
Bashkëjetesë dhe Integrim (Coexistence and integration), 126
begging, 106, 120, 127, 128, 131, 132, 136, 141, 142, 143
Bejko, Julian, 35
Berisha, Sali, 35–36, 37, 70, 95
Berlant, Laurent, 38
Berlin Wall, 34
besa ("honor"/"oath"), 77, 78, 142–43
Besson, Sébastien, 157
Binaj, Florian, 165–67, 171. See also *Portokalli*
birthday parties, 44–46, 68–69, 74–75
Bjelić, Dušan, 87, 159
blackface, 60–61, 161–70
blackfishing, 164
Black football players, 151, 165–67, 170
Black movements for equality, 136–37
blackness, 109–14
  arixhi, 114–17, 120, 121
  commodification of, 164
  and distinguishing of Roma and Egyptians from Albanians, 107–8
  dorë e zezë (the "black side"), 138–42, 146
Egjiptian, 133–38
gabel, 116–21

213

INDEX

blackness (*continued*)
  jevg/jevgjit, 127–33, 134, 137, 139
  meanings of, 106–7
  multifaceted meanings of, 142–46
  Rom/Romë/Roma, 121–27
  and shaping of social worlds, 146–47
  as tied to space of margins, 140–41
Blanc, Cristina Szanton, 158
Bllok/Blloku, 196n8
Blumenbach, Johann, 10, 193n6
Blumi, Isa, 31, 83, 93
Boatcă, Manuela, 114
bodies, and race and racialization, 7, 12
Bogdanov, Ivan, 154
Boletini, Isa, 154, 156, 157
Bonilla-Silva, Eduardo, 14
bookseller, 43–44
Boym, Svetlana, 193n2
Braverman, Suella, 15
brownface, 161–70, 171–73
bunkers, 32, 33*f*
Bunzl, Matti, 10
byrek, 166, 170, 193n7

Cana, Lorik, 155
capitalism, racial, 14, 102–3, 187
"Caucasian," 10, 193n6
Çekrezi, Konstandin, 89
census, 6, 96, 193n4
Chang, Felix B., 118
China, 32, 33
classification, 9
Clinton, Bill, 152
coffee, 83
collecting, 1, 43–44, 74, 75, 106, 125, 129, 138–39, 141, 167, 168, 174
collective shame, 78–79
Collins, Patricia Hills, 184
Committee for National Minorities, 126
communist afterlife, 25–27
  in Albania, 2–7
  arrival of democracy in Albania, 35–36
  Besa's family's perspectives on and experiences in, 47–54
  and cruel optimism, 38
  as entanglement, 55, 193n2
  ethnographic narratives of, 54–55
  historical and local contextualization of, 55–56
  impact of pyramid schemes, 36–37
  Mimoza's perspective on, 40–44
  rise and regime of Hoxha, 29–34
  Shpresa's experiences in, 44–46

Costache, Ioanida, 113, 114, 126
Courthiade (Kurtiade), Marcel, 6, 113, 121
Court of Arbitration for Sport (CAS), 156–57
COVID-19 pandemic, 168–69
cruel optimism, 38
Çuno, Rivelino, 144
curiosity, versus racism, 59

death, 53–54
Decade of Roma Inclusion, 176, 179, 180, 196n5
Dejijer, Vladimir, 67
democracy, 35–36
Democratic Party, 35, 38, 41
desire
  brownface as tied to, 172–73
  and commodification and devouring of race, 165–67
diaspora, Albanian, 15, 35–36, 37, 50–51, 66, 97, 98–103
Digitalb, 156, 165
displacement, 179–82
dorë e zezë (the "black side"), 138–42, 146
Drakulić, Slavenka, 15
drone incident, at Euro Cup qualifying game, 153–56, 158
Drumba (fictional character), 60–61, 165–67, 169–70
Du Bois, W. E. B., 67
Duijzings, Ger, 137, 196n10
Durham, Edith, 87

Ebron, Paulla, 20
education, 50, 51, 126, 172, 196n4
Egjiptian, 133–38
Egyptians
  African origins of, 135
  brownface portrayals of, 163
  collectively racialized as "black," 111–12, 133–38
  differentiation of Roma and, 135–36, 144–45
  displacement of, 179–82
  identity of, 137, 196n10
  pervasiveness of racism against, 179–80
  racialization of, outside of whiteness and Albanianness, 61–62, 65, 80, 106, 107–8, 140, 143–45
  segregation of, 105, 140–41
  treatment of, under Hoxha, 33, 93, 119
Ekspozita Shqipëria Sot, 26
Elsie, Robert, 102
El-Tayeb, Fatima, 10

employment, 118, 172. *See also* begging; collecting; unemployment
entanglement, 5, 55, 193n2
Essed, Philomena, 182
ethnic conflict/ethnic hatred, 151–52
ethnicity
    versus race, 8
    relationship between race and nation and, 158–59
    and 2011 national census, 6, 96
ethnocentricity, 21
ethnography, 18–19, 20–21, 67, 112–13, 184–85
Euro Cup (2016), qualifying game for, 152–57, 158–59
Europe
    Albanians' self-definition as Europeans, 83–86
    Balkans as periphery of, 87
    marginalization of Albanians from, 12–14, 15–16, 79, 83–84
    and nation-building projects, 88–92
    racial projects, 158–59
European Union membership, 95
European Values Study (EVS), 103–4, 105, 190–91
exclusionary incorporation, 144
executions, 31, 34, 131

fading, 55
fantasy
    brownface as tied to, 172–73
    and commodification and devouring of race, 165–67
Fassin, Didier, 12
Fédération Internationale de Football Association (FIFA), 151
FIFA World Cup (Moscow, 2018), 157
fire, at Roma settlement, 175–78, 181
Fonseca, Isabel, 131
food, 34, 40, 41, 45, 49–50, 68–79, 166, 170, 193n7
Football Association of Serbia (FFS), 155
forced labor, 31–32, 39
Forest People, The (Turnbull), 18–19
fortune telling, 143
Friedman, Eben, 196n10
furgon journey, 47–48
*furgon*s, 193n1

gabel, 116–21
Ghegs, 93, 195n5
Ghodsee, Kristen, 4, 21

Gilmore, Ruth Wilson, 8, 187
Gjermeni, Eglantina, 36
Gobineau, Joseph-Arthur, Count de, 9
Goldberg, David Theo, 10
Golemi, Marinela, 91–92, 195n4
Greece
    Albanian migrants in, 15, 66, 97
    anti-Albanian sentiment in, 79
    positionality within Balkans, 195n9
    relations between Albania and, 95–96
    return migrants from, 98–103
Greeks
    Balkan mentality of, 195n9
    as racist, 61, 96, 97, 98
    relationship between Albanians and, 61
Green, Sarah, 195n9

Hall, Stuart, 8, 107, 137, 152, 170
Hancock, Ian, 134, 146
Hartman, Saidiya, 5
health care, 52–53
Heng, Geraldine, 9
Hogan, Patrick C., 195n4
hooks, bell, 165
hospitality
    in relation to race, 68–78
    and shame, 72, 75, 76, 78–79
housing, 37, 174–75
Howard, Winant, 170
Hoxha, Dritan, 173
Hoxha, Enver, 29f
    death of, 34
    grave site of, 28–29
    imagination's role in regime of, 55
    national narratives under, 92–94
    restrictions on movement under, 97
    rise and regime of, 2–4, 29–34
    treatment of Roma and Egyptians under, 118, 122
Hughes, Langston, 67
Humor. *See* jokes
"hunger games," 22, 68–78
Hysenaj, Xhevrije, 176

identity
    Albanian, 77, 78–79, 89–91, 101
    of Albanian return migrants, 101
    denial of racialized, in Albania, 139–40
    as tied to authenticity, 78
    as unstable and conjectural, 137
ignorance, 62, 65–66, 100, 189–90
Illyrians, 85, 92
imagination, in Hoxha's regime, 55

INDEX

in-betweenness, 27. *See also* communist afterlife
INSTAT (Albanian Institute of Statistics), 6
Institute for the Studies of Communist Crimes and Its Consequences (ISKK), 39, 96
International Day of Balkan Egyptians, 137
International Monetary Fund (IMF), 36
Islam, 42, 90–91, 116, 158–59
Ismajli, Genta, 163
isolation, 61, 63, 64
Italian occupation, 116–17

Jackson, Esther Cooper, 67
Jackson, John, 21, 78, 190
jevg/jevgjit, 127–33, 134, 137, 139
Jewish population, 11, 78, 118
jokes
  author's experiences with racist, 160–61
  and racial depictions in sketch comedies, 159–74
  regarding police, 159–60

Kaçiu, Ervin, 113
Kanun of Lek Dukagjini, 77
Khrushchev, Nikita, 32
King, Russell, 15, 97, 195n9
Kipti, 134
Klubi i Futbollit Tirana (KF Tirana), 149–59
Koci, Tracy, 139–40
Kóczé, Angela, 111
Kombinat, 127–28
Konica, Faik, 90–91
Kosova, 152, 153, 157, 159, 196n1
Kosova-Serbia war (1999), 38, 152
Kreshtë, 124–25, 140–41

labor, forced, 31–32, 39
language, and race, 111
law no. 96/2017, 125–26
leeks, 34
Lemon, Alaina, 12, 111, 131
Lila, Andi, 154
Linnaeus, Carl, 9, 87
Liqeni, 174–75, 179–80
longing, of Albanian return migrants, 101–2

Mai, Nicola, 15, 97, 195n9
Mann, Stuart, 131–32
marriage, 51, 115
Marushiakova, Elena, 134
Mbembe, Achille, 5
Mbuti people, 18–19
Mëhilli, Elidor, 30, 31, 127–28

mërzit/mërzitur, 77
migration, Albanian, 15, 35–36, 37, 50–51, 66, 97, 98–103
minstrel shows, 162
Mitrovic, Stefan, 154
Mladenova, Radmila, 163
Morina, Ismail "Ballist," 156
Morrison, Toni, 193n2
Moss, Carlton, 67
Mos u mërzit, 77
mourning, 53–54
Musaraj, Smoki, 4, 36, 37, 194n3
music, 45, 46
Muslims. *See* Islam
Mustafa, Shkelqim, 177

naming practices, and understanding racialization and nationalization, 111
National Liberation Movement, 29
nation-building projects, racial belonging and, 88–92
nation/nationalism, relationship between race and ethnicity and, 8, 158–59
Nefreta, 134
'97, 36–38
Nixon, Nicola, 78
Noli, Fan, 90, 91–92
nomadism, 116, 117, 118
nostalgia, 193n2

Olli, Leonard, 180
Omari, Abaz, 31
optimism, cruel, 38
Ora, Rita, 164
Organization for Security and Co-operation in Europe (OSCE), 176
Othello (Shakespeare), 91–92, 195n4
Ottoman Empire, 30, 49, 86, 88–89, 115, 116

parë filxhan, 143
pariah, 146
Partridge, Damani, 8, 144, 147
Party of Labor, 34, 35
Parvulescu, Anca, 114
Pelasgian theory, 89
Penal Code, Article 256, 176–77
peripheral whiteness. *See* whiteness, peripheral
Picker, Giovanni, 180–81
Pierre, Jemima, 21
Platini, Michel, 156
police, humor regarding perceptions of, 159–60
Ponzi schemes, 36–37, 194n3

Popov, Veselin, 134
Portokalli, 60–61, 161, 162, 165–70, 171–73
prisoner camp, 31–32, 39
Pyramid, 58
pyramid schemes, 36–37, 194n3

Qemali, Ismail, 90, 154, 156, 157
Qesku, Pavli, 129, 194n9
quantum mechanics, 5

race
  Albania as case study for, 188
  as associated with malice or hate, 10
  author discusses, with *Wake Up Tirana* representatives, 58–62
  as commodified and devoured, 164–65
  conceptualization of, 7–13
  configuring and reconfiguring of, 27
  cultural forms of respect and hospitality in relation to, 68–78
  denial of, in Albania, 1–2, 7–8, 10, 11, 139–40, 161, 187, 189
  versus ethnicity, 8
  as hiding, 152–59
  idea of, 109
  issues in conducting ethnographic research about, 148–49
  and language, 111
  naturalization of, 187–88
  racial belonging and nation-building projects, 88–92
  and relationship between Albania and Greece, 96
  relationship between ethnicity and nation and, 158–59
  as shaped by World War II, 11, 77–78
  and shaping of social worlds, 146–47
  as socially and politically constructed, 7
  spatialization of, 146–47
  study of, in Central and Eastern Europe and Eurasia, 186
  unmaking of, 190–91
racelessness
  assertion of, in Albania, 1–2, 7–8, 10, 11, 161, 187, 189
  as driving segregation, 181
  as epistemological tool, 10
racial capitalism, 14, 102–3, 187
racialization
  of Albanian-Greek border, 95–96
  of Albanians, 13–14, 80, 87–88, 103
  author discusses, with *Wake Up Tirana* representatives, 58–62
  conceptualization of, 7–13
  effects of, 12
  and ethnic conflict in Balkans, 158
  and exclusion from whiteness, 141–42
  factors shaping, 110
  globalization frameworks in examining, 56
  history of, 9
  processes of, 12, 182–83
  and relationality, 12–13
  of Roma and Egyptians, 61–62, 65, 80, 106, 107–8, 140, 143–45
  and segregation of Roma, 123–24
  in socialist period, 92–94
  of space, 146–47
  as textured, 27
racism, 148–49
  against Albanians in Greece, 99–100
  author discusses, with *Wake Up Tirana* representatives, 58–62
  author's experiences with, 59–60, 64, 66, 196n4
  in context of race, nation, and sport, 149–59
  curiosity versus, 59
  denial of, in Albania, 1–2, 11, 58–61, 105–6, 190
  and depictions of black- and brownface in sketch comedies, 159–74
  and displacement and segregation of Roma, 180–82
  as hiding, 152–59
  versus ignorance, 62, 65–66, 100, 189–90
  misperceptions about, in Albania, 182
  naturalization of, 187–88
  negation and normalization of, 181
  public interview regarding, 64–65
  against Roma and Egyptians, 126, 179–80
  and segregation of Roma, 174–75
  in Soviet Union, 67–68
  structural, 182
Radio Televizioni Shqiptar (Albanian Radio and Television), 170
Rama, Edi, 70, 155, 196n2
Rama, Olsi, 155, 156
real estate, and Ponzi schemes, 37, 194n3
relationality, and racialization, 12–13
religion, 32, 93, 99
respect, in relation to race, 68–78
Rexhepi, Piro, 10, 103
ritualized degradation, 170
Robeson, Paul, 67
Robinson, Cedric, 14, 102

Roma
  arixhi and marginalization of, 114–16, 120, 121
  brownface portrayals of, 163, 167–69, 171–73
  collectively racialized as "black" with Egyptians, 111–12
  differentiation of Egyptians and, 135–36, 144–45
  discrimination against, under Hoxha, 33, 93
  displacement of, 179–82
  employment of, 172
  enslavement of, 114–15, 117
  exclusion and perception of, as stranger and outsider, 116–21, 175–78
  pervasiveness of racism against, 179–80
  racialization of, outside of whiteness and Albanianness, 61–62, 65, 80, 106, 107–8, 140, 144
  racism against, 126
  recognized as national minority, 125–26, 193n4
  segregation of, 105, 123–24, 140–41, 174–75, 180–82, 196n3
  self-designation and social activism of, 121–27
  settlements of, 174–75
  treatment of, under Hoxha, 118–19, 122
  viewed as at fault for their marginalization, 175–76
  violence experienced by, 126–27, 175–78
  weddings of, 176
Rom/Romë/Roma, 121–27
Rrapi, Salsano, 165. See also *Portokalli*
Rromani Baxt, 121–22, 123, 126
Rromano Kham, 123
Rucker-Chang, Sunnie, 118, 163, 169–70

Said, Edward, 159
Saideman, Stephen, 105
salvaging, 1, 43–44, 74, 75, 106, 125, 129, 138–39, 141, 167, 168, 174
Schiller, Nina Glick, 158
Seeman, Sonia T., 9
segregation, 105, 123–24, 140–41, 146, 174–75, 180–82, 196n3
Serbia, 152–59, 196n1
Serbian Academy of Sciences, 88
Shakespeare, William, 91–92, 195n4
shame, hospitality and, 22, 45, 46, 52, 56, 72, 75, 76, 78–79

Shaqiri, Xherdan, 157
Shehu, Mehmet, 118–19
Shehu, Xhemi, 167–69, 172
Simmons, Kimberly, 158
sincerity, 78, 190
Skanderbeg (Gjergj Kastrioti Skënderbeu), 89–90, 93, 94–95
Skrapi (fictional character), 167–69, 171–72
slavery, 114–15, 117, 162
soccer, racism in context of, 149–59
social issues and activism, 123
Socialist Party, 38, 41
Soviet Union, 31, 32, 67–68
spatialization of race, 146–47
sports, racism in context of, 149–59
Stalin, Joseph, 4, 31, 32
Stewart, Kathleen, 21, 193n2
Sude/Sudja, 122
Susser, Ida, 20–21
Switzerland, 157

Taço, Xheladin, 121–22, 123, 136
taxi driver, 98, 105–6, 175
television
  blackface and brownface on Albanian, 60–61, 161, 162, 165–70, 171–73
  during communist period, 170
  See also *Wake Up Tirana*
Tepelenë labor camp, 31–32, 39
Tochka, Nicholas, 91
Top Channel, 173
Top Media Group, 173
Tosk, 195n5
train station, destruction of Romani settlement at, 175–78, 181
Trubeta, Sevasti, 134, 137, 145
Tufa, Agron, 39
Turnbull, Collin, 18–19

unemployment, 126, 172. See also begging; collecting; employment
Union of European Football Associations (UEFA), 152–53, 155, 156, 157, 158
United Kingdom, Albanian migrants in, 15
urbanization, under Hoxha, 30–31

Valdi, Klodian, 176–77
Varrezat e Popullit (the People's Cemetery), 28–29
Vasa, Pashko, 32, 47
Vatra, 90–91
Veliaj, Erion, 177–78, 180

Vende dhe Popuj (Places and People), 170
Verdery, Katherine, 4
violence, experienced by Roma, 126–27, 175–78
Vladi, Besmir, 176–77
von Hahn, Johann Georg, 87

Wake Up Tirana
  arrangements for author's appearance on, 57–58
  author meets with representatives of, 58–62
  author's appearance on, 62–66
  collective shame and author's appearance on, 79
  outcome of author's appearance on, 66–68
  and racism versus ignorance, 189
Washington Post, 104–5
weddings, 176
Wekker, Gloria, 164, 169–70, 173
whiteness
  Albanians' assertion of, 103–8
  longing for, 82
  meanings of, 106–7
  racialization and exclusion from, 141–42
  racialization of Albanians outside of, 13–14, 80, 103
  racialization of Balkans and formation of European, 188
  as shifting category, 87, 94, 95
  as strategic, 82
whiteness, peripheral, 13–16, 81–83

and Albanians as perpetual outsiders, 82, 83–84, 87–88
and Albanians' self-definition as Europeans, 83–86
and marginalization of Albania, 95
production of, 188
and racial belonging and nation-building projects, 88–92
and socialist period, 92–94
and socioeconomic disparities across Europe, 102–3
World Cup (Moscow, 2018), 157
World War II, 11, 77–78, 117–18
Wright, Michelle, 5
Wynter, Sylvia, 9–10

Xhaka, Granit, 157
Xhaka, Taulant, 154
Xhufi, Pëllumb, 39

Ypi, Lea, 4
Yugoslavia, 117–18, 196n10

Zemon, Rubin, 135, 136–37, 140, 144
zezak/zezake, 194n9
zezë (black), 139, 140. *See also* blackness; *dorë e zezë* (the "black side")
zezoj (blacken, ruin, defame), 139, 144
Zog I, King, 89, 93, 117
Zwarte Piet (fictional character), 164, 173

www.ingramcontent.com/pod-product-compliance
Lightning Source LLC
Chambersburg PA
CBHW030647230426
43665CB00011B/995